The Minute-by-Minute Saga of the Most Spectacular Rescue of Our Time!

The doomed passengers jammed into an African airport terminal . . .

The specially trained hijackers bargaining for the freedom of convicted terrorists—with the blood of 105 hostages . . .

The government leaders agonizing over a desperate decision . . .

A proud Israeli commando force rehearsing for the surprise attack that would stun the world . . .

This Is the Full, Incredible Story of the Astonishing and Triumphant Entebbe Rescue

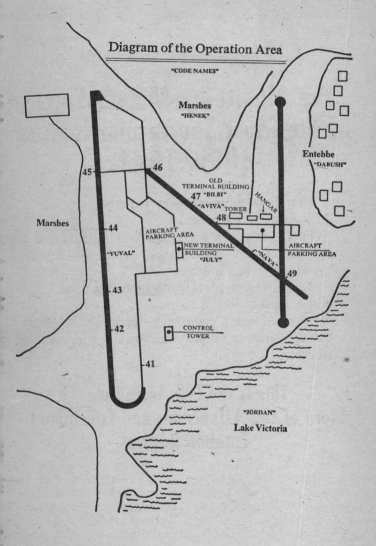

Diagram of the Operation Area

"CODE NAMES"

Marshes
"HENEK"

Marshes

Entebbe
"DABUSH"

45

46

OLD
TERMINAL BUILDING
47 "BILBI"

"AVIVA"

TOWER

48

HANGAR

44

AIRCRAFT
PARKING AREA

"YUVAL"

NEW TERMINAL
BUILDING
"JULY"

"NAVA"

AIRCRAFT
PARKING AREA

49

43

42

CONTROL
TOWER

41

"JORDAN"

Lake Victoria

ENTEBBE RESCUE

YESHAYAHU BEN-PORAT,
EITAN HABER and
ZEEV SCHIFF

A DELL BOOK

Published by
Dell Publishing Co., Inc.
1 Dag Hammarskjold Plaza
New York, New York 10017

Originally published in Hebrew
by Zmora, Bitan, Modan Publishers, Tel Aviv, Israel
Copyright © 1976 by Zmora, Bitan, Modan Publishers

English translation copyright © 1977
by Zmora, Bitan, Modan Publishers

Dell ® TM 681510, Dell Publishing Co., Inc.

ISBN: 0-440-17304-3

Printed in the United States of America
First Dell printing—January 1977
Second Dell printing—March 1977

Contents

Preface

This book was written because of the authors' sincere belief that Operation Thunderball—or "Jonathan," as it is now called—can teach the free world that it need not be helpless to prevent or powerless to stop the satanic games of ruthless terrorists, who endanger all the principles in which modern man puts his faith.

We dedicate the book to the men of all ranks and many echelons who worked around the clock in a superhuman effort that led to success, to the two-hundred-odd officers and men who embarked on the long journey into Africa, and to the government of Israel which had the courage to make the right decisions, though its members risked national tragedy and personal political oblivion.

We have interviewed hundreds of people and studied mountains of documentation, and have spared no effort to verify every detail and tell all that can be told about the fifty-three dramatic minutes at Entebbe and the week that led up to it. Some things still cannot be told. Israel is still at war against Arab terrorism. For this reason we cannot prejudice coming campaigns by laying all our cards on the table now. For this reason also, with the exception of Lieutenant Colonel Jonathan Netaniahu and Sergeant Hershko Surin, all persons with ranks below brigadier general appear under assumed names. Having done them this necessary injustice, we are confident that they will find compensation in the knowledge that they saved the lives of other human beings, in an operation that restored hope and pride to the hearts of mankind.

The story is theirs, yet we would be remiss if we did not acknowledge our debt to the many men and women whose willing cooperation made this book possible. There are far too many to list by name, and we therefore trust that they will forgive us if we only mention a few:

Yitzhak Rabin, prime minister of Israel.

Shimon Peres, defense minister.

Yigal Allon, foreign minister.

Haim Zadok, minister of justice.

Gad Yaakobi, minister of transport.

Lieutenant General Mordechai Gur, chief of staff of the Israel Defense Forces.

Major General Rehavam Zeevi, advisor to the prime minister on intelligence and counter-terrorism.

Brigadier Ephraim Poran, military secretary to the prime minister.

Brigadier Arye Braun, military secretary to the defense minister.

Amos Aran, director general, prime minister's office.

Professor Shlomo Avineri, director general, foreign ministry.

Eli Mizrahi, chief of bureau to the prime minister.

Dan Patir, communications media advisor to the prime minister.

Naftali Lavi, spokesman of the defense ministry.

Ehud Gera, personal assistant to the minister of transport.

Haim Braun, personal assistant to the foreign minister.

Mrs. Patricia Martel-Hyman.

The family of Lieutenant Colonel Jonathan Netaniahu:
    Prof. Ben-Zion, Zila, Binyamin, and Edo.
The sons of Dora Bloch: Ilan Hartuv and Danny Bloch.
Hadassa and Yitzhak David.
The family of Jean Jacques Maimoni.
Hana Cohen, widow of Pasco Cohen.
The Davidsons: Uzzi, Sara, Ron, and Benny.
And, last but not least, Air France.

Introduction
by
Yitzhak Rabin
Prime Minister of Israel

On the morning of July 4, 1976, when an Israeli force returned from the longest-range commando raid in history, the nation that is Israel knew that right was on its side. The force had ventured out into the night to reclaim from the claws of death 105 men, women, and children, who had committed no crime—the victims of a ruthless act of terrorism. Their only "fault" was that they were Israeli citizens. They had spent a week in Entebbe, wavering between hope and despair, between the brink of death and the faint chance of redemption from a terror served by international gangsters and Ugandan soldiers alike.

From the distance of two thousand miles, the people of Israel had watched in growing anxiety the events in the Old Terminal of Entebbe International Airport. There was not a moment of doubt, neither in the government of Israel nor the nation, that the obligation to rescue the captives, one way or another, rested with us. During those terrible days and hours, we had to face our own truths, alone. We did not delude ourselves. Nor did we place much hope in international organizations, whose silence in the past has encouraged the terrorists and the Arab countries that back them.

Israel's battle in the Entebbe hijacking was, first and foremost, against the hands of the clock. The decisions, political and military, were taken under growing pressure of time, and in constant sight of the mortal peril of a great many Israelis. This was a great hour for the people of Israel, no matter of what political persuasion. An hour in which the nation ascended to heights above the daily differences of opinion, and became one—in the face of a need either to negotiate with terror or in resolve to pick up its gauntlet.

The Entebbe hijacking was not the first terror action nor, sorrowfully, will it be the last. Events since Entebbe have confirmed that. Yet we are steadfast in our determination not to allow terror to harm us. We shall strike at them, in any place and at every opportunity. Arab terror is a cancer in the body of the free world, and Israel sees it as her duty to lop off the malignant tentacles. In this campaign Israel must be aided by active partners, and we want to see together with us on the front line the enlightened and freedom-loving nations of the world.

Operation "Yonatan"—as we now call it in memory of an outstanding young officer who gave his life to save the Entebbe hostages—has a historical significance. It is to be hoped that its influence will not die away, that the terror organizations will understand the capability that is the fist of the Israeli army. This was one battle in a protracted war, the end of which is not in sight—but we do not for a moment doubt that we will be victorious.

This perfect operation was the fruit of imagination, initiative, boldness, and many years of training. It was performed by young men, both conscripts and regular army, who traveled a long way in a very short time after a minimum of preparation. In its entirety it was of the Israel Defense Forces. And only a government with absolute faith in the dedication and capability of its army can afford to take decisions on missions like this one.

The officers and men who took part both in planning and performance are deserving of the compliments and admiration of all of us. This tribute is the least we can do for the anonymous soldiers of the intelligence community, the stout-hearted paratroops, the brave infantrymen of the Golani Brigade, the air force pilots, and all the others who made the impossible come true. It also the due of the hostages, who faced their captors with pride and dignity, and of the state of Israel—in that we are blessed by men, women, and children like these.

We do not bask in the glory of such victories. We do remember, in sorrow and pride, the men who gave their lives—at Entebbe and elsewhere in the defense of Israel—that this nation should live in peace and dignity in its land.

Epigraph

Jonathan Netaniahu led the Israeli paratrooper raid on Old Terminal, Entebbe International Airport, to free the hostages held by Palestinian terrorists on July 3, 1976. The following is an excerpt from his farewell speech to the armored corps of which he had been battalion commander:

—I believe first of all in common sense, which should guide everything we do.

—I believe that there can be no compromise. Never compromise with results that are less than the best possible, and even then look for improvements.

—I believe, with absolute faith, in our ability to carry out any military task entrusted to us.

—I believe in Israel and in the general sense of responsibility that must accompany every man who fights for the future of his homeland.

—I leave with the feeling that much still remains to be done, and I admit that it is difficult to leave. But I also know that I am leaving the battalion in good hands.

—I would like you to know that I believe in you—the

officers and men of this battalion. With a battalion like this, a man could go to war.

The basic assumption in our work is to prepare for war in the best possible fashion, in order to stand quietly on the day of judgment, when it comes, in the knowledge that we did everything we could in the time that we had.

CHAPTER ONE

Flight Number 139

Dora Bloch absolutely refused to fly to the United States for her son's wedding. "I'm old, I can't travel that far," she told him.

Danny Bloch refused to listen. The youngest of Dora's sons, he was, a political correspondent on the staff of Israel's daily *Davar*. The State Department had invited him on a tour of official Washington, and Danny—chairman of the National Association of Israeli Journalists—accepted the invitation. He was to marry Phyllis Kabakov, a young Jewish New Yorker, on July 11. Now, as he packed his bags, he was still trying to convince his mother, but Dora Bloch was adamant.

Finally the seventy-five-year-old woman proposed a compromise: "Instead of flying to the United States, I'll buy you a present equal to the value of the ticket."

"Mother, there will be so few of the family in New York to share my joy. I would like you to be there. . . ."

Dora Bloch knew when she was beaten: "All right. I'll go."

*   *   *

Benny Davidson really wanted this trip to America. He had turned thirteen in May, but his grandfather died just before his bar mitzvah, and the long-awaited celebration was cancelled. His parents—Uzzi and Sara—promised him a vacation in the United States as a consolation prize, but only after the end of the school year. That was a long time off, and Benny was impatient. As the days of waiting drew to a close, tension peaked in the comfortable Davidson home in a pleasant north Tel Aviv suburb. Cut-rate tickets for the two boys, Ron and Benny, were only possible if the final departure for America was from somewhere in Europe. On the night before they collected their tickets, Benny fought for Paris as their pretransatlantic stopover; Uzzi, Sara, and Ron conceded.

Jean Jacques Maimoni wanted to fly to Paris on Saturday, June 26, to complete his baccalaureate before the new academic year started. Meanwhile, the nineteen-year-old made the most of the beach at his resort town home in Natanya. Much of his time was spent with Thiery Sicker, son of the French consul general. Their parents were good friends, and Jean Jacques' father—an ex-French police officer—treated Thiery like another son. It was Thiery who suggested that Jean Jacques fly with him on the Sunday plane, though Mr. Maimoni argued that he had already cabled relatives to be at Orly on Saturday.

Yosef and Lisette Hadad wanted to reach Paris, yet they preferred that no one know about it. Yosef worked long hours, starting his daily bread delivery at 2 A.M., and finishing, exhausted, at 1 o'clock each afternoon. He, Lisette, and their three children lived in a modest apartment in Holon, near Tel Aviv. Worried that hard work for such little money was breaking her husband's spirit, Lisette wondered aloud about the possibility of leaving Israel. They were going to Paris to examine possibilities to live and work there. "We'll make a little money and come back," Yosef Hadad told himself and his wife.

The Labor Union Sick Fund couldn't help Pasco Cohen, even though he was the Fund's branch manager in his home town of Hadera. Pasco, now fifty years old, had heart trouble. The Cohens spent the winter dreaming of a summer trip to Europe, with their two children—eight-year-old Zippora and twelve-year-old Yaakov. They planned to visit Mrs. Cohen's brother who was to be married in July, in Paris, and then they would spend three weeks on the classic grand tour: England, Switzerland, Italy, and Germany. Hana Cohen intended to lock up her women-and-children's clothing store in Hadera. The intoxicating smell of a vacation was already in her nostrils.

Yitzhak David, from Kiriat Bialik, a kibbutz near Haifa, had been to Europe many times before. A director of a mining firm, he traveled frequently on business. In his spare time he also served as head of the local council. But this was one trip that Yitzhak had promised his wife Hadassa long ago. They were to start out on Sunday, June 27, 1976.

Sunday, June 27, was a hot day in Israel—88 degrees Fahrenheit in the shade. It was also a day "low on news," as the foreign editor of *Yediot Aharonot*, the evening paper, described it. Nothing of any real importance happened the day before. The morning papers were a good indication of Israeli summer boredom and reaction to the oppressive heat. The chief news editor had a hard time finding the lead headline for his paper: "United States Allows PLO Rep at UN to Leave New York for Information Trip to Washington." The most sensational item of the day was the arrest of a French tourist—a woman known for extreme leftist leanings and suspected of links with terrorist groups.

In Montreal, an American broke the world decathlon

record in last-minute pre-Olympic trials with a score of
8,538 points, but the news was shunted into a corner of
the front page. As on previous days, there were strikes in
Israel. The Land Registry was closed for three days by a
walkout. The report that caused the most concern was
tucked into a box on an inside page: "Unprecedented Heat
Wave in Western Europe." Not very encouraging for the
quarter-million Israelis who intended to flood the cities of
Europe this summer.

Beirut was still a disaster area. Headlines noted total
blackout by night—no electricity and a severe water shortage. Hundreds of dead and wounded—but that was nothing new.

Sunday morning was the time for the Israeli Cabinet's
routine weekly session. This Sunday's agenda was hardly
likely to excite any of the participants: first, a report on
the situation in Lebanon, then President Ford's decision to
increase interim foreign aid to Israel from $75 million to
$275 million, Foreign Minister Allon's visit to Germany,
and finally, review of a previous decision not to institute
daylight savings time this year.

Nineteen ministers convened at 10 A.M. in a wood-
paneled conference room on the second floor of Yitzhak
Rabin's Jerusalem office. Prime Minister Rabin took his
seat at the Cabinet table. He also seemed bored by the
dreariness of this Sunday. Rabin is not a poker-faced politician; it was clear from his expression that he expected no
excitement during this session. Cabinet Secretary Gershon
Avner sat by his side. To his left, a stenographer was
struggling to keep pace with the ministers' comments. A
large clock in the center of the room reminded speakers
that their time was limited. From time to time, a minister
ducked out to the anteroom for a quick cigarette.

This Sunday, the chairs reserved for ministerial advisors
around the Cabinet Room stood empty, as the agenda was
of no interest to them. The session dragged on quietly.

*   *   *

By the time that Michel Bacos landed in Israel on Saturday night, he had clocked 17,307 hours of flying time. He was to pilot Air France 139 from Ben-Gurion Airport to Orly, via Athens, this Sunday morning. Michel had flown for twenty-one years—first for Air France, then as a pilot on loan from them to the Moroccan national airline, then again for Air France. After flying a variety of aircraft, he received his license as captain of an Aerobus, the latest addition to the French passenger fleet, on February 18, 1976. Born in Port Said, Egypt, this pilot had flown the Paris–Tel Aviv route several times during his career.

Michel's Aerobus was parked on the apron at Ben-Gurion Airport between aircraft of TWA and Alitalia. The craft (which first flew the Tel Aviv route in 1974) is the French answer to the American jumbo 747 and can carry 250 passengers. Flight 139 this Sunday was only one of eleven weekly flights on Air France's summer schedule.

Dora Bloch sat in the taxi between her sons, Ilan Hartuv and Binyamin Bloch. They raced down the hills from Jerusalem to the airport, arriving ninety minutes before take-off time for the thorough security checks required.

Dora and Ilan parted from Binyamin. Ilan's wife would be following a few days later, together with Binyamin and his wife. The two couples would take a tour of Spain, leaving Dora to continue alone to New York. At the Air France check-in counter, a uniformed hostess informed Dora and Ilan that there would be a stopover at Athens. Ilan objected, but it was too late to do anything about it. Within five hours flying time, Mrs. Bloch would be meeting her French brother, an author, and she was looking forward to it.

A long row of baggage separated the four Davidsons from the check-in counter. The line moved forward inch by inch as a woman security officer probed the interior of each bag. Uzzi Davidson heard of the Athens stopover just as he was digging into his billfold to pay the six-dollar air-

port tax. His wife, Sara—attractive, forty years old, and
secretary to the director general of the Israel Electric Corporation in Tel Aviv—also heard it, and told herself that
had she known this previously she would have insisted on
a different flight. She remembered the Air France sales
clerk in Tel Aviv, who described the delights of the Aerobus as if there was no better craft in the skies: "Good
Lord, he told me about every nut and bolt, but couldn't
mention a stopover in Athens?"

Pasco Cohen prodded Zippora and Yaakov along, as he
was sure they were late. Hana, his wife, had been slightly
behind schedule in leaving home this morning.

Almost on the dot of 8:15, Daniel Lom entered the
spacious cockpit of the Aerobus. Daniel, a thirty-four-
year-old French air force veteran, was one of twelve in the
crew. He had already chalked up 4,105 hours flying time,
to which he was now about to add five more as first officer
on board this plane. Behind him in the cockpit sat flight
engineer Jacques Lemoine, a man who had left the armored
corps of the French army to become a navigator, and at
last, a flight engineer. His log showed 6,078 flying hours,
two thousand more than thirty-six-year-old Bernard Cotte,
the chief steward.

Ann Franking greeted Dora Bloch in the hatchway of
the aircraft. Ann, a Swede with a French passport, was the
youngest and least experienced crew member, having joined
Air France in February 1976. She led Dora and Ilan down
the gangway to their seats in row 25. The loudspeakers
were providing soft music as the Davidsons moved into
their seats.

Stewardess Christine Bouchard guided Zippora and
Yaakov Cohen to their seats near the door, helped them
fasten their belts, then handed them some sour balls before
moving on to offer her tray to the other passengers. Outside the sun was beating down, but the cabin was pleas-
antly air conditioned.

At 8:54 the doors of the Aerobus were locked, and Michel Bacos taxied his heavy craft to runway 26/08. At 8:54 the passengers were looking down on the rooftops of Tel Aviv, and at the Shalom Tower which loomed high above the gray-white city.

This Sunday, like every other, the patriarchal delegate prayed alone. Bishop Hilarion Capucci occupied an Israeli prison cell in Ramla, far from his 4,500 congregants of the Greek Catholic Church in Jerusalem. The tall, bearded bishop, dressed in white cassock even in prison, had lost none of his arrogance and intolerance. Indeed, he behaved towards guards and inmates alike as though they were members of his flock. It was as though prison walls did not exist for him; one could certainly see no hint of remorse for the actions that had brought him here to serve a twelve-year sentence. It would be difficult for an outsider to believe at first glance that this man was one of those the Palestinian terrorists wanted freed; that he was, in fact, a prize for which they would risk hundreds of innocent lives.

Capucci, Syrian by birth, had commuted regularly between Jerusalem and Beirut. The frontier guards treated him with the respect due a senior churchman, even—or perhaps particularly—one in the Jewish state. As his black limousine drove through the barrier without stopping for inspection, policemen on both sides saluted the bearded dignitary, or at least the church he represented.

He had often exploited the circumstances of his office: in April 1974, the suitcases in the trunk of his black Mercedes contained demolition "brick," hand grenades, sub-machine guns, and even Katyusha rockets. These rockets exploded against the walls of Jerusalem homes a few days later. In May 1974, the bishop transported 150 detonators and delayed-action fuses across the international frontier into Israel.

His ambition to be a messenger of terrorist organizations rather than of the church knew no bounds, and finally led him into the hands of Israel's security services. When he was caught early in August 1974, the walls of his limousine contained pistols, Kalashnikov carbines, magazines, 400 detonators, and 448 pounds of explosives.

There are 2,600 "security prisoners" in Israeli prisons, mostly Arabs, but no other like Hilarion Capucci. While still in the courtroom before being taken to prison, he arrogantly announced that he wouldn't spend twelve years behind bars. Unlike other convicts, Capucci refused to work, and the prison authorities did not insist. Capucci in fact enjoyed special treatment: he had a cell designed for six all to himself. Anyone who knew how crowded Israeli prisons really were could appreciate the gesture that the Directorate of Prisons made to its august inmate.

Capucci's whole day was spent in prayer, rest, and incitement of other prisoners to action. He was rarely silent, and when he was, it was because he was writing complaints to the authorities and initiating legal action against the wardens for denying him what he considered reasonable conditions. Capucci had a high opinion of himself. He treated those around him as his personal servants, and they (perhaps from lack of alternative) served his every need from morning till night. Capucci's prestige peaked when the terrorist organizations put his name at the head of the list for release—if and when they had hostages to trade. But, regardless of others' opinions of him, this representative of God on earth considered himself at least the equal of the deity he served.

Kozo Okamoto had never heard of the Holocaust that decimated the Jewish people, nor would he have been interested in it. He did not differentiate between Jew and non-Jew, between African or Asian, between Arab and Israeli. He sat in a well-guarded cell of the security prisoners' wing at Ramla Prison indifferent to his warders and making no contact with the other inmates. Occasionally his crazed eyes focused on the few books and brochures supplied by the Japanese embassy in Tel Aviv. He spoke to no one, and no one spoke to him. Three times a day a bowl of food was placed before him, and he ate without a word. An iron curtain seemed to separate him from the rest of the world.

Kozo Okamoto, twenty-nine, was a student of agriculture when in February 1970 his brother recruited him for the Japanese "Red Army." He was offered military training in Beirut, under the auspices of the Popular Democratic Front for the Liberation of Palestine (PFLP), and he agreed. In contrast to his present behavior in an Israeli prison, Kozo then showed constant alertness and interest in the intricacies of underground activity. The PFLP sent him to New York to board an El Al jumbo jet and study the security arrangements. He couldn't get a seat on the jumbo, so he flew to Paris in an El Al Boeing 707 instead. From Paris he went to Beirut to meet two Japanese colleagues and the three of them moved on to Baalbek for weapons and demolition training, as well as an intensive physical-fitness course. Shortly afterwards, Kozo traveled to Frankfurt, Germany, on a fake passport in the name of Namba Kisoka and under the code name of "Ahmad." His next destination was Rome where, together with his two Japanese comrades, he boarded a flight to Lod Airport on May 30, 1972. In Lod passenger terminal, the three opened fire on the crowd waiting for their baggage from an Air France plane, killing twenty-four and wounding seventy-two.

On Sunday, June 27, 1976, Kozo Okamoto finished breakfast at 7:30, moved to his bed—the only furniture in his cell—and fixed his glassy stare on the ceiling.

An hour after the beginning of the Cabinet meeting, Commerce and Industry Minister Haim Bar-Lev was in the middle of a spirited defense of his own proposal to institute daylight saving by moving the clock one hour forward. At the end of his presentation, Tourism Minister

Moshe Kol followed him with a question to Prime Minister Rabin: "How are we to understand President Ford's expression of thanks to the PLO, when their men murdered the American ambassador in Beirut?"

Foreign Minister Yigal Allon said quickly: "The Israeli embassy in Washington has registered a reservation about the gratitude expressed by the State Department to the PLO on the evacuation of Americans from Lebanon. The U.S. government explained, in response, that they transmitted verbal appreciation to all who took part—including the PLO—but this is not to be seen as recognition, direct or indirect, of the PLO."

Twelve miles west of Tel Aviv, Air France 139 entered flight path "Green 18," on course for the island of Rhodes at an altitude of 33,000 feet. Ann Franking, Christine Bouchard, and their colleagues served a Continental breakfast to the passengers. The skies were blue and cloudless—typical late June weather over the Mediterranean. A pleasant flight with no problems. Children were playing in the three aisles, but they weren't disturbing anyone.

In the twenty-six-seat first-class cabin, the stewardesses had already served champagne in long-stemmed glasses. Some Israeli passengers were surprised to see that the flight-deck door was unlocked, offering an occasional view of banks of switches and colored lights whenever someone went in or out.

Dora Bloch felt very relaxed. She had flown before and, despite her age, she was not at all worried. She chatted with her son about her coming visit to France. Dora stood out among the passengers. Her aristocratic features, platinum hair, and upright posture seemed more appropriate to a nineteenth-century English lady than a twentieth-century Israeli. Her seventy-five years in Israel had done nothing to dull the English patina. Dora had actually acquired her British manner from her late husband, Aharon—an English Jew who came to Palestine in the early 1920s.

Aharon, a violinist, met Dora at the home of the Russian postmaster in Jerusalem. When he wasn't making music, he worked in a bank. Even though he was one of the pioneers of modern Palestine, he held on to his English traditions and British passport even when he acquired his Israeli document after independence in 1948. The Bloch household made of their Jerusalem and later their Tel Aviv home a little corner of London.

It was rather strange, this mixture of Aharon Bloch's meticulous British politeness and Dora's pioneering Israeli background. Her parents' home had rejected all things foreign to the renewal of the Jewish nation in the "Promised Land." Dora was the daughter of Yosef Feinberg, scion of one of the most respected Palestinian families. Yosef, an early member of *Hovevei Zion* ("Lovers of Zion")—forerunners of the Zionist movement—bought the land on which Rishon Le Zion, one of the first colonies of renewed Jewish settlement, was built. He was the one who convinced Baron de Rothschild to finance the colonization of Palestine in the early 1900s, but he also led a campaign against the baron's corrupt administrators, after which Rothschild wrote to Yosef Feinberg: "In my eyes, you are dead."

Yosef paid the price of his war on the baron's representatives. He was driven from Rishon Le Zion and moved to Jaffa where he worked first as a carter, then at other occupations. Dora was born and brought up in their Jaffa home, which doubled as the center of the *Hovevei Zion* Committee. Some claim that Naphtali Herz Imber, a frequent visitor to the Feinbergs both in Rishon and in Jaffa, wrote the verses of the song that would become Israel's national anthem—"Hatikva"—under Yosef's roof.

Yosef Feinberg died when Dora was one year old. Dora and her brother Mark eventually moved to Egypt. Mark became court physician to the king of Egypt, and saved the monarch's sister's life when she was stricken by smallpox—a disease for which, in those times, there was no sure cure. Dòra, who spoke seven languages, married Aharon Bloch after her return to Palestine. She filled her day with charity work, but her pride and joy were her three sons and her grandchildren.

The galley between the first-class and tourist cabins served in free moments as the "clubroom" of the stewards and stewardesses on Flight 139. It was late morning, and Air France 139 was over Rhodes—where Israeli and Arab peace delegations had met twenty-seven years earlier at the end of the War of Independence. Empty trays were now stacked on carts in the galley, and the flight crew was preparing for landing at Athens, even though the plane was still at 33,000 feet.

Yitzhak and Hadassa David were impatient to reach Paris, although Hadassa was already feeling twinges of homesickness for her son and daughter. It made little difference that the "boy" was twenty-five and the "girl" a nineteen-year-old soldier and student of computer sciences at the Technion. Hadassa didn't travel abroad frequently, unlike her husband who had a special affection for Paris, the city he was now looking forward to seeing again.

Twenty-two years ago, when he had escaped from the Buchenwald concentration camp, Yitzhak David offered his services to De Gaulle's Free French army, which happened to be nearby. He acted as interrogator of German prisoners and interpreter for the Frenchmen. When the job was over, the French soldiers offered to take him back to France with them, but Yitzhak chose to move toward Hungary, in the hope of finding his parents and brothers who, like Yitzhak himself, had been taken to a concentration camp.

Michel Bacos, captain of Air France 139, could see the Greek island of Kos 33,000 feet below. This was the point at which he took his heavy plane on to flight path "Red 19" to approach Athens. The thirty-eight passengers due to disembark at Athens were already assembling their hand baggage. The others knew they would remain in Greece fifty minutes, and have another three hours in the air to Charles de Gaulle Airport near Paris.

As the Aerobus began its descent on "Red 19," the passengers settled back in their seats, ready for landing. Uzzi Davidson told Ron and Benny to fasten their seat belts. Uzzi, forty-three years of age, an ex-IDF (Israeli Defense Forces, or army) officer was born in Rishon Le Zion, the one-time home of the parents of Dora Bloch. Ron, at seventeen the eldest son, was an excellent high school pupil. His blond-haired, smiling brother Benny sat beside him and both did at once as their father had asked.

Regina and Yehuda Gottlieb from Ramat Gan were in a hurry to get to Boston. July 7 was the second birthday of their granddaughter Billi, whom they had never seen. Before leaving, Yehuda had turned his shop over to another barber so as not to lose his regular clients while he was away.

Jocelyn Munir was going home to Paris, after visiting Morris Ben Shimon's parents in Bat Yam. Jocelyn and Morris had become engaged in Paris a few weeks previous, and she had spent fourteen days in Israel to get to know her in-laws-to-be.

Just after eleven o'clock, the kitchen in the prime minister's office was preparing sandwiches for the ministers. The consumption of food at Cabinet meetings was always in direct proportion to the length of the session. The government of Israel was discussing the "Kadoum settlement" affair for the seventh time. On this occasion, it was Liberal Minister-without-Portfolio Gideon Hausner who was needling the prime minister. Kadoum was an attempt by several dozen Israeli youngsters who wished to establish legal settlement in the Occupied Territories. The enterprise had won a temporary and doubtful approval from the government, but many people saw it as an obstacle in the path of dialogue between Jordan and Israel. And so some ministers made it a weekly habit to remind the prime minister that approval was only temporary. "What about Kadoum?" Hausner asked, and no further elaboration was necessary on the question.

At 11:35 A.M., the ten wheels of Air France Aerobus 139 from Tel Aviv to Paris touched down on the runway of Athens Airport.

CHAPTER TWO

"Mother, Does It Hurt to Die?"

Air France 139 was due at Charles de Gaulle Airport, Paris, at 2:35 P.M. Two hundred and fifty-one minutes more of flying time, but first fifty minutes on the tarmac at Athens. The passengers loosened their seat belts, waiting for the big craft to brake to a halt. Soft music was playing as the thirty-eight Athens-bound passengers disembarked. The others remained in their seats. A mobile generator stood below the plane to supply power for the air conditioning, but the sound of its motor barely interfered with the music.

Ilan Hartuv and several other passengers expressed their surprise at not being allowed off the plane for a few minutes in the transit lounge. After all, fifty minutes wasn't a short stop. Hartuv spoke to hostess Lydie Devine and she suggested that Ilan should refer the question to the steward, Gerard Gabas, her senior in the Air France hierarchy.

Gabas was firm: "Security. The Greek government doesn't allow transit passengers to get off." Ilan, satisfied, returned to his seat.

There are two terminals at Athens International Airport.

The eastern one serves all flights of Olympic, the national airline. The second is used by all the other airlines flying to and from Greece. Old-fashioned, small, and cramped would be the most accurate way to describe this crossroads of the eastern Mediterranean.

Air traffic at Athens was very heavy, particularly since the civil war in Cyprus had paralyzed Nicosia Airport. Nicosia control tower had been the traffic policeman for aircraft flying over a troubled area. Flight controllers in Beirut, Damascus, Amman, and Cairo were not willing to exchange a word with Lod control, even in emergencies. Now, Athens handled the added burden.

No day went by at Athens without its few flights from the Arab countries and Israel, en route to Western Europe and the United States. From morning to evening of every day, the terminal building transit lounge looked like an Oriental bazaar, with passengers milling around waiting for planes to finish refueling. Jet fuel is cheaper in Athens than at other airports.

All in all, the conditions were ideal for terrorists: two hours flying time from the Arab countries and Israel, and the terminal was crowded around the clock. The slow-moving Greeks were well known for their apathy, and their security provisions were no exception. The airport was packed, the work hard, and the strikes frequent. Who could think about checking passengers and their belongings—and transit passengers as well? Few security officers circulated in the terminal, and even fewer outside. Suitcases were usually checked in small rooms so bustling and noisy that the examiners quickly became impatient. They spent more time chatting among themselves than in probing the interiors of passengers' bags. There was an X-ray machine for hand baggage, but on the morning of June 27, 1976, the policeman on duty was more interested in sniffing the flower in his hand than in watching the fluoroscope screen, and nobody was on duty at the metal detector in the passenger corridor.

Among the scores of planes that put down and took off from Athens on that summer morning was an overnight flight from Bahrein, which stopped at Kuwait before continuing to Greece. Singapore Airlines 763 landed at 6:45. Among the five passengers off the Boeing 707, four headed for the transit area to check in for Air France 139. Two of them appeared to be Europeans—a young man and woman.

There were fifty-six people in line for passport and customs inspection before boarding the Paris flight. A young woman, about twenty-five, with attractive though acne-scarred features, a ponytail, and glasses, produced her Ecuadorian passport in the name of M. Ortega. When a Greek policeman returned the document, she walked quickly through the gate to a waiting bus. A few places behind her in the line, a young, light-skinned blond with blue eyes handed over a Peruvian passport identifying him as A. Garcia. The policeman studied it a moment, comparing the man to his photograph, and handed it back with a polite "thank you." The man moved out toward the waiting plane carrying a handbag that weighed 38 pounds. Had anyone bothered to compare their tickets, he would have found that both first-class reservations had been made in Kuwait on June 20, 1976. Pure coincidence?

Two or three more passengers passed through the barrier, and then two dark-skinned youngsters offered passports from Bahrein and Kuwait, in the names of El-Davih and Ramin el-Shatti. Their tourist tickets were also purchased in Kuwait, on June 22.

The fifty-six newcomers shuffled slowly down the narrow aisles of the Aerobus, looking for empty seats. It took ten minutes until they were settled in their places—the two dark-skinned youngsters were assisted by an Air France steward. The outer door swung slowly into position and was locked. Stewards and stewardesses walked down the aisles checking that all seat belts were fastened. Pierrete Violet's soft musical voice welcomed aboard the new pas-

sengers and wished them a pleasant flight; then the twenty-
six-year-old Senegalese stewardess replaced the microphone and picked up a straw basket of sour balls.

"Some of our cousins have come aboard," Yitzhak
David remarked to his neighbor in seat E20, Dr. Hirsch.
Yitzhak didn't like the newcomers' looks at all. In row 25,
Dora tapped Ilan on the elbow, and with her eyes indicated
the two youngsters in row 28: "I don't feel right about
them, somehow."

"They're not to my liking," Hana Cohen whispered to
her husband in their seats near the door. It was the boy
holding the package that aroused her suspicion. "I'm telling you, that one is a terrorist. . . ."

Pasco Cohen did not hesitate. Catching the eye of a
stewardess, he quietly repeated Hana's suspicions. The girl
headed for the flight deck, while Moroccan-born Hana
used her Arabic to strike up a conversation with the boy:

"Tell me, what have you got in that box?"

"You tell me, do you have children, madam?"

"Yes. Two of them—here on the plane."

"Then, I've got candies for you and a little dynamite for
your kids."

The grisly joke silenced Hana. The two who had attracted Dora and Hana's attention nodded politely to Yosef
Abugadid when they took the vacant seats next to him.
Forty-nine-year-old Yosef had come to Israel from Tunis
fifteen years ago. He lived in Atlit on the Mediterranean
coast. Yosef was on his first trip out of Israel since his
arrival in 1961, and hadn't felt comfortable about it when
he left home this morning. He had told his wife, Yehudit,
he had had a premonition that the plane would blow up
in the air. Nevertheless, he kissed her and his seven children goodbye and left for Ben-Gurion Airport. Now, he
was feeling better about it. Half the flight was over and
nothing had happened. He chastised himself for conjuring
up such nonsense and nodded in reply to the polite smiles
of the two strangers. Meanwhile, they shoved their leather

shoulder bags under the seats after pulling out two tins of dates.

For a fraction of a second, something flashed across Yosef's mind. He could both speak and read Arabic, and the tins were clearly marked "Produce of Iraq"—an unusual sight to someone living in Israel. But this nervousness faded as fast as it had come. As he relaxed, one of the youngsters leaned over to offer him some fruit. Yosef smiled and extended a couple of fingers to fish two dates from the tin.

Sara Davidson was worried. The two youngsters didn't appeal to her either, and she said so to Uzzi who waved the apprehension away with a flick of his hand, as if to say: "You're imagining things. Forget it!" The boys, Ron and Benny, were tense, ready for takeoff, and trying to catch a last look at Athens Airport through the windows of the plane. A British airliner was crossing the tarmac ahead of them on its way to takeoff point.

At 12:25 Air France 139 was airborne. In less than a minute, the passengers on one side of the cabin were looking down on the white rooftops of Athens, while those on the other side had a view of the blue-green waters of the Mediterranean. As the plane leveled off to a more steady climb, the "Fasten Seatbelts" signs flickered off.

"Did you see the big handbag that those two Arabs brought on board?" Dora Bloch asked her son, adding, "I'm scared."

Lisette Hadad hoped she was going to feel better on this leg of the flight. She had vomited on the way from Tel Aviv to Athens. Still, at most there were only 130 minutes more to suffer.

In the cockpit, Michel Bacos put the plane on automatic pilot at 2,000 feet. Now, his $27 million craft was climbing steadily to 31,000 feet. The stewards and stewardesses were crowding into the two galleys to prepare lunch for the 246 passengers.

Eight minutes out of Athens, the flight was smooth,

though the passengers could no longer see anything except grayish clouds. The stewardesses had completed their demonstration of the plane's safety equipment. At 12:33 two people got up from the front row of the twenty-six-seat first class cabin. The girl with the ponytail turned to the door which separated the flight deck from the passenger cabin. The blond blue-eyed youngster raised high his champagne glass—the signal agreed on—then followed her. His six-foot bulk blocked the doorway.

It seemed to Michel Bacos that the passengers' voices were growing louder. For a moment he thought perhaps there was a fire on board. As he turned his head, flight engineer Jacques Lemoine heard a scream, and the cockpit door was kicked. Bacos told Lemoine to go see what was happening. Jacques was already on his feet when the door burst open to reveal a blond young man, clutching a revolver in one hand and a hand grenade in the other.

The two dark-skinned young men were also on their feet, and no longer bothered to be polite to Yosef Abugadid, their neighbor. They brushed past his outstretched legs and for a second or two he couldn't understand their hurry. "Where the hell have they got to rush to now?" Then it was suddenly clear. The long-haired one in the red shirt, gray pants, and beige sweater was waving a gun in his right hand. A similar weapon, a little darker in color, was in the hand of the other boy with the thick mustache and yellow shirt. The two raced down the gangway towards the service area, then turned and "red shirt" yelled, "Hands up!"

A woman's scream rang out in the cabin.

"Uzzi, we've just been hijacked," Sara Davidson mumbled.

This was the moment Yosef Hadad chose to stand up. The bread-van driver from Holon thought at first that a passenger had gone mad, but suddenly he understood what was happening. As a reserve soldier, Yosef decided he would try to stop the hijacking. Lisette knew what must be going through his mind, and tugged him hard to get him back in his seat. But Yosef was too excited for that. He wanted to tackle the hijackers, though he didn't know how many there were. Lisette shouted: "What are you going to fight with? Your empty hands? They'll blow the plane up because of you! It's idiotic!"

Lisette grabbed the only thing near to hand, a glass of water, and flung it in her husband's face. That did the trick. Yosef, the man who was going to France to look for a job—and a way out of Israel—cooled down. He twisted his head to peer over the seats, but there was no way of seeing what was happening in the cockpit.

The terrorist with the gun shoved Jacques Lemoine aside, and pointed his weapon at the other crew members.

"Raise your hands," he ordered.

He began a quick body search of the second pilot, Daniel Lom—including his shoes. At that moment the girl also burst into the cockpit. The plane meanwhile was still responding to the automatic pilot. Michel Bacos was worried—and showed it. His craft, now steady at 21,000 feet, was picking up speed. That could be dangerous.

An alarm bell began to ring in the cockpit, startling the terrorist, who thought it was some kind of signal that the plane had been hijacked. He panicked.

"Sir," Michel Bacos, "I must reduce the engine speed immediately!"

Lemoine, gathering what was happening, added his voice: "Sir, we must deal with it."

The plane flew steadily on towards Benghazi, while the terrorist watched every move made by the pilot. For a moment it seemed to Michel Bacos that the man's attention had wavered. He gently moved the joystick over to a new course.

"No tricks," said the man—and Michel could do nothing else but correct back to course for Benghazi. The young man continued to watch him, while occasionally glancing at the map he held in his free hand.

In one more minute, precisely at 1 P.M., Pierre Leon, the Air France station manager in Israel, was going to end his work day. He gathered the papers from his desk in his pleasant office at 32 Ben-Yehuda Street. His home was five minutes away, but in slow-moving Tel Aviv traffic it might take a few minutes more. He had promised his wife he would be home early today to enjoy Sunday dinner with the family.

At exactly 12:59, Israeli time, the teleprinter began to chatter in Air France communications center a few steps from Mr. Leon's office: ALERT CABLE NUMBER ONE. RADIO CONTACT LOST WITH FLIGHT 139. AIRCRAFT VANISHED FROM RADAR SCREENS. SEEN SOUTH OF SUDA CRETE.

The message was rushed into Mr. Leon's office as he was about to leave. This was the last thing anybody could have expected at noon on a hot Sunday.

Ezra Blass dialed 02-6 0251 himself. He had been airport manager at Ben-Gurion Airport for three months, and there had already been plenty of dramatic moments at Israel's single international terminal. The knowledge he gained in aviation experience made him understand instantly that something serious had happened—serious enough not to wait for a secretary to put him through to the transport minister's office in Jerusalem.

"The minister isn't here," said his secretary, Aliza Eshed, from the other end of the line. "He's at a Cabinet session."

Ezra was momentarily at a loss, then Aliza's voice cut in again: "Hold on. I'll put you through to Ehud."

Ehud Gera was the transport minister's assistant. He and Gad Yaakobi, the minister, were not only partners in running one of the most problematic government departments, but were also good friends. They were coauthors of *The Right to Choose*, a political-sociological study of Israel's electoral system.

At forty-one, Gad Yaakobi was the youngest minister in the Israeli government. Born in a *moshav*—a cooperative agricultural community—he started his career of public work quite young, becoming deputy minister of transport during Shimon Peres' term as minister. Gad was just beginning his third year as a full-fledged cabinet minister, but transport was not his only interest. Like Shimon Peres, he had inherited from Ben-Gurion an ambition to make drastic changes in Israel's political system. For years now, Yaakobi had headed up a movement to reform the election system from country-wide proportional representation to local constituencies. He was considered by his colleagues to be an efficient and dynamic technocrat. And Ehud Gera was a loyal and devoted assistant in politics and ministerial matters.

"Ehud," Ezra Blass began, "Nicosia control tower picked up a message from Athens a few moments ago. They've lost contact with the Air France plane that left Lod this morning. There are Israelis on that plane. . . ."

Ezra, sitting in his second-floor office in the terminal building, was getting the reports direct from the control tower by intercom. While he was talking to Ehud, a message was placed on his desk.

"Hold it, Ehud. I've just been told that the plane has changed course for the southeast. It could also come back here. We must go on full alert!"

"Okay. I'll report to the minister straight away."

One floor below the cabinet conference room, in a spacious office facing the prime minister's room, sat Ephraim Poran, Rabin's military secretary. The Polish-born, forty-five-year-old advisor to the prime minister was entitled to sit in at Cabinet meetings, but on this Sunday at 1:32 P.M., he was more interested in reading the classified material that had arrived on his desk. He was interrupted by a call from the report center of the General Staff in Tel Aviv. Their news was brief: Athens Airport had lost contact with an Air France plane en route to Paris from Lod.

Ehud Gera was busy dialing the prime minister's office.

"Shula," he demanded of the receptionist, "call Gad out!"

Poran picked a paper out of the holder on his desk, and wrote in large firm letters:

P.M. [Prime Minister]:

CONTACT LOST WITH AIR FRANCE PLANE CARRYING MANY ISRAELIS. PLANE WAS ON WAY FROM ATHENS TO PARIS.

Transport Minister Gad Yaakobi left the Cabinet Room, where another minister was reviewing measures against the Arab boycott, and walked over to the telephone on Shula's desk. "Gad," Ehud said, "we have trouble." He told Yaakobi all he knew up to that point.

"Put Lod Airport on immediate alert," said the minister.

"Already done. . . ."

"Ehud, keep me in the picture. Shalom."

Yaakobi stood by the phone to write the essentials on a piece of paper, then returned, a little pale, to the conference room and put the note in front of the prime minister. Poran's note was brought to him a moment later. Yitzhak Rabin read both messages, then looked up at Defense Minister Peres, who had also received copies. Rabin cut short the minister who was speaking and reported the loss of contact with Air France 139 to the Cabinet:

"We do not yet know how many Israelis are on the plane, but it is clear there are a great many, and almost all the other passengers are Jews from France."

The prime minister promised to report any further news as it arrived, then resumed the routine discussions. The debate went on as if nothing had happened, though many of the ministers were obviously more interested in the plane, now somewhere over the Middle East, than in whether or not Israel would go on daylight savings time.

It was 1:57 P.M. when the bell of a teleprinter interrupted the *Yediot Aharonot* editorial offices in Tel Aviv.

The wire services use the bell to call attention to unusual news items as they arrive in client newspaper offices. The announcement coming in to the Tel Aviv evening paper had originated with Itim news services at Lod. Editorial secretary Katia Vered ripped the message off the teleprinter and rushed to phone the home of senior news editor Moshe Vardi.

Vardi's day normally started at four in the morning. Noon for him was religiously devoted to a nap, but not today. The telephone awakened him and from the other end, an excited Katia read him the message just in from Itim.

"Who's in the office?"

Usually, there were no journalists in the office at noon, but the sports editor of the paper was putting together a dummy of the Olympics Special that would be attached to a coming issue. Summoned to the telephone, he took the text of a banner headline for a special extra of *Yediot Aharonot* from Moshe Vardi: "Air France Plane Hijacked with Scores of Israelis."

Hysterical screams were coming from the first-class compartment of the Aerobus as it winged southeast across the Mediterranean, but the passengers hadn't noticed the change of course. They were being shoved back into the front rows of the tourist cabin.

Ruthi Gross was more than a little panic-stricken. When she realized that the plane had been hijacked, she suddenly remembered last night's parting from her good friend in Tel Aviv. The woman had hugged her and, instead of "happy landings," had said half-smilingly: "Watch out for terrorists." Now Ruthi, her husband Baruch, and their son Shai were in the hands of four of them.

The Grosses were on their way to the United States—their first trip abroad—to celebrate their twentieth wedding anniversary. One week earlier they had been on the verge of giving up the idea, after standing in line for hours at the American embassy to get an entry visa. The summer of 1976 saw tens of thousands of Israelis flying over to help America celebrate its Bicentennial.

A minute or two after the hijacking, while the uproar in the cabin was at a peak, the women and children were suddenly ordered to the front of the plane. Fearful for her young son, Ruthi stuck him between her knees, and covered him with her dress.

"Mother, what's happening?"

Ruthi was silent for a moment. Then she said: "There are terrorists on the plane."

The six-year-old Shai peeked out from the folds of the dress, and asked: "Mother, does it hurt to die?"

Ruthi heard but didn't answer. She would have liked to appear tough, but she found her voice choked with tears.

Not far from the Grosses sat Patricia Martel, Israeli citizen and resident of Petach Tikva. She was very sad. On Thursday night, she had picked up the phone to hear that her mother, Pearl Hyman, had died at home in Manchester, England. At eight o'clock the next morning, Patricia and Haim Martel were at the El Al offices in Tel Aviv—but El Al wanted $833 cash in advance, and the Martels didn't have that kind of money with them. Haim Martel, a technical photographer from England, and Patricia, a nurse at Sharon Hopital in Petach Tikva, looked for a quick way to Manchester at any price, but the planes were full until Sunday, and even then, only Air France had space. Patricia Martel didn't know that the Aerobus was scheduled to stop in Athens, but it wouldn't have made any difference. She was sunk in her own private thoughts when the two young men raced hysterically down the length of the aircraft and screams rent the air.

"Somebody must have gone crazy," Patricia murmured to herself. At that moment, a steward stopped in front of her, and seemed to confirm her diagnosis. "Someone has gone mad," said the distraught steward, "please stay calm."

Patricia understood almost immediately that she was mistaken. She suddenly felt cold and terrified.

Ron Davidson's eyes were frightened. From his seat in the middle of the tourist cabin, he watched the activity forward in first class. Stewards and passengers were rushing around in panic. Two dark-skinned young men were brandishing Beretta revolvers and hand grenades—their safety pins hanging from a little finger. Sara Davidson looked at her sons and heard, through all the tumult, the voice of her son Benny: "I don't want to die yet. It's so early."

The Davidson family had known plenty of troubles recently, and their trip abroad was designed to calm and relax them after the death of Sara's father and after her own serious surgery. Now Uzzi Davidson was holding her hand while she gripped Ron, who held on tight to Benny. "Boys, you'll see, we'll still go home to Israel and be together," Sara said. Then, Uzzi added a terse instruction: "If they separate the men from the women, the two of you stay with your mother!"

Sara, Ron, and Benny didn't answer, but their eyes told Uzzi all he needed to know: they understood him perfectly.

There had been twenty-six passengers in first class, but the compartment was now empty except for a few champagne glasses and some paper napkins. The hijackers pushed everyone into the tourist cabin, and those who couldn't find a vacant seat squatted in the aisles—an extra discomfort for people who had paid to fly to Paris in luxury. All the passengers were equal in their feelings of anxiety and fear.

Suddenly, the loudspeakers screeched—as if operated by somebody who was not sure of how they worked—and a voice boomed through the plane: "This is Captain Basil el-Koubeisi of the Che Guevara Force, the Gaza Commando of the Palestine Liberation Forces. The plane has been hijacked, and from now on will be called 'Haifa,' and

will answer only to that name. I would advise you to behave quietly for your own sakes, and no harm will come
to you."

El-Koubeisi? Che Guevara? What was the connection
between the two, and who was this Captain Basil el-
Koubeisi? Uzzi Davidson tried to remember where he had
heard the name before. A faint memory surfaced. If he
was right, then Dr. Basil Rauf Koubeisi was an Iraqi-born
professor at the American University in Beirut. According
to various sources, he was also a terrorist leader in Europe,
and apparently a member of the top brass of the Popular
Front for the Liberation of Palestine. He had been killed
by gunshots, fired by two strangers, in Paris on April 5,
1973. The terrorist organizations had claimed that Israelis
did it.

The voice over the loudspeaker was talking a stilted
English, with a German or perhaps South American accent, and the words were being translated into French by
one of the stewards. Patricia Martel tried to identify the
accent, and finally decided that the man must be South
American. Neither she nor any of the others had yet seen
his face. Patricia looked around and realized that, unlike
some of the others, she was in control of herself. There
were hysterical voices on all sides, speaking a variety of
languages: "They'll kill us! They'll slaughter us!" The passengers who weren't hysterical were trying to calm the
others, but not always successfully.

From up front, Patricia Martel was ordered to come to
the nervous, almost-hysterical young woman who was
standing in the service area by the entrance to first class.
As she approached, Patricia noticed the gun and hand
grenade in the girl's hands. It was her first meeting with
the terrorist, but Patricia noted something strange: this
woman terrorist was manly, a little bulky for her sex, yet
very femininely dressed and turned out. The thought
flashed across Patricia's mind that masculine appearance
and feminine dress didn't belong together.

The terrorist ran her hands over Patricia's body, looking for possible weapons, and the close proximity only served to strengthen Patricia's impression that here was a woman who looked and behaved exactly like a man. She wore silver-rimmed glasses and was very pale, gripping the pistol and grenade nervously. "Dear God," Patricia thought to herself, "if that grenade drops on the floor. . . ."

She felt the barrel of the pistol in her back, and the woman said in a metallic voice: "Okay, go back to your place!"

As she turned, the woman ordered her into the forward compartment, telling her to sit with her hands on her head. "That's also not an English accent," Patricia noted as she dropped into a seat and lifted her arms.

One by one the passengers were ordered up to the hijackers for a body search. It took a long time and it wasn't done too politely. The terrorists started with both men and women, but ended up checking only the men. They seemed to suspect that there were security men on board. A demand for all weapons to be thrown into the aisles yielded a poor crop: a few pocket knives, a kitchen knife left behind from an earlier meal, and a few forks.

One red penknife belonged to Yaakov, Hana Cohen's twelve-year-old son. The nervous terrorist girl hauled it roughly from the boy's pocket.

"You obviously have no children of your own," Yaakov said in halting English.

The girl was furious. She struck the child, then kicked him back toward his seat.

The tall, blond commander of the hijacking stayed in the cockpit, watching every move made by Captain Michel Bacos. The two did not talk unless it was absolutely necessary.

At 32 Ben-Yehuda Street, Pierre Leon already knew that this would be a terrible day. Immediately after "Alert Cable Number One," his secretary brought him "Alert

Cable Number Two," also from Air France at Athens Airport. This one read: POSITION OF PLANE NOT YET LOCATED. ASSUMING IT IS FLYING MALTA OR BENGHAZI. TIME IS 1:30.

Mr. Leon ordered his secretary to call his wife and tell her he wasn't coming for lunch, then asked her to get French ambassador Jean Herli on the phone immediately. Meanwhile he prepared a cable to Air France head office in Paris: REQUEST INSTRUCTIONS.

The prime minister's military secretary, Ephraim Poran, was in constant touch with the report center of the General Staff. A little after 2 P.M., the hijacked aircraft radioed Benghazi control tower in Libya demanding fuel sufficient for at least four hours' flight. Sometime later the hijack commander told Benghazi control tower: "This is 'Haifa.' Please have the Popular Front representative come to the airport."

"Assumed that Benghazi isn't the last stop," Poran wrote on a note to the prime minister.

"Libya will apparently only be a refueling stop," Yitzhak Rabin reported to the nineteen ministers.

The prime minister was already assuming this was going to be a tough and prolonged affair. He passed a note to his head of bureau: "Please convene Peres, Allon, Zadok, Galili, and Yaakobi in my office immediately after this session." Eli Mizrahi did as ordered. Rabin was following an already established practice of setting up a small ministerial team to deal with an urgent problem.

Patricia Martel asked the terrorist girl for permission to lower her arms, which were aching and cramped. The girl peered nearsightedly at her and asked: "Have you already been examined?" Apparently she had forgotten that she checked Patricia herself. Patricia answered in the affirmative and was allowed to lower her arms. She took a cigarette from her bag and lit it. Next to her was a young girl from Canada. They struck up a conversation in English, while Patricia occasionally glanced forward to the flight deck, looking through the open door. She could clearly see all the dials and lights as well as the blond hijacker who was holding his gun on Michel Bacos. The first officer was sitting among the passengers not far from Patricia.

Uzzi and Sara Davidson watched the two dark-skinned boys placing canisters by the emergency exits. A yellow-white fuse poked out of each. Uzzi was intrigued: were these really bombs or merely fakes? But 31,000 feet up, in a crowded plane, was no place to find out.

The terrorist in the cockpit was quiet and cool. He, unlike his comrades, had iron nerves. He seemed completely sure of himself in his elegant, light-colored suit. He picked up the loudspeaker and made an announcement to the passengers.

"I speak to you on behalf of the Popular Front for the Liberation of Palestine," he said in halting English, his gaze moving around the cabin. His speech was certainly not polished, but the hostages clearly understood the meaning of his words. "This hijacking is being carried out because of the Zionist crimes in Palestine and throughout the world," he said forcefully. "Israel has taken it upon herself to usurp territories and suppress peoples who are only fighting for their freedom, and she has had the vicious support of hostile nations such as Germany, France and the United States. France is a culprit!" the terrorist fairly screamed into the loudspeaker. "France has cooperated with the *Mossad*, Israel's intelligence agency, she has sold planes to Israel, and she has given Israel help in building atom bombs. It is therefore only just that the Popular Front retaliate."

These scathing accusations surprised the Israeli passengers, who knew that France was in fact supporting the terrorist's views, and that they in turn were trying not to harm French interests or operate on French soil.

Sara Davidson turned to Uzzi with a look of anger on her face. "I don't understand this airline. How can they let things like this happen?" Uzzi merely shrugged.

Close by the Davidsons was sitting a pale-faced Air France steward. Sara turned to him and asked in a cold tone: "Do you think you did enough to prevent the hijacking? Where are your security people?"

The miserable steward turned even paler: "We don't have security men! It's the policy of Air France!"

"And why was the flight deck door open? To help terrorists?"

"That's our policy! We don't lock the door."

The aircraft slowly quieted down. The two dark young men paced back and forth in the tourist cabin, keeping an eye on the passengers. From time to time, the woman called them over and gave them fresh instructions, but never mentioned their names. She called one of them "Comrade Thirty-Nine" and the other "Comrade Fifty-Five," referring to herself as "Comrade Ten."

By now, the Arabs were supervising a steady stream of passengers to the toilets. They were allowed to go one at a time, keeping their hands above their heads but, as the traffic increased, they were no longer escorted but merely watched over from the side.

The voice of "Captain Basil el-Koubeisi" again crackled over the speakers: "We are stopping in Libya to refuel, and will continue immediately to our next station."

Looking out of the window, Patricia Martel could see a vast expanse of sand. Realizing that they were very close to their first destination, she suddenly decided that she was going to get out of this: I must be there to sit *shiva* (the traditional week of mourning) for my mother, she thought to herself. She concentrated on becoming absolutely sure of herself and in believing that, in any case, after this she wasn't ever going on a plane again. Now she had nothing to lose.

Patricia was a hospital nurse, and she knew patients and illnesses. Forcing herself to remain calm and cool, she reviewed every detail of what she had to do, deciding that the critical "medical" stage would be presented only to the woman terrorist. "She's a woman—and only a woman would understand, if anybody will."

Patricia Martel screwed up her face in simulated agony. She blanched, perspired, began to twist and turn with pain, then called to the terrorist girl in a tortured voice: "I'm pregnant . . . second month . . . I think something's happened to me. . . ."

She again contorted her features and held her breath in agony. The terrorist was showing signs of sympathy. Apparently Patricia had made a good choice.

"I'll call a doctor," the girl said, meanwhile moving Patricia farther forward in the plane. In her new seat, Patricia again twisted around. She was pale and sweating—seemingly on the verge of coma.

It was a minute or two before a doctor, who looked like an American to Patricia, stood by her side. This was Dr. David Bass, and the nurse was partly right: he was American, but also head of gastroenterology at Kaplan Hospital in Israel. Patricia murmured: "I'm bluffing. I must get out of here. . . ."

There was a moment of silence and then the doctor said coldly in English: "You're better off on the plane than in Libya." The young Israeli woman from Petach Tikva suddenly felt as if condemned to death and on her way to the gallows.

The announcement about imminent landing at Benghazi, Libya, again created an uproar in the plane. Most of the Israelis thought of Libya as a backward Arab country ruled by a cruel and insane dictator. Some of the passengers also remembered that there was an open account for revenge. A Libyan Arab Airlines plane had been shot down over Sinai in February 1973, when the Libyan craft penetrated Israeli airspace and Israeli Phantoms were scrambled to intercept. They had signaled the pilot to follow them in to a military airfield, but he ignored them. Afterward it turned out that he thought he was near Cairo, and believed the jets to be Egyptian MIGs. His behavior became more and more suspicious and the Israelis, aware that Palestinian terrorists intended to hijack a plane and blow it up over Israel, opened fire as a warning. The Libyan crashed in flames, and 104 passengers and crew died in the wreckage.

Now, in the hijacked French plane, some of the Israelis were shrieking: "They'll slaughter us in Benghazi!" The quieter among them were trying to calm their hysterical companions.

The new uproar was depressing Uzzi, Sara, Ron, and Benny Davidson even more. The children clung to their parents, who were holding tightly to each other. The faces of the members of this family reflected everything that was going through their minds. Uzzi tried his best to calm the others: "The hijackers don't want to die either. They'll get the plane down safely."

Ilan Hartuv was looking out over parched landscape, a breakwater, and one runway. The plane circled for half an hour before coming in for a soft landing.

Patricia Martel decided that she wasn't going to spend another minute on board this plane. She was still pale and perspiring, looking for all the world as if she would faint at any moment, and the terrorist was obviously worried about her. She stroked Patricia's arm, and said: "The doctor will be here in a minute."

To ease her condition as much as possible, the girl now transferred Patricia into the empty first-class compartment and settled her carefully into a seat as though fully aware that it would be a terrible experience to miscarry in a plane in the middle of a hijacking. For a moment, the terrorist leader also came out of the cockpit to see the passenger who was ill. Patricia fixed him with a glassy stare, as if she did not know what it was all about. Every moment was precious, so she kept on calling for a doctor.

Her mind was made up—she wasn't going on with this crazy flight. She had to get off in Libya, no matter what it cost, and every added minute of waiting lessened her chances. Salvation came in the person of a Libyan doctor, who climbed aboard the plane which was now parked at the end of the runway. Patricia was very nervous. She knew that this man's ruling would determine whether or not she had succeeded in bluffing the terrorists.

The doctor laid his fingers across her left hand to feel her pulse. Patricia, a highly experienced nurse, felt like laughing. The doctor had put his hand at the wrong place. In the midst of all this, she couldn't help wondering about the standard of medical services in Libya if indeed this man was typical of the country's doctors.

Then the blow fell. The Libyan straightened up and said: "There's nothing wrong with her. Just frightened, that's all."

Of course, all the passengers were frightened. For no apparent reason the terrorists were exhibiting greater nervousness while the plane was on the ground. They had placed a round tin by the left-hand door of the plane out of which protruded a delayed-action fuse. Next to the right-hand door was a square tin, also complete with fuse. The terrorist in the yellow shirt—the one called "Comrade Thirty-Nine"—told the passengers that the doors were booby-trapped. Perhaps the tins were empty, but nobody was in the mood to check, particularly because of the drawn guns and hand grenades.

The Libyan authorities had no interest in the hijacked plane. Apart from their terse instructions on refueling the aircraft, there was no conversation between the Aerobus and the control tower. Air France 139 was parked on the most remote runway, supplied with a generator to keep the air conditioning working, fuel tankers to replenish its needs for a long flight—and a few crates of Egyptian mango juice. The anxious passengers met one of the ground crew, a man with uncombed hair who was wearing sandals, when he came aboard for a moment and introduced himself as representative of the government of Libya. He exchanged a few words with the hijackers and chatted with some of the passengers, but clearly the local government wasn't behind this—or even cooperating with the terrorists.

The temperature in the plane was pleasant, but the toilets were beginning to stink. Meanwhile, fuel continued to pour into the plane's tanks.

Patricia Martel held her breath. The Libyan doctor appeared ready to leave the plane. Then, as though in last-minute reprieve, she heard the doctor say: "I think the girl needs clinical treatment. I'll take her with me!"

There was a moment of silence in the plane. The terrorist girl listened to the doctor, but said nothing. It was "Comrade Fifty-Five" who agreed to let her go. Before she left, he asked for her passport.

Patricia almost panicked. She handed him the British document. Although she was now an Israeli citizen, she held two passports, having been born in England. He thumbed through it once or twice and wanted to keep it. She objected. "I don't get off without the passport!"

There was a short argument, then finally "Comrade Fifty-Five" gave in and handed her the British travel document. Taking it, she opened her bag and placed it carefully inside. She glanced at her Israeli passport and identity card as she slowly inserted the British passport next to the other documents and closed the bag.

Instead of moving toward the exit hatch, Patricia asked to go back to her original seat in the tourist cabin. Permission was given. Pushing through the crowd of passengers, she retrieved her cigarette case, then—without a glance at the sad faces of the other passengers—walked out the door escorted by the Libyan doctor.

Patricia Martel reached the doorway and didn't believe her eyes. No steps had been wheeled into place. For a fraction of a second she wondered whether the terrorists were testing her. A pregnant woman doesn't jump five feet from a plane hatchway to the ground below. She looked at the asphalt—and jumped. The Libyan doctor followed.

She was taken immediately to Benghazi Airport clinic, where she asked to see the British consul in Benghazi. She was informed that he was in Tripoli and had already been told that she was off the plane. Patricia would not be placated. She was afraid for her life as long as she didn't see a representative of Her Majesty's government. The Libyan doctor tried to console her, but couldn't.

After some time, she was transferred to a luxurious, carpeted, well-lit room, and was surrounded by Libyan policemen. They were most courteous and attentive, making a conscious effort to calm her—but it didn't help. Patricia Martel became increasingly pale and scared. First of all she was terrified at the thought that someone might go through her handbag and find the Israeli passport and blue identity card, so she decided on a preventive tactic. When one of the Libyans told her that, as a British subject, she had nothing to fear, she blurted out: "Yes, but I live in Israel."

In any case, the fact was recorded in her British passport, which the Libyans were passing around from hand to hand, reading it, handing it back, taking it again, and repeating the cycle.

Patricia didn't protest. Rather that than have them go through her handbag—which even held a membership card of the Labor Union Sick Fund in Israel. The Libyans behaved marvelously. They brought her an armchair, and placed it where she could see the portraits of Qadaffi and Nasser that hung on every wall. They brought her drinks and cigarettes, and smiled all the time as though their expressions might soothe her jangled nerves. But Patricia still didn't know what to expect.

At 3:10 P.M. "Alert Cable Three" landed on Pierre Leon's desk. It was slightly longer than the earlier messages: ATHENS CONTROL TOWER HAS JUST RECEIVED NEWS OF THE LANDING OF AEROBUS FLIGHT 139 AT 2:58 HOURS AT BENGHAZI AIRPORT.

"As we assumed," Yitzhak Rabin told his nineteen colleagues, "the plane has landed at Benghazi."

The Cabinet meeting was nearing its end, but the ministerial team appointed to deal with the crisis would obviously convene in the prime minister's office for a short session after this meeting was over.

Close to 4 P.M., the government session in Jerusalem came to an end. The ministers and their advisors dispersed, but only after the prime minister promised to keep them informed about forthcoming developments.

Within five minutes the six members of the special ministerial team were closeted with their advisors in the prime minister's own conference room, which was next to his office, a large, carpeted room on the first floor of the building, decorated with antiques. One of the walls bore a large map of the world, and the table covered in green cloth was amply stocked with ashtrays, pads, and pencils. One particularly noticeable decoration was a satellite photo of Israel in full color taken by astronaut Walter Schirra in October 1968.

Yitzhak Rabin's choice of team seemed natural. The prime minister and foreign minister were at any time the senior political persons for preparation of any particularly difficult security or diplomatic decision. The minister of justice often joined them because of his experience and familiarity with international law. Minister-without-Portfolio Galili, in this government as in the one before it, was considered to have exceptional talent in framing political formulations, and had been known on occasion to keep Israeli governments out of serious trouble. The new addition this time was Gad Yaakobi, although this wasn't the first time in his career that he had participated as part of a limited ministerial body. Yaakobi had been chosen because as minister of transport, he bore the public responsibility for civil aviation to and from Israel.

The six ministers convening for their first session had very little information with which to work. Their senior advisors were also seated at the long narrow table: the director general of the Prime Minister's Office Amos Eran, director general of the Foreign Ministry Professor Shlomo Avineri, military secretary to the prime minister Brigadier Ephraim Poran, the military secretary to the defense minister Brigadier Arye Braun, the chief of bureau and political advisor to the prime minister Eli Mizrahi, and Rabin's spokesman Dan Patir.

A number of decisions were taken at this first meeting as the ministers obviously feared for the safety of the Israelis on board Air France 139.

1. The foreign minister will contact his French counterpart to clarify to the government of France the position of the government of Israel, according to which the responsibility for the safety of all the passengers is that of France, since she is the owner of Air France. The foreign minister will demand that France do everything in its power to release all the passengers without any discrimination.

2. The minister of transport will urgently approach the president of the ICAO (International Civil Aviation Organization) and will demand vigorous action for the release of the passengers.

3. The ministry of transport will set up a special liaison office to deal with the families of the hijacked passengers.

4. The managing director of El Al, Mordechai Ben-Ari, will bring pressure to bear on the president of Air France, and on IFALPA (International Federation of Airline Pilots Association), by means of the Israeli Pilots Association.

5. The security network, through all its arms, will take the necessary steps against the possibility of the plane landing in Israel after its takeoff from Benghazi.

6. The minister of transport will take on himself the contacts with communications media in Israel, and will approach those responsible for communications media, to prevent publication of news that is not based on government intentions in the affair of the aircraft. The minister of transport will also demand of all the media in Israel to desist at this stage from publishing a list of the passengers. The names are to be given only to members of their families.

Against all predictions, it was a very short meeting.

Before the ministers and their assistants dispersed, Yitzhak Rabin asked Foreign Minister Allon and Transport Minister Yaakobi not to publish any communiqué without coordinating it with him, and without his prior approval. He instructed his spokesman, Dan Patir, to stay in touch with the two ministers to assist with any official pronouncement.

Rehavam Zeevi seemed pensive as he came down the steps from El Al Boeing 747 on flight 016 from New York to London on Sunday, June 27, 1976. Zeevi was a general on the IDF reserve list, appointed two years ago as the prime minister's advisor, and therefore the senior Israeli official on intelligence and counter-terrorist warfare. He brought considerable experience to this job from his years in the IDF as commanding general, Central Command. He had succeeded in sealing the Jordanian border against infiltrators and had caught hundreds of members of the terror organizations in the occupied areas under his jurisdiction.

In Israel, Rehavam Zeevi, fifty years old, was known to all as "Gandhi" because somewhere back in his youth he had dressed up as the Indian leader for a costume party, and had appeared complete with a goat on a leash. For twenty-seven years, he had been party to some of the most important security decisions, and had taken part in more than 120 manhunts after the terrorist teams—in which he developed the techniques used along the Jordanian front.

"Gandhi" came to London from Montreal, where he had been checking the security arrangements for the Israeli Olympic delegation, which was due to arrive in Canada in a few days. He went there to do some final checking so that there would be no repetition of what happened in Munich in 1972.

He came down the steps from the El Al jumbo at Heathrow Airport to find an airline security officer waiting for him.

"Shalom. They took an Air France plane out of Athens this morning."

Gandhi listened to the few available details and asked to be taken to the security officer's room in order to phone the Prime Minister's Office in Jerusalem for instructions. Then he asked permission to continue home, instead of making his planned visit to a few European countries. He was given orders in the prime minister's name: stay in London for operational reasons.

In the evening, Gandhi had wanted to visit friends but his mind was elsewhere—on the steps being taken in Israel, without him.

Four bored Libyan soldiers were standing some tens of yards back from the Aerobus. A number of fire engines stood by—just in case. A generator was supplying power for the air conditioning, but that was the total extent of Libyan involvement with the plane. They simply did not seem to be interested in the plane or its human cargo. From the little that Captain Michel Bacos overheard, all the Libyans wanted was for the plane and its passengers— including the terrorists—to move on from Benghazi as soon as physically possible.

Inside the plane, the passengers were finding it difficult

to stay seated. Almost twelve hours had passed since the plane had left Lod. People were trying to find a comfortable way to sit, to stretch out, but it just wasn't possible. Any activity in the plane had become an intolerable nuisance and the situation was not helped by the fact that several passengers were forced to sit in the aisles. The trip to the toilets was an obstacle course. The lavatory basins were blocked. It was difficult to maintain any kind of cleanliness, and the interior of the Aerobus was fast becoming a rubbish dump.

Some of the exhausted passengers fell asleep in their seats, possibly as an escape from the nightmare. But even the few sleepers were awakened by the loudspeaker. Apparently the terrorist up front had pressed the wrong button. His voice reverberated through the cabin: " 'Haifa' calling Benghazi tower. . . ." The announcement cut off abruptly as he realized what he had almost done, then— after a few minutes of silence, his voice came through again with a series of crisp orders for the passengers: "You are required to hand over all your documents. Every paper that gives evidence of your identity must be given to us, and anyone who doesn't comply and who is caught hiding any paper will be punished without mercy."

A steward translated into French, and the hijackers began to move along the aisles collecting the papers. They were handed passports, driving licenses, identity cards, military identification, all of which was crammed into a big nylon bag.

The stewardesses served a cold but tasty dinner accompanied by cans of mango juice. There were all the signs of imminent takeoff. Again, the terrorist officer spoke from the flight deck. He courteously asked the passengers' forbearance for the discomfort, and promised that they would be moving on very soon. "I thank you for your patience in the first part of our flight. I hope you will continue to behave the same way for the continuation."

The Libyan soldiers moved back from the Aerobus parked at Benghazi.

Patricia Martel marveled at the luxurious and spotless lounge of Benghazi Airport, which resembled an Oriental-style guest room. She was still sitting there when a Libyan civilian arrived and shook hands with her: "I'm your friend. I'm Ahmad," he announced.

Ahmad was the driver assigned as Patricia Martel's escort until she left Libya. He also brought her an airline ticket, and told her that she would be flying out the next morning at 8:30. There was still a whole night ahead of her, and once again she demanded to see the British representative in Libya. He finally appeared, late that evening, meticulously dressed in an elegant black suit as befitted the emissary of the United Kingdom. "You are being looked after by Her Majesty's government," he told her in cool, reserved, and official tones. After exchanging a few words, he left, partly because the Libyan authorities wouldn't let him stay. But Patricia Martel had calmed down. Having seen him, she knew that it would be difficult to come to harm in Libya.

After he left, Ahmad suggested that she move to a Benghazi hotel for the night. She didn't want to leave the airport, and was scared of missing the plane next morning. She already knew that there were only two flights a week from Benghazi to London, and she couldn't afford to miss the next one. Ahmad and the other Libyans were insistent, and most politely, they suggested that she move to a hotel. Finally, Patricia agreed and was taken to the Geneira Palace Hotel in town.

This was another surprise for Patricia. The Geneira Palace was five-star luxury. The Libyans arranged a pleasant room for her and, after a day of tension, anxiety and fear, she sank down gratefully onto a well-sprung bed and—within seconds—was asleep.

* * *

Israeli security forces still waited at Ben-Gurion Airport.

In Jerusalem, the prime minister suggested that there should be an interdepartmental staff set up for information collection and coordination of activity with the ministerial team. The suggestion was accepted. The staff now included the prime minister's military secretary, the director general of the Foreign Ministry, the defense minister's military secretary, and the transport minister's assistant.

It was difficult to foresee with any certainty the degree of cooperation and coordination in the ministerial team and that of their assistants. Poran had been brought in by Rabin when he needed a loyal colleague and efficient liaison with the security agencies within his jurisdiction. All the criticism leveled at Rabin in recent months had not weakened Poran, or detracted from his loyalty or faith in the prime minister. In fact, quite the opposite. As the criticism grew, Poran took on a job that seemed almost impossible—to win over friends. He was the man who pointed out Rabin's successes to journalists. His wit and special sense of humor, his natural warmth and endless devotion, eased the common labor and opened up the access to the media whose support Yitzhak Rabin so badly needed.

Brigadier Arye Braun's activity on behalf of the defense minister was less noticeable than Brigadier Poran's, but was no less effective or efficient. It would have been difficult to find anyone more loyal or devoted than Arye Braun in Shimon Peres' entourage. He had fulfilled a similar function for the previous minister, Moshe Dayan.

Ehud Gera was a friend of his superior, Gad Yaakobi, but was also close to the defense minister and his staff. He could indeed be classified as a member of the Peres camp, while Professor Shlomo Avineri was a close confidant of his minister, Yigal Allon. His appointment as director general of the Foreign Ministry, three months before the hijacking, had been the subject of sharp controversy in

Israel because Avineri was known for his liberal views on the Palestinian question.

At the time of the Air France hijacking, the government of Israel could count on only limited support among the Israeli public. The weaknesses of the regime were noticeable. When the government was formed in June 1974 under Yitzhak Rabin, the man who had been chief of staff in the Six Day War and Israeli ambassador to Washington, its watchword had been "continuation and change"—continuation of the policy of the previous government, while making changes without causing tremors.

Two years later, there were some who—rightly or wrongly—saw Rabin's government as continuation without change. Quite a few were ready to argue that the prime minister had not displayed the expected qualities of leadership, and had not succeeded in infusing new life into the trust and self-confidence that had been characteristic of Israelis up to the Yom Kippur War in October 1973. That faith and confidence had been hard hit in the war. More and more was now being written to the effect that Rabin and his government had wasted the vast fund of credit that the public had been prepared to extend when they came to power.

There was a continuing personal rivalry between Rabin and Peres, which did not derive from fundamental differences over policy or security, but rather from differences in mentality. This rivalry had been greatly responsible for creating the sterile atmosphere in the upper ranks of Israeli politics and government over the last year, and had weakened the public image of the government. A year and a half before general elections, due in the fall of 1977, it was already clear that Peres and Rabin would be competing for the premiership when the electoral list was presented by their party to the voters. The previous competition between them had been in May 1974, when Rabin had won a majority of the Labor party vote, but beat Peres only by a narrow margin.

On June 27, 1976, as the government of Israel was called on to deal with the affair of the hijacked Air France plane, it was clear to all the ministers and political observers in Israel that this affair could spell the downfall of the government, and of the men who led it. Bad handling would put an end to the political careers of the ministers. A success could restore the public faith that had been lost over the past year.

In the evening, Prime Minister Rabin returned to his Jerusalem home and received the latest information from Brigadier Poran over the phone. Across town, at the Foreign Ministry, one of the deputy directors general remained on duty right through the night on the instructions of Foreign Minister Allon.

El Al managing director Mordechai Ben-Ari phoned the minister of transport. He had a message from the management of Air France: "There are on the plane seventy-seven passengers of Israeli nationality."

In the Air France sales department on Hayarkon Street, right near the company's head office on Ben-Yehuda, Pierre Leon had long forgotten his missed lunch and the dinner he never had. He had been working since the early afternoon with a dozen employees of the company to inform the families of passengers about the hijacking of Air France 139. In almost none of the cases had the families been taken by surprise. They had already spent half the day, ears glued to their radios listening for news on the whereabouts of the French Aerobus.

At Benghazi Airport, after taking on forty-two tons of fuel, the hatches of the plane again swung into place. Michel Bacos started his engines. The dull throb penetrated the cabin, and the renewed activity of the terrorists also served to waken any passengers who had dozed off. The familiar voice again crackled out of the loudspeakers: "We are taking off and will be flying for about three hours. Sit quietly and no harm will be done you."

As the plane rolled out to the runway, Michel Bacos applied full throttle. Within a minute, they were airborne, with the lights of Benghazi twinkling below.

The hands of the clock stood at 9:35 P.M., the evening of June 27, 1976.

CHAPTER THREE

"The Taste of Jewish Blood"

Arye Chizik, an employee of Israel's national water utility, was the first Israeli to meet Arab terrorism in its modern reincarnation. That was on January 3, 1965, eleven years before the first Hercules landed at Entebbe Airport. That morning, a sack floated down the waters of the national network toward where Arye was standing. Bending over, he pulled it from the canal and found an explosive charge, complete with detonator.

Chizik promptly called in the security services. It wasn't clear who had dropped the sack in the water or why. Few people in Israel, and they mostly professional intelligence agents, even knew of the existence of a terror organization called "Fatah." The country had been living more or less in peace since the 1956 Sinai Campaign, which had eliminated the Egyptian-sponsored *fedayeen* sabotage and murder squads. But for the various incidents on the Syrian frontier, there was nothing to worry the average Israeli.

The water-soaked sack of explosives at once stirred the headquarters of Israel's security services to action. Arab armies and organizations had made no secret of their intention to sabotage the canals and installations of the water network, contending that the waters were "stolen" from Syria. The precious fluid was vital to Israel, and her security forces had promised to protect it—no matter what the price. A special border police detachment watched over mile after mile of canals and concrete spillways, and the Sea of Galilee pumping station was turned into a fortress.

Investigation showed that the sack of explosives had been put in the canal near the Netufa Valley in northern Israel by saboteurs who came on horseback from Jordan, and returned there when their job was done. A day or so later, Fatah claimed responsibility.

Fatah's first appearance on the terrorism scene was thus totally mismanaged. The demolition charge itself and the way it had been placed gave evidence of inexperience and primitive tools. The tendency in the Israeli government was to be contemptuous of this operation but in order to discourage any encore, military censorship moved in to prevent general knowledge of the event. However, the Fatah announcement in Damascus, and pressure brought to bear by Israeli military correspondents allowed the curtain to rise on the new terrorist organization's first attempt at sabotage.

Security officers reopened the files of IDF Intelligence Branch and discovered that a Fatah cell had been created in the universities of Cairo and Alexandria as long ago as the early 1950s, by one Yasir Arafat. Its formal foundations were laid in 1958, when the group began to publish a newsletter in Beirut entitled *Our Palestine*. Syria allowed the Fatah to begin military operations only early in 1965.

Arab terrorism had been the companion of Jewish settlement ever since the turn of the twentieth century. No single year had passed without clashes and blood spilled on both sides. On occasion, there were outbursts of violence that involved thousands. For the most part, the Jewish settlers held on tenaciously and gained the upper hand. This was the case in the round of bloody clashes that followed the UN decision to partition Palestine on November 29, 1947, which lasted until David Ben-Gurion declared Israel's independence in May 1948. The local Arab gangs dragged the regular Arab armies into a full-scale invasion of Israel that began on the night of May 15 of that year.

When the war ended in March 1949, the marauder gangs once again began terrorizing the settlements, particularly those on the borders. Thousands of Israelis, many of them new immigrants, forgot what it meant to sleep at night. Infiltrators penetrated the farming communities, broke into homes, murdered men, women, and children, stole anything and everything that was movable, sowed land mines, and ambushed traffic on the roads.

Arab terrorism reached a new peak in the mid-1950s when suicide squads were formed in the Gaza Strip and Jordan at Egyptian instigation. They were trained for bold guerrilla operations, and units of these *fedayeen*—which translates as something akin to "fighters prepared for sacrifice"—succeeded in infiltrating Israeli daily life. They murdered children in schools, watchmen in orange groves, families in their homes. Israel retaliated with a series of raids into Egypt and Jordan, which reached their peak in the war of 1956 in which the IDF occupied the Sinai Peninsula and the Gaza Strip, and methodically wiped out the nests of *fedayeen*. Major Mustapha Hafex, the commander of these squads, lost his life when a book delivered to him exploded in his hands. The Arabs obstinately claim that Israel was responsible for that "execution."

The eight years of post-1956-war tranquility ended with the appearance of Yasir Arafat's Fatah. The first incidents were unimpressive: demolition charges placed next to houses, warehouses, and pumping stations well clear of the watchful eyes of Israel soldiers. The Fatah saboteurs obviously did not want to take any chances, and were so wary, in fact, that many of their explosive packets were installed in deserted hovels and near remote telephone poles. Israel's reprisals, at the insistence of then Chief of Staff Yitzhak Rabin, were basically warnings: the IDF demolished fuel stations, water wells, and houses that offered shelter to the saboteurs.

The sabotage and terror missions became bolder, but without much success, mostly because the terrorists' equipment was so primitive and they lacked the essential willingness to risk their lives. Many of them were criminals released from Jordanian penitentiaries who agreed to undertake missions in return for a handful of dinars: the going rate was 15 dinars per job, about $42. However, the growing number of incidents, in which Israeli lives were being lost, moved the IDF to take more vigorous action, almost entirely against Jordan, which was extending patronage, home bases, and training facilities to the saboteurs.

The Six Day War swelled the chest of the average Israeli. In a 140-hour whirlwind, the IDF crushed the armies of Egypt, Syria, and Jordan, and occupied vast tracts of Sinai, the West Bank, and the Golan Heights. Stupendous victory dazzled Israel and put a temporary end to terrorist activities, since the various groups were in a state of shock. And it seemed to Israelis, after the elimination of three well-equipped regular armies, that the amateurish terrorists didn't stand a chance against the fist of the IDF.

Nevertheless, not long after the war, the terror organizations were back at work with growing intensity and efficiency. Many youngsters from the West Bank escaped to Jordan to join the ranks of Fatah, then returned, equipped with demolition materials, to an area where they knew every home and pathway. Israel responded firmly, but terrorist activities were still of minor import, evidencing the very limited capability of those in charge.

In the third week of July 1968, the El Al office in Rome was visited by a priest who wanted three tickets from Rome to Lod. An El Al clerk asked for passports. The priest produced his own Indian document and the two

Iranian passports of his companions. For the record, the clerk noted that the three passengers could be reached if necessary at the Imperial Hotel in Rome.

Nobody checked baggage at Fiumicino Airport. Nobody asked any questions. Thirty-eight passengers and ten crew members boarded an El Al Boeing 707, on flight 426 from Rome to Tel Aviv. The date was July 23, 1968. On board were twenty-eight Israelis and ten others, of whom seven were Italian priests making a pilgrimage to the Holy Land.

Twenty minutes after takeoff, three of the passengers stood up and walked down the aisle into the unprotected cockpit of the Boeing. A shot was heard, startling the other passengers. The cockpit door opened and first officer Maoz Poraz came out, his face streaming with blood.

Poraz, who died five years later in the Yom Kippur War, was the first to notice the three men as they entered the flight deck. Since they did not seem like the type who show casual curiousity about flying, he tried to block their way. One of them shot him. Their takeover of the aircraft was complete within two minutes. The hijackers ordered Captain Oded Abarbanel to change course for Algeria. They were obviously all extremely nervous, and told the passengers to raise their hands, the youngest among them adding a suggestion to the priests that they pray. "Perhaps God will hear you," he said. Turning to the other passengers, he added: "If you don't sit quietly—we will all go!"

As the plane flew on toward Algeria, the same youngster stood beside Maoz Poraz, dipped his finger in the still-streaming blood, and put it to his lips. "How tasty is the blood of a Jew," he said.

The hijacking of an El Al plane en route from Rome to Lod shook the Israeli public. Until July 23, 1968, the average Israeli had shown little or no interest in newspaper stories about hijacked aircraft. Indeed, most of the reported cases were American domestic flights diverted to Cuba, and these incidents seemed more to cause more in-

convenience than actual danger. Passengers, crew, and
planes were always released, usually after a pleasant overnight interlude in a Havana hotel. The human cargo had
never been used as hostages.

The first hours after the news of the El Al hijacking
reached Israel were bewildering and difficult. Though intelligence data had indicated the possibility of a hijacking,
nobody really thought it would happen. Israel was not
equipped, and certainly not ready, for this kind of terrorism.
It wasn't even clear who in the government of Israel was
responsible: was it in the jurisdiction of the Transport
Ministry or the Defense Ministry? Did it concern El Al,
or perhaps the country's security service, the *Shin Bet*?

Israel was confused, but the hijackers knew exactly what
they were doing. Within an hour of landing at Maison
Blanche Airport outside Algiers, the Israelis among the
passengers and crew of the El Al Boeing were separated
from the others. Within a few more hours the non-Israelis
were free to leave Algeria, and the Israelis were housed
in an army camp. In return for their release, Dr. George
Habash's Popular Front for the Liberation of Palestine
was demanding the liberation of a number of convicted
terrorists who were serving time in Israeli prisons.

The hijackers hadn't asked Algerian government permission to land at Maison Blanche. As far as the Algerian
government was concerned, they were presented with a
fait accompli, but they promptly accepted the role that
the hijackers expected of them. The official Algerian newspaper, *Al Mujahad*, praised the hijackers the next day,
claiming that El Al, unlike other civil air carriers, was
legitimate prey for Palestinian commandos.

Within thirty-six hours, Israel launched a campaign
aimed at world public opinion, foreign governments, and
airlines. Official spokesmen stated that hijacking of aircraft was an international matter, that the El Al incident
would only be the beginning of a wave that would strike
at every airline in every country, that this act of piracy

would serve as a model for other terrorist groups, and that international restraint in the face of this kind of extortion would turn out to be an expensive luxury. There was also talk of international law and order. Israeli ambassadors requested, explained, almost begged, but the free world was busy with other matters. England, France, Germany, and the United States acted deaf, dumb, and blind. Apart from a few noncommittal statements, nothing was done. Israel was alone in the face of the first real attempt at piracy in the skies.

Israel began secret government-level deliberations on whether to give in to the hijackers' blackmail. The hostages themselves made the decision much easier when they told the Israeli authorities that they were quite willing to remain in captivity a lot longer, rather than see convicted terrorists walk out of prison. Other countries tried to bring pressure to bear on the rulers of Algeria, but the answer was adamant insistence on an exchange for imprisoned terrorists.

Israel tried to gain time and postpone surrender. She suggested aerial boycott of any country that supported or helped the new breed of pirates, but nobody took the suggestion seriously. The world remained silent, while Egypt, accused by Israel of instigating the entire affair, crowed delightedly: "The Israeli accusation does us great honor."

Meanwhile the days were passing by. Since the plane had been hijacked just out of Fiumicino, the Italian government was called in to mediate between Israel, Algeria, and the Popular Front. Finally, with no other alternative, the Israeli government decided to trade fifteen terrorists for the hostages. The Israeli passengers and crew returned home on August 31, 1968, after forty days of captivity.

The El Al hijacking suddenly confronted Israeli security with the dreadful fact that the country's air traffic was vulnerable. With hostile neighbors on three sides, Israel was all the more dependent on free air and sea access. Three unknown members of the Popular Front had made

Israel appear vulnerable. After a brief panic, the security services again proved their ability to improvise.

Almost immediately after the hijacking, telephones began to ring in homes throughout Israel. Veteran soldiers, mostly paratroopers, were recalled to form a special unit for the protection of El Al aircraft. The response of the "old warhorses" was all that could be desired. With no time for planning, they were armed with pistols and dispatched to El Al stations everywhere in the world. No more El Al planes were going to fly without security men on board.

After the first rush and a number of discussions and consultations, a special training course was started, volunteers were invited, instructors were chosen, and detailed methods were prescribed for the protection of passengers, crew, and aircraft.

There were serious problems. Although foreign governments were understanding, they could not permit aliens— including Israelis—to carry weapons in their territory, even if only for self-defense. And Israel was at a disadvantage. The Arab countries could always disown terrorists on the contention that they did not represent their nation, but Israel could not hide behind the skirts of unofficial organizations. The defenders had to have full and unreserved official backing.

Some countries, particularly in Europe, did cooperate with their own security agencies and police forces, but almost all of them insisted that Israel say nothing about it, lest it invite the terrorists' attention. Israel also asked Interpol to help, and forwarded secret information to their Paris headquarters, only to discover that the Arabs had gotten hold of it and they in turn had passed it on to the terrorist organizations.

For a short while the whole world, but again particularly the Europeans, were in the grip of a psychosis on the subject of terrorism. Anyone with a dark skin was suspect, and police forces were flooded with thousands of worried phone calls. But the concern eventually passed and the world once again became apathetic.

This apathy, of course, only encouraged the terrorists. Freedom and the concept of open frontiers were exactly what the underground cells thrived on. Fatah and the Popular Front established bases in almost every country of Europe and went on to appoint commanders, train men, and prepare secret arsenals of weapons and sabotage materials.

The worst thing the terrorists could do was hijack aircraft, and twentieth-century technological development made air piracy quite easy. Any flight would be loaded with passengers and would have tons of highly inflammable fuel on board, so it was extremely unlikely that passengers or crew would offer any resistance. Almost immediately after the Algerian incident, some airlines made a point of announcing publicly that they had no interest in waging airborne battles with terrorists, and that their crews had been ordered not to resist. Others stated that they would not allow armed security men on board. What had seemed to be one of twentieth-century man's greatest advantages had become a potential nightmare. But Israel could not allow herself the luxury of aircraft which would be unprotected against terrorism.

Meanwhile, newspapermen representing the world press were manufacturing banner headlines on the security measures adopted by El Al. Much of the detail was purely imaginary but occasionally there were factual items. It was reported, for example, that armed Israeli security officers were sprinkled among the passengers. According to the journalists, these boys could pick off a terrorist with one bullet, fired the length of the passenger cabin. And then, of course, there was the steel wall separating the crew from the passengers, and all the electronic-surveillance paraphernalia installed in the planes.

The considerable data published in the world press was

also read by the terrorist organizations, who realized that El Al aircraft had become "Flying Fortresses." Next time it wouldn't be so easy to hijack one of the blue and white Boeings.

Members of Dr. George Habash's Popular Front planned their second strike against El Al in the light of the lessons of the first. Assuming that there was no chance of hijacking from inside, they decided to try from the outside.

On December 26, 1968, two terrorists attacked an El Al plane on the ground at Athens Airport. They opened fire and threw hand grenades, killing one Israeli passenger and wounding two stewardesses. The terrorists were arrested by Athens police, but released later after the hijacking of an Olympic Airlines plane. Israel reacted with terrible fury. An IDF force descended on Beirut Airport and destroyed thirteen aircraft.

Dr. Habash's organization staged a similar action in February 1969, at Kloten Airport, Zurich, this time with four terrorists. When they moved in to attack the El Al plane which was taxiing to takeoff point, a young Israeli security officer jumped from the plane and shot the leader. He was tried before a Swiss court and found innocent. But the fast reaction of the security officer, Mordechai Rahamim, confirmed that there were indeed Israeli security agents "riding shotgun" on El Al aircraft.

The Popular Front officers had another lesson to learn from their next two attempts to hit El Al on the ground— once parked and once taxiing to takeoff: this method was no easier given present security conditions. And so, in August 1969, they chose to strike at an unexpected and less-protected target: a TWA flight from Rome to Lod was hijacked by two terrorists and forced to land at Damascus. There were only two Israeli men among the passengers, but Israel was asked for—and gave up in return for their release—two Syrian pilots who had landed by mistake in her territory.

Strikes at planes destined for Tel Aviv while still on the

ground resulted almost immediately in increased security measures around the aircraft. Israeli agents were now stationed on the ground. Every El Al landing and takeoff began to look almost like a military operation. On the runways, a plane would be escorted by police vehicles, sometimes armored cars, soldiers or armed police, vast numbers of weapons, and a lot of communications equipment. At Addis Ababa, for example, an El Al landing involved 800 Ethiopian paratroops as guard detail. El Al seemed totally inviolate, though there were still many headaches for airport security police.

Terrorist intelligence agents were quick to detect this frantic activity in and around the planes. Obviously, they would have to find a new point of attack to hurt Israel's air traffic. The battle of wits between Israeli security and Arab terrorist squads was on in full fury and, as always, the attacker with his unconventional methods enjoyed somewhat of an advantage.

They found a weak point. In February 1970, three terrorists attacked a Munich airport bus that was carrying passengers out to a parked El Al airliner. One Israeli was killed and eight were wounded, among them Hana Meron, a star of the Israeli theater. Shots were fired at the terrorists, and all three were caught—yet there was no doubt that they had found a security loophole. The guards were doubled in and around the planes, on the airport buses, and at the El Al desks in the terminal buildings.

The Israeli hierarchy now set their minds to the task of determining where the terrorists could still strike. Tens of millions of dollars were invested in men and installations in an attempt to outguess the adversary, but not even the most wildly imaginative mind could have foreseen the next horror.

On February 21, 1970, only eleven days after Munich, a breakaway faction of the Popular Front led by Ahmad Jibril planted a package of explosives on board a Swissair plane en route from Zurich to Tel Aviv. The charge was detonated at a given altitude by a pressure-sensitive device. The Swiss pilot tried to land his burning plane, but it was impossible; all thirty-eight passengers and nine crew were killed. That same day, another package—also the work of Ahmad Jibril—exploded in the cargo hold of an Austrian plane; damage was done, but the plane landed safely.

The Swissair and Austrian Airlines packages were a relatively cheap and easy solution for the terrorists. They were not risking their own lives this way and could cause the deaths of a great many people for only the cost of airfreight charges on a small parcel.

One successful and one unsuccessful attempt at blowing a plane and its passengers out of the skies caused world public opinion to react in horror at the lives lost. There was obviously no limit to the ruthless inventiveness of the terrorists, which was proving to be far beyond the worst predictions of Israeli intelligence. This time the airlines were also badly shaken. Overnight, the security procedures of airports were augmented. Agents began to probe passenger baggage and search their pockets. Unaccompanied bags and parcels were thoroughly checked. Air cargoes were subjected to varying pressures in specially prepared chambers. Instruments to detect firearms and explosives were installed at passenger and baggage check-in points. Another crack was sealed, but the terrorist groups were not ready to give up on air traffic to and from Israel.

In September 1970, George Habash put in motion the Popular Front's biggest operation yet, on the justified assumption that nothing short of a huge demonstration would remind the world of the piteous state of the Palestinians. On September 6, three planes were hijacked in the space of one day—one to Cairo and two to Zarka in Jordan. Four hundred human beings were trapped in terrorist hands. This time the world was outraged: there had been nothing on such a scale before. Old people, women, and children were held on an improved airstrip in the Jordanian desert, waiting and praying for salvation. And before the world had time to draw its breath, on September 9, a BOAC airliner en route from Bahrein to London was hijacked to Zarka to join the other three.

On the day that the first three were taken, another attempt was made on an El Al plane flying from Amsterdam to London. A terrorist using a Colombian passport made out in the fake name of Patrick Arguello, and an Arab girl named Leila Haled, who had commanded the TWA hijacking to Damascus, tried to take the Israeli jet. In a short clash inside the plane, the Colombian died from a gunshot wound. Leila Haled was overpowered and could easily have been killed, but the Israeli security officer who caught her brought her back to London's Heathrow Airport. Leila was handed over to the British police, only to be released a few days later. The security officer lost his job.

The wholesale seizure of aircraft and passengers who were in no way involved in the war between Israel and the Arabs created chaos on the international airways. All of civil air transport might actually be in peril.

Israel's situation was particularly grim. Though there were no Israelis among the hostages at Zarka, the perpetrators obviously intended to whip up British, American, and Swiss pressures on Israel to release convicted terrorists. Meanwhile, the passengers spent a few days under the desert sun, penned in by machine gunners. The IDF began to plan a military operation to rescue the four hundred captives. However, on the recommendation of the General Staff, and with the blessing of then Defense Minister Moshe Dayan, a decision was taken to work through nonmilitary channels for the time being. Within one day and night, Israel's security forces detained hundreds of relatives of Popular Front leaders. The relatives were picked up in towns and villages on the West Bank, and six of them were taken to the Jordanian border. Once across, the delegation lost no time in contacting Popular Front headquarters and informing the terrorists that their kin were in

Israeli prisoner pens. The hint was clear: if anything happened to the four hundred hostages at Zarka, the lives of the terrorists' relatives in Israel would also be in jeopardy.

There was no need for more than that hint, which was also leaked to the government and king of Jordan. Acting on the instructions of King Hussein, the Jordanian army moved in against the terrorists and liberated the hostages, but not before the hijacked aircraft were demolished.

Meanwhile Hussein had begun the counter-measures and massacre of the terrorists that was to give birth to "Black September."

CHAPTER FOUR

The Dentist

The soldiers in an IDF forward position, overlooking the River Jordan and the Hashemite Kingdom on the other bank, were astounded. They could see the heads of several Arab youngsters poking out from among the reeds on the waterline and the boys were shouting in terrified voices: "Help! We want to cross to your side!"

The officer on the spot didn't know what to do. There were standing orders on how to deal with people who approached the waterline. There were also orders on when to open fire—but nobody had told him what to do with Arabs who wanted to turn themselves in to Israel.

He phoned the area commander for the Jordan Rift Valley, who in turn called the commanding general, Central Command. Back down the line came an order to help the Arabs across, and to transfer them to the Israeli rear.

Once in Israeli-controlled territory, the Arabs seemed no longer in fear for their lives—no longer the hunted animals they appeared to be minutes before. These boys, who a day or two previously had been planning murder in

Israel, were now asking sanctuary and shelter from their intended victims. September 1970 had become a black month indeed for the terrorists in Jordan. King Hussein's soldiers were massacring them without mercy, dealing with them just as brutally as the Syrians did six years later in Lebanon. Jordanian soldiers were amputating limbs, burning bodies, standing terrorists before firing squads without hearing or trial. Whoever could get away was running to Syria, Lebanon, or across the frontier into Israel. Scores of them, ironically enough, found sanctuary in Israeli prisons.

Fourteen months later, in November 1971, Jordanian Prime Minister Wasfi Tal was shot and killed during a visit to Cairo. The assassins identified themselves as members of "Black September." This was the public debut of an organization that, for more than a year, was at the forefront of terrorism in the Middle East. Though it tried to pose as an independent group, Black September was merely a cover for the "Revolutionary Surveillance System" or, in other words, Fatah Intelligence. The man responsible for the group was Salah Halaf, better known among the terrorist community and throughout the Arab world as "Abu Iyad."

Exactly two years after the massacre in Jordan, seven strangers hurdled the security fence at the Olympic Village in Munich and moved quickly toward the building at 31 Connolly Street. At first light they occupied the building, which housed the Israeli Olympic delegation. A few Israeli athletes got away, but eleven remained trapped in the hands of Black September. While the building was being taken over, one athlete was killed, and another was murdered two hours later.

The terrorists demanded the release of 250 of their comrades imprisoned in Israel and of the German anarchist Ulrike Meinhof. The ultimatum they delivered to the government of Israel specified that the liberated prisoners were to be flown to Arab countries other than Jordan and

Lebanon. Exhausting negotiations went on from early that morning till nine in the evening, when the Olympic team members and their captors transferred to helicopters for a flight to Munich military airport. A Lufthansa plane was waiting, ostensibly to transport them out of Germany. Fearing a trap, the terrorists checked the aircraft, and were then fired on by German snipers stationed at various points around the field. The shooting started while some of the captors and their hostages were still in the helicopters. The terrorists did not panic. A hand grenade was thrown into one of the craft, which caught fire. Bullets from automatic weapons ripped through the second helicopter. Nine Israelis, four terrorists, and a German policeman were killed. The other three terrorists were captured.

The Munich massacre, in full view of television cameras and thousands of newspapermen assembled to cover the Olympiad, deeply shocked the world. Trapped Israelis being led to their death in Germany, of all places, aroused associations better forgotten. The average Israeli, not being particularly well-informed on security affairs, had assumed that the government had taken all the necessary measures to prevent, or lessen, the effects of terrorist strikes. Munich punctured that illusion within the space of one day. There was suddenly a horrible realization of cracks in the security wall. Indeed, a commission of inquiry appointed after the tragedy found that there had been negligent arrangements, lack of appropriate supervision, and a great deal of government apathy. Some of the security personnel concerned were found to be at fault.

The morning after Munich, Israel went into action. Huge budgets were suddenly available to the security services. Agents went scurrying to the four corners of the world to build an impenetrable security system unlike any other existing today.

Countless millions were invested in the protection of installations and persons outside the frontiers of Israel. Every Israeli office overseas became a fortress, equipped with and protected by the most modern instrumentation, and this included embassies, airline ticket offices, and even the stall of the Citrus Marketing Board at a trade fair. They had it all: bullet-proof steel doors, closed circuit TV, microphones, explosives detectors, cubicles for body searches. And at the same time local security police doubled their own forces on duty outside the Israeli "potential targets." The measures were extended to ships at anchor and on the high seas. Prominent personalities and emissaries of Israel were ordered to fly only on El Al, and some were required to take other protective measures.

The trauma of Munich was not quickly forgotten. There was a wave of demands from the Israeli press, from political leaders and retired senior officers and from the public, to apply active methods against terrorism instead of passive protection: fight terror with terror!

Adel Wahil Zueitar was entering his home in a Rome suburb, on October 16, 1972, when a dozen revolver bullets were pumped into his body. At first the Italian newspapers were surprised at the killing of this junior interpreter in the Libyan embassy—but then the Fatah itself chose to reveal Zueitar's true identity. Translating newspaper clippings for the embassy was only a cover for this thirty-eight-year-old from Nablus, Palestine. He had been Fatah representative in Italy since 1968 and, as such, had been picked up a number of times for interrogation by Italian police. Fatah issued an obituary notice for "one of the best of warriors."

After a couple of days of speculation and editorials in the Italian and Arab press, the first guesses began to surface: Israel was involved in the killing. Israel never admitted it, just as she never admitted any connection with the deaths of eight other Arabs in Europe and Cyprus, although in almost every case the victim proved to have been living a double life. Muhamad Boudia managed a Paris theater, but also recruited terrorist operatives. Basil Rauf Koubeisi was a university professor, but also head of a terrorist base in Europe. They all died under more or less similar circumstances: a bomb in their homes or cars, or a bullet in the street—always when they were alone. No one but the candidate for execution was ever hurt.

The last to die was Ahmad Boushiki, a resident of the Norwegian resort town of Lillehammer. Boushiki was a waiter. The morning after he died, it was already obvious that a fatal mistake had been made: he was the wrong man. A group of men and women were rounded up by Norwegian police. They held passports of different countries, but there was a common thread linking them. Under interrogation, and in their later trial in Oslo, they were shown to be Israelis on a mission for the *Mossad*—Israel's Central Institute for Intelligence and Special Duties. The wave of executions came to an abrupt stop.

Black September, unlike other terror organizations, was not discriminating in its strikes during the summer of 1973: Jew or non-Jew—it didn't matter. They operated against Jordanians, Saudis, Americans, Italians, Dutch, and West Germans. In March 1973, they even invaded the Saudi embassy in Khartoum, Sudan, to kill three diplomats from the United States and Belgium.

The world, which had ignored previous attacks against Israel, spoke out against Black September. Sensing such widespread hostility, the Fatah leadership took no public responsibility for the group's activities, though they did make sure that Black September got loud and sympathetic publicity. Yet the strikes were detracting from the support accorded the Palestinian cause. Arab governments and other organizations applied pressure on the group to stop its murder rampage. Consequently, shortly before the Yom Kippur War, Black September faded away from the world scene, although the widows and orphans they left in their wake remembered them all too well.

Not for a moment did the Israeli authorities believe their security wall to be impermeable. They knew the Arabs had new schemes more devious than blatant terrorist attacks. For example, when they were foiled in attempting to put bombs aboard aircraft, the terrorists resorted to the use of innocent non-Arab girls.

The first to fall into the Arab trap was the young daughter of the Dutch chief of staff. A young man charmed the girl with all the courtesy of the Orient during a brief courtship in Rome, and invited her to accompany him on a visit to his parents in Israel. He bought her a ticket for a flight to Lod, but at the last minute came up with an urgent excuse why he could not join her on the same flight. He asked her to take a suitcase on to his parents, promising to join her as soon as possible.

The young Dutch girl fainted when the false sides of the suitcase were ripped out at Lod Airport. She had no idea that her lover had packed it with explosives, and that only a faulty mechanism had prevented it from detonating in the plane between Rome and Tel Aviv.

One failure was no reason for the Arabs to give up this scheme. They tried again and failed again, with a young Peruvian girl coming from London. One day in August 1971, there was an explosion in the cargo hold of an El Al plane flying from Rome to Lod. Little damage was done, but investigation showed that it was a matter of pure luck. Agents of Ahmad Jibril's terrorist organization had given a record player to two English girls, who had been charmed off their feet by the Arab boys after an encounter in a Via Veneto cafe. They also had no idea what they were carrying on board the El Al airliner.

Israeli security moved in fast. Passengers to and from Israel were ordered to report any package received from strangers, and were warned what it might contain. Souvenirs bought from Arabs in the Occupied Territories were examined thoroughly before being cleared for flight. It was no longer possible to take a jar of preserves or a bottle of perfume on board a plane without having it checked.

Undaunted, the terrorists looked for new techniques. In September 1973 the unbelievable happened in Rome. A raid on a house not far from Fiumicino Airport uncovered an arsenal of Soviet-made Strella ground-to-air missiles, designed to home in on the heat of aircraft engines. These weapons were to be used in an attack on an El Al plane after takeoff, but a tip brought Italian security to the house before the terrorists could act.

The use of missiles was proof, for anyone who needed it, that there were no limits to what the terrorists would do to interfere with Israel's air traffic. The incident caused immediate efforts by police forces to prevent any possible missile launching against aircraft, but everyone knew they still had no foolproof preventive techniques.

On January 7, 1975, bazookas replaced missiles as Orly Airport, outside Paris, was turned into a battleground. The assailants this time succeeded in firing rockets at an El Al plane moving on the ground, but they missed their mark, hitting a nearby Yugoslav plane and injuring three people. Only six days later, they tried again at the same place. They opened fire with light arms, threw grenades, injured twenty people, and seized six hostages from among the crowd in the main concourse of the terminal building.

Perhaps the most horrifying attack occurred on May 30, 1972, when three young Japanese arrived at Lod Airport on a flight from Rome. Once on the ground and in the passenger hall, they tore up their passports and turned toward the baggage carousel. Opening their bags, they pulled out Kalashnikov carbines and hand grenades, to the astonishment and shock of the crowd. Twenty-four people died as the Japanese sprayed the hall with automatic fire.

The Lod massacre was shocking, not only because of the large number of victims, but because there were now non-Arabs allied to the terrorist cause. Israel would have to fight on a much wider battlefield—no longer against Arabs alone. The thoroughness with which Arab passports had been checked on entry into Israel was now extended to all incoming passengers. Everyone was suspect until proved otherwise.

The Israeli "respect but fear him" approach bore fruit. At Lod Airport, Haifa Port, and inside both the Occupied Territories and Israel proper, a number of men and women were caught. Most of them were Europeans, holders of passports from non-Arab countries, sent by the terrorist organizations, but basically by Dr. George Habash's Popular Front.

The most noteworthy "foreign assistance" extended to the Popular Front in the early 1970s (apart from that of the Japanese) was given by an elderly French couple, a young French girl of German origin, and two beautiful Moroccan sisters. Recruited by Paris "theater manager" Muhamad Boudia, the four women and the old man were to carry out one of their dispatcher's most ambitious schemes. Boudia, who died some time later when his car mysteriously exploded, was a senior officer of the Popular Front in Europe. He sent his five recruits at different times, by different planes, but with one purpose: to blow up nine Israeli hotels.

Boudia's function could be be described as "organizer"—a rather strange function for a terrorist officer, but then he was not using his own Palestinian Arabs for the job. To get the explosives through Israeli security checks, they were soaked into the fibers of clothes, including underwear and even sanitary napkins. The elderly couple, who received a small fee for their effort, carried the delayed-action fuses hidden in a transistor radio into Tel Aviv. The group was caught and sentenced to long terms of imprisonment, but pardoned after a while and sent back to Paris.

A connection among the various practitioners of international terrorism was discovered in the early 1970s, but Interpol and the European police forces could prove nothing. Eventually the organizations themselves confirmed the existence of a "Terror Internationale"—a kind of terrorism syndicate, with tentacles stretching from West Germany to Ireland, from Turkey to Japan, South America, and Lebanon. Though it was difficult to understand the nature of the bond between Baader-Meinhof and the Japanese Red Army, the hunted terrorists were obviously communicating with each other, trading arms and information, and cooperating in each other's missions.

Most of the help emanated from the Popular Front for the Liberation of Palestine. George Habash's organization is affluent and regularly finances the activities of others who have no special interest in fighting Israel. The Popular Front opened the gates of its main training base at Nahar el-Barad, near Tripoli in Lebanon. Here, terrorists from Turkey, Germany, Ireland, South America, Holland, and Iran found a common roof and all the facilities they lacked. Apart from training in Syria and Lebanon, members of the Popular Front and of other organizations were offered facilities in the army camps of East Germany, the Soviet Union, China, Algeria, and Libya. Many of those who came to Nahar el-Barad were revolutionary socialists and alienated kids who had been rejected by their families and society. Occasional gun battles broke out among them, and at least twice the IDF raided the camp, killing Arab and foreign terrorists—and even bringing a Turkish prisoner back to Israel.

While the average terrorist is usually of medium to low intelligence, the heads of the organizations present a totally different picture. In fact there have been periodic debates in Israel on whether to chop off the head of the terror octopus by striking at the above-average intellectual leadership. The prevailing opinion, however, has been that it is better to leave those in charge alone lest they retaliate in kind against Israeli leaders.

The facts speak for themselves. There have been several attempts to assassinate PLO and Fatah leader Yasir Arafat, yet on each occasion he has managed to evade his attackers.

Dr. George Habash was to have flown from Iraq to Lebanon one August day in 1973 in an Iraqi airliner. As the
plane descended toward Beirut, Israeli fighter planes swept
past and ordered the pilot to change course for Israel.
When the plane landed at a military airport in Israel, the
Israelis were furious. Habash wasn't on board, apparently
having changed his plans at the last moment. The terrorist
doctor, himself the pioneer of aircraft hijacking in the
Middle East, was enraged at this attempt to catch him in
the air. Many governments across the world sided with
him. Israel, the constant victim of air piracy, was condemned, while the man who had stated in public interviews that his objective was a "mass grave for Israelis" was
the recipient of congratulatory telegrams and messages.

The men who attempted to strike at terrorist leaders
lived a furtive existence—surrounded by bodyguards, constantly changing their places of residence, never spending
more than two nights in any bed. Their flights from country
to country are still kept a tight secret, and are subject to
frequent scheduling changes. They enjoy neither night nor
day, and cannot permit themselves the luxury of relaxing.

At 2:15 on the morning of a July day in 1970, Katyusha
rockets were fired into an apartment in the heart of Beirut.
The tenant, his wife, and young son were slightly injured,
and the apartment was badly damaged. The next day Dr.
Wadia Elias Hadad made one of his rare public appear-
ances. He claimed that the rockets were fired at the apartment by "Zionists and their helpers in American intelligence."

The apartment belonged to Wadia Hadad. This man is
today the most dangerous terrorist on Israel's list. Unlike
other arch-terrorists, he observes all the rules of the underground: he is not seen in public, and according to Israeli
security officers, his photo has never been published. The
picture that appeared on the pages of world newspapers
in July 1976 after the Air France hijacking to Entebbe was
a fake. Hadad is wary of assassination attempts. Since the

1970 incident, he and his family have been constantly on the move. After all, Hadad knows that in recent years he has caused more damage and pain to Israel than any other single terrorist leader.

Some of the old-timers in the Israeli town of Zefat still remember Hadad's father, who taught in the Scottish College, as a handsome, courteous man who wore pince-nez glasses. Hadad senior taught Arabic, geography, and mathematics. His son, Wadia, was born in Zefat, but lived in Jerusalem for many years. After high school he went on to study medicine, and ironically enough, took the Hippocratic oath to save life.

Dr. Hadad is a dentist. He became friendly with an eye specialist named George Habash and, in the late 1950s, the two doctors started a medical practice together and also launched their political campaign. They opened an eye clinic in Amman, and wrapped the drugs they dispensed in handbills of the *Kaumion el-Arab* ("Arab Nationalism Movement"), of which they were leaders.

After the Six Day War, the movement underwent a drastic change, becoming the Popular Front for the Liberation of Palestine, with Habash as leader and commander. Hadad, who is now sixty-four, became Habash's operations officer. Most of his activity over the years has gone into the planning of PFLP terror operations abroad, and he has had a hand in all strikes outside Israel. He planned the first overseas operation—an attempt to assassinate David Ben-Gurion—and then moved on to hijacking aircraft, including a Lufthansa plane. He demanded—and received—$5 million for its release. The ransom was used to finance the operations of the terrorist group he now leads.

Hadad despised all publicity, and hoped that Israeli security would find out absolutely nothing about him, and therefore the bombing of his Beirut apartment came as a complete surprise to him. The rockets hit the lounge and master bedroom while Hadad was sitting in his study.

Within minutes he discovered that the rockets had been fired from an adjacent building, where a man holding an Iranian passport had taken a lease and then vanished.

The two doctors parted ways in 1972 following the Japanese massacre at Lod Airport. Habash had not sanctioned the Lod hit, which was apparently planned by Hadad, who believed that Israel must be fought by every possible means and in every possible way. Hadad moved to Iraq and set up the Popular Revolutionary Front for the Liberation of Palestine, with himself as commander, head, and operations officer. In almost all his operations so far, he has used women, even for the most murderous of missions, presumably because they attract less attention and can more easily cross the stiffest security barriers.

In the last week of June 1976, the dentist who had given up his career as a healer landed at Mogadishu Airport in Somalia with two or three days to spare in planning the final details of the hijacking of an Air France Aerobus. In a room in the Somalian capital, Hadad prepared his next blow against Israel.

CHAPTER FIVE

Number 12346,
Left Arm

The plane took off from Benghazi, and the passengers were enormously relieved, even though their final destination was still unknown. Six hours on the ground, trapped in the plane, had created an illusion of a world suddenly standing still. Flight seemed to start the clock all over again. In the passenger cabin, all was quiet.

Sara Davidson was worrying about their French pilot: "He's been locked in that cockpit almost twelve hours. He must be terribly nervous. How can he possibly stand it?" she remarked partly to herself and partly to Uzzi.

Michel Bacos was indeed tired. He said nothing about it to the terrorist next to him, however. Michel suspected that the man was not unfamiliar with flying. He was studying the dials and checking the compass, with an occasional glance at the navigation charts. Captain Bacos dimly remembered cases of hijackers who knew navigation and at least the theory of flight. "He must be one of them," he murmured to himself, as he stole a look at the terrorist commander, who was still holding an aerial route chart.

The man was far more active now. From time to time

he told the passengers, in a very quiet, very confident voice over the intercom: "The danger is over. We'll soon be in a safe place. I ask you to remain calm. . . ."

"Remain calm. . . ."

Yitzhak David had already heard those words, or something like them, in exactly the same tones. It was only too familiar. Turning to his wife, Yitzhak commented: "That boy is using psychology on us. He knows his job!"

Again the voice over the loudspeakers: "Remain calm. . . ."

Suddenly remembering, Yitzhak David shivered.

He was fifteen when the armies of Nazi Germany stormed across Europe—a fourth-year student in a Hungarian high school. Yitzhak's family were observant Jews. His father, Herman David, was a cloth merchant. Herman David brought his children up to know the Bible and its commandments, but he also insisted that they learn a profession. Yitzhak was studying dentistry—though he would never practice it. He felt a revulsion for it, probably because his father forced him to learn it.

Yitzhak was born in Satmar, a big Jewish center, and home of the extremist *Neturei Karta*, a very devout sect of Judaism. Yitzhak's own inclination was to Zionism—anathema to the *Neturei Karta*—and he joined the local Zionist youth movement. As World War II progressed, he began to hear news of a vast holocaust that was engulfing the Jews of Europe. Like some of his friends, Yitzhak David decided that he was not going to be a victim. They organized to defend themselves and built bunkers. Meanwhile, he prepared a private hideout in the garden of the local synagogue.

The Davids lived under the German heel for a few years, while they heard about the deaths of hundreds of thousands of Jews. But Yitzhak had other ideas, and prepared himself a set of fake documents. When the day came, he told his father: "So far we have been together, but now I must escape."

Herman David encouraged him, but had a request to make: "Yitzhak, take your sister Klari. You will always be able to manage—even if she doesn't have papers. You can say she's your wife."

Regina David urged him, "Go! Go!" and then burst into tears. Yitzhak hesitated only for a moment. Then he gave up the idea. He stayed at home in Hungary with his family, telling himself: "My end will be the same as theirs."

In 1944, the David family arrived in Auschwitz. The boy was taken almost immediately to a cell where his scalp was shaved and he was issued a striped concentration-camp uniform. Coming out of the cell, he caught a glimpse of two of his sisters—one of them for the last time.

Auschwitz was calm. The Germans did everything possible to keep it that way, to alleviate doubt and fear among the hundreds of thousands of Jews.

"Remain calm. . . ."

Now, in a hijacked plane somewhere between Benghazi and who knows where, the phrase terrified Yitzhak David. He couldn't be calm.

"We'll soon be in a safe place," the voice repeated, "remain calm. . . ."

Dora Bloch was ready for anything. She was relaxed, even though the hours of sitting in the aircraft hadn't been easy for her. She exchanged a few words with her son Ilan, and followed every movement of the terrorists as they prowled back and forth down the cabin, holding their grenades and pistols.

"I've had a good and full life," she told Ilan. "I'm already seventy-five and I don't mind dying. I only want that you should return home, safe and sound, to your wife and daughters."

"Where are we going?" Sara asked Uzzi Davidson. He shrugged. All around was a hubbub of questions and guesses on the same subject.

"I think we're flying to Israel. They'll do there what they tried to do with the Sabena plane. . . ."

"We must be going to South Yemen. I'm sure of it! The Yemenites have been helping the terrorists recently. The newspapers said so. . . ."

"Sudan! Do you remember how they killed those diplomats in Khartoum? That's where we're flying. . . ."

The man to the left of another passenger, Rina Kipper, was studying an Air France map. When the little man with his green eyes came on board at Athens, Rina knew immediately that he was Arab. Now, as he studied the map, trying to guess where the Aerobus was taking them, Rina plucked up the courage to talk to him. She was right—the accent gave him away. He said he was a chemical engineer, had studied in Philadelphia, and was living in Amman. His pregnant wife hadn't wanted him to fly.

As the conversation progressed, Rina said: "Look, here we are, you an Arab and me a Jewess, chatting in a hijacked plane just like people should chat. It's a pleasant talk. Why shouldn't it be the same between our countries?"

The chemical engineer from Amman said she was right—it should be, and Israel could help the Arab countries, if and when peace came.

Suddenly Rina's face changed. She was so frightened: "I think they will kill us, the Jews on this plane, but they won't kill you. You're Arab."

"You mustn't think about it."

Yitzhak David didn't doubt for a moment that the commander on the flight deck was German: that voice, the behavior, the speech and clumsy language, the maddening "remain calm. . . ." He murmured to himself: "This is exactly how the Germans brainwashed Jews in the Holocaust."

How could one forget? He sank back in the padded Air France seat and remembered his meeting with Yeri Pihota. Yeri was a Jew whom Yitzhak had smuggled out of a ghetto. When the David family arrived in Auschwitz, the two met again. Yeri was already a veteran in the camp. He led Yitzhak toward the gas chambers and showed him the end of the line for hundreds of thousands of Jews.

"If you don't want to get there quickly, tell them that you have a trade in building."

The advice was gratefully accepted. Herman David told the Germans he was a glazier, while Yitzhak said he was a plumber. The Davids began their life in Auschwitz with every hope of getting out. Herman worked as a glazier, while Yitzhak sorted valuables and jewelry that the Germans took from their Jewish victims. Later on, his father joined him and their days were spent collecting gold, silver, precious stones, watches—and gold teeth.

Herman David: 12345, left arm.

Yitzhak David: 12346, left arm.

At Lod's Ben-Gurion Airport, there was much speculation about where the plane was headed. Lieutenant General Mordechai Gur waited in the airport manager's office for news of further developments. There was a new element in the flight path: the plane was moving away from the Middle East—the home base of the terrorist organizations. General Gur phoned Shimon Peres, who decided to come to the airport himself. A call to the prime minister in his Jerusalem home confirmed government approval for action at Ben-Gurion Airport if necessary. But the plane was moving away, even though it was still within range. A quick check with Air France offices in Tel Aviv established that this model of Aerobus could fly 2,500 miles without refueling—as opposed to the other model, which had a range of only 1,560 miles. Was it conceivable that terrorist intelligence knew this already?

There was an unpleasant feeling in the plane though the atmosphere was calm enough, mostly because of the repeated announcements from the cockpit. The lavatories had jammed long ago and the stench was intolerable.

Many passengers settled down to sleep, perhaps in the hope that they would awake to find the nightmare over.

The air odyssey in its second act was already into the fourth hour. Sara Davidson persevered with her anxious guesses. Captain el-Koubeisi, or whatever he called himself, had promised three hours, but they were still going. How much fuel did the plane carry? Would it just drop from lack of gas? Uzzi shared her anxiety. Perhaps the terrorists were trying to land but no one wanted them: "Two hundred and fifty lepers looking for somewhere to put their feet. What a long way to go. . . ."

Yitzhak David was remembering his long way through the Holocaust nightmare. Sunk in the now-uncomfortable orange armchair, he was reliving a train journey from Grosshausen to Buchenwald extermination camp. There were two thousand like him on the death train. Six days never to be forgotten. Not a drop of water nor crumb of bread. People died like flies, one after the other. There was no room to move, and no way to throw bodies out of the cars. To make space, they stacked and bent corpses and sat on them. For the final forty-eight hours, Yitzhak David did not sit a single moment. He chose a corner, since it was protected on two sides. He stood, and stood, and stood. . . . Hunger and thirst were tormenting him. He was helpless, semi-comatose, and exhausted to the point of death.

Of two thousand passengers that boarded the slow cattle train, only five hundred arrived at the final destination. Some of them were insane. Yitzhak remembered how, at the last stop, a starving man tried to eat the foot of another. He remembered the terrible screams. He remembered the mad rush into the shower cubicles of Buchenwald to drink water. Men clung to the pipes and wouldn't be budged. Six days without food and water had done that.

He stretched his legs and twisted around to find a more comfortable position. The cabin was quiet. Many of the passengers were asleep, and he was free to ponder the two worst experiences of his life. The first was that train to Buchenwald, without food and water, standing amid a sea of dead bodies. The second was still going on in a hijacked plane. Thirty-two years had passed, but he was making the same journey into the unknown, perhaps to death. The only difference was that, this time, he was traveling there in an upholstered seat at jet speed in the tourist cabin of an intercontinental airliner. "What a luxury," he muttered to himself. His wife, Hadassa, sat beside him. Yitzhak had known her from childhood. She, like him, had been incarcerated at the age of fifteen in the Auschwitz extermination camp. The mediation of the Swedish Count Folke Bernadotte had gotten her out of German hell into Swedish neutrality.

"This business of Che Guevara and the Palestine problem doesn't matter right now," Yitzhak David remarked to his wife and the couple next to them. "What matters is that Germans are doing it again." The Davids' neighbors, Dr. and Mrs. Hirsch, were also concentration-camp veterans.

Flight 139 seemed endless. For five hours the aircraft had been forging on into East Africa, and there was still no sign of descent for a landing. Those who were awake still puzzled over the question: where were they going? China? Perhaps Albania?

The Aerobus had logged 3,750 miles since leaving Ben-Gurion Airport the previous morning on its way to Paris, via Athens. Now the tanks contained enough fuel for another twenty minutes. Captain Bacos, tired as he was, knew that he was responsible for the fate of his passengers and crew. The aerial odyssey would be over within twenty minutes, for better or worse. There was no way to stay in the air without refueling.

Yitzhak David didn't sleep. He estimated that the tanks must be almost dry, and asked himself when and where the craft with its hostages would touch down.

He well understood the meaning of "hostage." He could

remember almost every minute of his last day under Nazi rule. He had been working in a coal mine in the path of German retreat. The end of World War II was very close— they could even hear the thunder of Allied guns. One night, Yitzhak overheard a conversation between two Frenchmen who slept beside him. He pretended to be asleep, but understood from what they were saying that General Charles de Gaulle's Free French were approaching. His two neighbors were planning their escape from the barn where they slept under German guard between shifts in the coal mine.

He decided to follow them. He watched them go, and minutes later was on their tail. When they entered a house, he followed and, from the shouting, he understood that they had found weapons belonging to the German house-holder, and were now holding his daughter hostage.

"You turn us in to the Germans, and we kill your daughter," one of the escapees threatened.

There was no need to kill the hostage. A few days later, French soldiers arrived, and Yitzhak joined the other two on the road to victory. He became an interpreter and in-terrogator of German prisoners. Once it was over, he headed for home to look for traces of his family. The David's home had been reduced to rubble by an air raid, but Yitzhak did find one of his brothers. His mother had died in the ovens of Auschwitz soon after entering the camp. Herman, his father, died of starvation in Dachau three days before the Allies liberated the camp. Klari, the sister Yitzhak was to have taken with him on his escape from Hungary, was also a victim of Auschwitz. One brother and one sister were still alive.

Yitzhak, as an active Zionist, turned to the work of rescuing the survivors of European Jewry. He personally brought to Palestine a group of fifty who had escaped the Nazis and evaded the British.

At this moment, Yitzhak needed someone to help him escape from this orange-upholstered, air-conditioned hell.

Had he escaped one death camp only to be killed years later in another?

The Holocaust of World War II that claimed six million Jewish lives had left a heavy shadow over the three million Jews of Israel and their brethren all over the world. But the Palestinian Arabs also claimed a "Holocaust" of their own —the 1948 war between Palestine and Israel. For them, the memory of 1948 is a black and bitter one—it is at the root of their personal tragedy.

The Palestinian Arabs began to develop a recognition of separate nationality amid the Arab nations in the 1920s. In 1976, they numbered three and a half million, though the Palestine Liberation Organization claims a figure nearer to five million. Most live in Jordan, Israel, the West Bank, and the Gaza Strip. A minority are in Lebanon, Syria, the Persian Gulf Emirates, and outside the Middle East. As a result of their failure in 1948, some six hundred thousand left the area that was to be Israel. Their political leadership disintegrated completely. An attempt made in 1948 to form a Palestine government in Gaza failed, mostly because of opposition from King Abdullah of Jordan, who had designs of his own on Arab Palestine. From 1952 to 1956 there were efforts by various Palestinian groups to reorganize politically and militarily for renewed war on Israel. They infiltrated with intent to steal and kill, and were aided by various Arab governments, but they could not gain wide popular support.

Following the 1956 Sinai Campaign, the trend among Palestinians was to ally with the Nasser camp and seek their own solution through Arab unity. The only remaining Palestinian organization of any significance was the "Arab Nationalist Movement" headed by Dr. George Habash.

The "Palestinian entity" regained its importance in 1959, becoming a regular item on the agenda of the Arab League, though Jordan vigorously disputed the idea and its terminology. Underlying the revival was a belief that the Palestinians must be the vanguard of the Arab struggle against Israel. This obviously required emphasis on national identity and independence in Palestine—or at least a representative body with its own military force. In 1963, the Palestine Liberation Organization and the Palestine Liberation Army were born.

In the early 1960s, there was noticeable opposition from groups of Palestinian intellectuals, who disliked the idea of an organization under the patronage of Arab governments. They preferred an independent "Palestinian entity" that could work for a more dynamic anti-Israel policy. These were the groups that spawned the terror organizations, but when the splinter terrorist factions gained control over the PLO in 1969, the circle was complete, and their original opposition no longer mattered. The PLO was committed to the "Palestinian entity" as a target of national revival.

The charter of the PLO is a document known as the "Palestine Covenant." Its text has been amended a number of times, the last occasion being in 1968 when the Palestinians inserted the most extremist terminology imaginable. The Covenant rejects political compromise. It views Zionism as a political movement linked to world imperialism, one which is hostile to all national liberation and progress. According to the Covenant, Zionism is "racist, aggressive, expansionist in its aims, fascist and Nazi in its means."

Faiz Abdul Rahim Jaaber considered himself a Palestinian refugee, even though he left his home in Hebron to live in Egypt in 1946, two years before the War of Independence. He married in Egypt and had six children. Occasionally he visited his parents in Hebron.

Jaaber didn't even finish primary school but his lack of education did not stop him from being active in many underground organizations. In 1964, he became a founding member of "Heroes of the Palestinian Return"—a terrorist group. As a colleague of George Habash, Jaaber was also active in the Arab Nationalist Movement and helped organize the Popular Front for the Liberation of Palestine.

Jaaber, aged forty-six in 1976, has held many senior positions in the PFLP, among others head of the political department, security officer, and chief operations officer. He recruited four members of his family in Hebron, and almost all became senior officers of the organization. Some were killed and others are now in Israeli prisons. In 1970, Jaaber fought in the "Black September" war in Jordan. He also participated in missions inside Israel. Jaaber went with Dr. Wadia Hadad to the new faction of the PFLP after the split with George Habash.

As a senior commander of a terrorist organization, Faiz Abdul Jaaber no longer participated in missions. Now he was on his way from Kampala to Entebbe, comfortably seated in his white Mercedes. Whatever was to happen, he could not disappoint his superior, Dr. Wadia Hadad. He had received instructions from Mogadishu in nearby Somalia to be at Entebbe Airport in Uganda. An Air France Aerobus was due to land at any minute.

The passengers were no longer in line for the toilets. All were in their seats, under the watchful eyes of armed terrorists. A Belgian Jew finished laying phylacteries, then moved along the aisles offering the older men his set and suggesting that they pray. No one refused, even though the majority were not religious or observant Jews. In times of distress, even the nonbelievers will put their faith in the God whose existence they doubt.

Uzzi, Ron, and Benny Davidson were in good spirits—a passing moment of optimism. Sara awoke from a short nap to hear the terrorist commander announcing: "We will be landing in a few minutes at Entebbe Airport, Uganda." He ordered all shades drawn over the windows.

"The Ugandan authorities will help us finish the affair," he said into the microphone. There was a moment of silence in the cabin, as though all the captives needed time to digest that news. Was it good or bad? Then a sudden burst of applause, in which the Israelis joined. . . .

The announcement of impending landing, and the round of applause, united the passengers with the terrorists in a feeling of relief. All signs of fear had vanished from the faces of their captors. For the first time since the plane had been hijacked, the passengers breathed easily. The terrorist in the red shirt had meanwhile dropped the safety pin of his hand grenade. Suddenly upset, he held the spring down firmly as he groped around on the floor for the pin. Then he calmed down and threaded a metal wire through the grenade as an improvised replacement.

The wheels of Air France 139 touched down on the runway at Entebbe Airport at 3:15 A.M. Two long rows of lights showed Michel Bacos the route he had to take to a parking spot. There were also lights on in the airport buildings.

"Well done," the German said, patting Captain Bacos' shoulder.

Many of the passengers sighed with relief. Takeoff from Benghazi had meant progress after long hours of waiting. Landing at Entebbe was now further progress after long hours of flying. The atmosphere in the plane was easier—almost freer. . . . Then the German girl, who was looking out the window, remarked, "They're waiting for us."

The curtains were drawn over the windows, but Ilan Hartuv pulled them aside for a brief look. He knew Old Terminal. He had been through this building in 1969 when he visited Uganda. He had, at that point, been serving as economic counselor in the Israeli embassy in Addis Ababa, Ethiopia, and had come to examine Uganda's economic problems. A long report of his was still filed somewhere in the Foreign Ministry in Jerusalem.

Now he saw a great many Ugandan soldiers on the lawn alongside the runway. In the first rays of a new morning, he could also see a large expanse of water: some of the 26,828 square miles of Lake Victoria spread out before his eyes. But he was not really interested in the view. With the unknown still uppermost in all their minds, no one on Air France 139 paid any attention to the beauties of the scenery becoming visible with the new dawn.

CHAPTER SIX

Mackinon Road—
The House at Number 17

It was still dark when Haled el-Sid came out of his home at 17 Mackinon Road, Kampala. El-Sid was resident representative of the Palestine Liberation Organization in Uganda, a frequent and welcome guest of President Idi Amin. In fact the house and surrounding gardens had been put at his disposal by Amin himself. Situated in a smart residential area, 17 Mackinon Road had served as the private residence of the Israeli ambassador until late March 1972, when Amin gave the Israeli colony a few hours in which to get out of Uganda. Two days after the last Israeli departed, Idi Amin announced that he was giving the house to the PLO. Now it served as the nerve center of Haled el-Sid's subversive activities throughout East Africa.

Haled's white Fiat glided down the deserted streets of the Ugandan capital toward the Entebbe airport. Wadia Hadad had instructed him to be present for the landing of Air France 139. The street lamps of Entebbe town still twinkled in the distance when he drove into the airport.

The passengers of Air France 139 would not be the

first members of the Jewish community in Uganda. At the end of the last century, a Ugandan army officer had converted to Judaism and persuaded the members of his tribe to do the same. A few years later, in 1903, Uganda became an important location for the Zionist cause.

Early in the twentieth century, the persecuted Jews of Czarist Russia and Eastern Europe were in need of urgent sanctuary. Dr. Theodor Herzl, a Viennese journalist, was promoting the idea of a Jewish state in Palestine, then part of the Ottoman Empire, when Joseph Chamberlain brought him a British offer of an autonomous Jewish colony in East Africa. The area offered was then part of Uganda, but is now inside Kenya, a few miles from the Ugandan border. Herzl listened attentively to Chamberlain's proposal. He wanted a solution to the immediate problem badly enough not to reject the offer out of hand. Following clarification of details, the "Uganda Plan" was formally submitted to the Zionist leadership in August 1903.

Uganda became a subject of frequent discussion in every Jewish home in Europe and Russia. Years of exile, persecution, and pogrom had taught the Jews to be cautious and suspecting, and the British motives were quite clear. Britain sincerely wanted to rescue Jews from Czarist persecution, but she also wanted to recruit white manpower and Jewish capital to develop her colonies in Africa.

Herzl was in favor of the "Uganda Plan," which represented to him both a way to save Jews and a stepping stone on the way to future colonization of the land of the patriarchs, Palestine. As a politician, he could also see the advantages of alliance with, and support from, the great British Empire. But it was Herzl's own colleagues who caused him bitterness and disappointment. The Sixth Zionist Congress, which convened in August 1903, could not support its leader's viewpoint and quickly reaffirmed its political goal of "Jewish settlement *only* in the land of Israel." Uganda aroused emotions so stormy that at moments it seemed as if the generous British offer would be the death of the infant Zionist movement.

Within two years the incident was completely forgotten. Herzl was dead, and a special commission sent to Uganda to investigate reported back unfavorably to the Congress. The word "Uganda" took its place in the Zionist lexicon as synonymous with betrayal of the cause.

Almost sixty years separated the Sixth Zionist Congress and the advent of Israelis in Uganda as representatives of an independent and sovereign state. It was the late 1950s. Israel badly needed to strengthen her political links with the outside world, including Africa. And the friendship of Uganda, not yet independent, a nation on the periphery of a hostile Arab and Moslem world, would be a treasure indeed.

The first foundations of Israeli-Ugandan entente were laid by Asher Naim, Israeli Foreign Ministry representative in Nairobi, Kenya. Naim, a dynamic and talented man, made direct contact with Dr. Milton Obote, who became the first president of independent Uganda. When, in 1962, the British flag was lowered from the mast above Government House in Kampala for the last time, an Israeli blueprint for diplomatic activities in Africa already existed. Its underlying principle was simple: Israel would not force her friendship on any African country, but was willing to share her rich experience in agricultural development, swamp and desert reclamation, youth organization, and the rudiments of the military arts necessary for basic security.

Israel's deputy defense minister, Shimon Peres, visited Kampala within twelve months. His hosts were asking help in organizing an army—and particularly an air force—and Peres had no reason to refuse. In April 1963, Foreign Minister Golda Meir signed a treaty of cooperation between Uganda and Israel.

Colonel Zeev "Zonik" Shaham, an IDF field officer, moved to Kampala to help train an army. Zonik was easily accepted by the Ugandans, and his Kampala home became open house for the entire "Who's Who" of Ugandan society.

Zonik Shaham was not an empire builder with grandiose personal ambitions, nor was he the kind of man to view Uganda as a mother lode to be milked dry. Though under pressure to produce fast results, he worked slowly and methodically. First he studied Uganda's military and security needs. When he arrived, the "Ugandan army" was a single infantry battalion—seven or eight hundred men— originally raised as part of the King's African Rifles for service in the World War II British army. The line soldiers were Ugandan, their officers British. The soldiers had not the faintest idea of how to use their weapons. The battalion's sole function was ceremonial, and they excelled only in "general salute" and "present arms."

Zonik called in Israeli reinforcements and, despite England's displeasure, he began to turn the ceremonial battalion into a real force to perform the military functions needed by the young state. With his officers, he began to train one company of the battalion up to the level of a good rifle company. Meanwhile, he sent Ugandan soldiers for intensive training at the IDF's Central Officer School in Israel and at the Israeli air force (IAF) pilot academy. The training was tough, but it produced fast results.

At that time, the Kampala authorities had no serious security problems. They needed an army primarily for intervention in intertribal squabbles, and to chase refugees who infiltrated in from neighboring countries. Most of the force was in fact designed to protect the regime and its leaders.

Milton Obote maintained a special police for the protection of his government. He began to fear a gap between the performance level of the army and that of his police, so he asked Zonik Shaham to train them, as well. To the Israelis this seemed an accolade for a job well done.

Their success was complete. Uganda's second Independence Day, in 1964, was celebrated with a military parade and a display of six Fouga Magister jets. Uganda's leaders were ecstatic. The planes, flown in close formation, were piloted by Israelis—but no one in Kampala knew that.

The most impressive Israeli success was with the air force. IAF personnel built the Ugandan air force up from the smallest bolt and the first pilot. Fouga Magisters and Dakotas were shipped in from Israel and pilots were trained to fly them. The Ugandans raved over advanced technology and rejoiced at the sight of planes shrieking through the skies.

Among Zonik Shaham's many friends were two Ugandan officers, both former British army sergeants. Captain Opoluto became commander in chief of the Ugandan army, but was dismissed and imprisoned by President Obote. The other officer, a man of impressive height and girth, if limited education, was—Captain Idi Amin.

Amin's official biography notes that he fought courageously in the Burma campaign, but Idi Amin was never on a frontline, nor has he ever risked his life in war. He spent World War II as assistant cook in a rear base. His personal psychiatrist, Dr. Marcel Ashael—an Israeli in Uganda as psychiatric consultant and as lecturer at Kampala University—claims that Amin is an uncommonly infantile, fearful man. He has a constant craving for the symbols of grandeur and dresses up in glittering but meaningless trappings. His uniforms are decorated with medals and orders, for which he pays a great deal of money. He delights in toys of the new technology, and loves cameras and film equipment, though he has little understanding of how they work.

Amin is ambitious, yet he lacks self-confidence. He clung to Zonik and the other Israeli officers from the moment he realized they were treating him as an equal. He suffered at the hands of the British, and hated them because, according to him, they failed him in a Command and Staff College course in England. He was so much at home in the Israeli colony in Kampala that the Ugandan chief of staff appointed him liaison officer between the military mission and the local authorities.

His liaison function brought him invitations to visit Israel. Each time, he returned to Kampala full of vocal admiration for Israeli dynamism. The Israeli officers were well aware of his weaknesses and fed his illusions of grandeur with frequent praise. He, of course, was incapable of deciding how much of this was sincere and how much stemmed from accepted Western etiquette. The Israelis joked about this gigantic Ugandan captain among themselves. Here was a man whose eyes almost popped out as he watched them put together jet planes from crated parts that arrived by air freight. Amin was present when the first Fouga was assembled, and volunteered to join Danny Shapira, the IAF's chief test pilot, on its maiden flight.

Amin progressed rapidly up the ladder of rank, at least partially because of the frequent purges in the Ugandan army. By 1965 he was already deputy commander in chief. Then, one morning, he took off for a routine inspection of a unit composed of West Nile tribesmen. While Amin was on his way there, Zonik was quietly informed that the tribesmen had decided to greet him with a hail of lead as he appeared in the hatchway of the aircraft.

Zonik did not hesitate for a moment. Grabbing a radio transmitter, he ordered Amin's Israeli pilot to return immediately to Kampala. Idi Amin didn't even notice that the Dakota had changed course. When they landed at Entebbe, Zonik told him what would have happened had he arrived at his destination. Amin thanked Zonik with emotional fervor, and Dr. Milton Obote also sent a letter of thanks.

Eventually Amin was appointed chief of staff of the Ugandan army and he was intoxicated with his victory. He asked Zonik, as a special favor, for a set of paratroop wings to adorn his dress tunic though he had never jumped out of a plane, at least not in Israel. To this day, years after breaking off diplomatic relations with Israel, Field Marshal Idi Amin still wears his twenty-cent Israeli paratroop wings.

Colonel Zeev Shaham was replaced in 1968 by Colonel Baruch "Burka" Bar Lev as head of the military mission. Lithuanian-born Bar Lev was a tank soldier. His last job in the army was as chief of staff in Central Command during the Six Day War. He was transferred by the commanding general, Major General Uzzi Narkis, and became military attaché and head of mission in Kampala.

Together with his new job, Bar Lev inherited the relationship with General Idi Amin. He continued Zonik's policy of encouraging the Ugandan, who was, after all, a friend of Israel. Bar Lev and Amin became firm friends. Meanwhile, the Israeli colony in Kampala had grown very quickly to some 170 families.

Outwardly, the picture of Israel presented in Uganda was united but, beneath the surface, there were sharp differences of opinion. One faction, led by Burka Bar Lev, was for offering Uganda military installations and other million-dollar projects. The second, led by economists, argued that Israel was involving Uganda in large and unnecessary investments, which the country would never be able to repay. However, Bar Lev had the support of major Israeli construction firms, including the General Federation of Labor's "Solel Boneh," the publicly owned "Vered," and private contractors who were establishing their own foothold and enjoying Uganda's new prosperity. Various economists wrote time and again to Jerusalem: "Uganda is at the end of her finances." But no one answered them.

President Milton Obote was scared enough of Amin to try to separate the ambitious soldier from his power base. At one stage, Amin was in a bad physical and mental state as the result of his drinking habits. To evade the watchful eyes of Obote's men, he disappeared with an army unit loyal to him. Bar Lev heard of it, and asked Professor Foster, a Jewish physician and lecturer at Kampala University, to get Amin back on his feet as fast as possible.

On another occasion, Amin was on a visit to Cairo at the invitation of the Egyptian war minister, when Obote phoned to order him back to Kampala. Amin's animal instincts told him something was wrong. He got an intermediary to contact Burka Bar Lev, who—despite his agreement not to interfere in internal Ugandan affairs—phoned the defense minister in Kampala. The minister, a loyal supporter of Idi Amin, managed to find out that the president was setting a trap for his commander in chief, on the grounds that he was party to the assassination of another senior Ugandan officer. Amin did return to Entebbe, but was met by friends who hustled him away to safety until the president's anger cooled. Amin never forgot the favor done him by the Israeli officer.

Burka suggested, at this point, that the commander in chief should have his own elite bodyguard—a proposal that was enthusiastically received by the status-hungry Ugandan. He promptly ordered the establishment of a guard battalion, to consist of two paratroop companies, a tank squadron, and a company of jeep-mounted recoilless rifles. From that moment on, Amin did not move without his impressive escort. Now he waited for his opportunity to overthrow President Milton Obote.

The chance came in January 1971. President Obote went to a British Commonwealth conference in Singapore and phoned instructions to the minister of the interior and the chief of Kampala police to arrest Idi Amin. That same evening, as a number of soldiers were being briefed in an officers' club on how and when to arrest Amin, four Ugandan parachute instructors loyal to Amin chanced by and overheard the briefing. They burst through the door of the briefing room and mowed down the group of assembled officers.

Bar Lev was the first to hear of it. Idi Amin phoned him with the details, adding: "The coup has begun. . . ." In the revolution that followed, hundreds of Obote's supporters were murdered, and Idi Amin nominated himself president of Uganda.

Idi Amin was conscious of a debt owed to Burka Bar Lev, whom he considered to no small extent responsible for his elevation to the presidency—something that Bar Lev does not deny. The friendship between these two men became even stronger as the new president of Uganda promoted himself from "General" to "Field Marshal" and consolidated his hold on the country.

Despite the closeness of their relationship, Bar Lev treated the president with a respect that impressed and flattered Amin, and this strengthened the friendship even more. Burka, for his part, was securing the Israeli position in Uganda and promoting project after project.

Surrounded by his private guard unit, Amin ruled Uganda with complete control. Anyone not to his liking vanished, usually under mysterious circumstances. Amin has openly admitted committing murder with his own hands, and ordering the execution of thousands of Ugandans without trial or even a moment of consideration.

Idi Amin's insanity could not be ignored. Indeed there was evidence that, even during his British army service, the president of Uganda had suffered from a mild case of syphilis which, with correct treatment administered in time, could have been cured, but wasn't. Amin had gone to Israel as guest of the government when it was suggested that he receive treatment. He was hospitalized at Tel Hashomer under a blanket of total secrecy. The doctors ran a series of tests, then prescribed a course of treatment—but the Ugandan president was contemptuous of pills and injections. Finally, since the patient refused all help, his time ran out. The Israeli doctors pronounced the disease incurable.

Amin's powers of rational judgment have vanished

completely. His behavior is no longer understandable, even to Africans. He is totally unpredictable, and prone to actions that conflict with each other and with the normal patterns of African behavior.

At the end of 1971, there were five or six hundred Israelis in Uganda. The embassy was manned by six or seven people—but their number did not at all reflect the intensity of activity. Both the embassy and Israel were rife with rumor about corruption among the Israeli residents in Uganda, but Israeli authorities never investigated. Indeed, the Israeli diplomatic offices were too wrapped up in a frenzy of enthusiastic creativity, even though it was at the expense of the Ugandan treasury.

Amin was still ecstatic about each new project. Any event in the Ugandan air force, or any opening of an airfield installation, housing project, or industrial plant, was reason for festivities and was fuel for the flames of his Napoleonic visions. He bragged frequently about his friendship with Golda Meir, Moshe Dayan, Burka Bar Lev, and other Israeli leaders.

His delusions of grandeur perhaps reached a peak on the day he demanded that the Israeli army instructors build and train a navy—even though Uganda is landlocked. In deepest secrecy, he revealed to Bar Lev and to Dr. Ashael that he holds nightly conversations with God, who also relays his instructions for Amin's new missions via angels who whisper in his ears as he sleeps. The doctor is convinced that these notions are symptoms of Amin's syphilis.

In the summer of 1971, Israel offended President Idi Amin. Four African heads of state went to Israel as emissaries of the Organization of African Unity to try and mediate in the dispute with the Arabs. The Ugandan, who was not popular with the other Africans, decided he wanted to visit Israel at precisely the same time. The Israeli government hinted, perhaps not delicately enough, that a visit at that moment would not be desirable. Amin's attempt to co-opt himself onto the African delegation had failed. For him this was a personal affront.

He was insulted again when he found out that the IDF intended to recall Bar Lev to Israel. He wrote to Moshe Dayan, Defense Minister of Israel: ". . . I am sending my defense minister to brief you on the needs of the Ugandan army. Our forces are undergoing basic and large-scale changes. For this reason I ask you most urgently to allow Colonel Bar Lev to remain in Kampala for at least two more years. His long experience will enable him to help us carry out the new projects that are now acquiring flesh and blood. . . ."

Meanwhile, the Israeli General Staff had heard rumors about the behavior of the head of the military mission in Kampala. A senior Israeli officer, Brigadier Raphael Vardi, was secretly sent to Uganda, accompanied by an auditor. Brigadier Vardi flew back to Israel bringing Burka Bar Lev with him. Although a great deal of evidence was presented, the investigation did not substantiate the accusations against him. Finally, chief of staff Lieutenant General David Elazar issued a letter permitting his return to Kampala, but he did not return the same colonel who had swaggered around Uganda as a close associate of Idi Amin. Nor were the relations between Uganda and Israel what they had been. Moshe Dayan had turned down another request. This time, Amin was asking for a squadron of Phantom jets to bomb neighboring Kenya and Tanzania as part of his campaign to claim tracts of land across the border as Ugandan territory.

The Israeli refusal sent Idi Amin straight into the arms of oil-rich Libya. Whatever was refused by Moshe Dayan was now given willingly by Colonel Muamar Qadaffi, who wanted the Israelis out of Uganda. Amin returned from a visit to Libya a completely different man. Suddenly he was making extreme anti-Israeli statements. It looked like Israel's days in Uganda were numbered.

The blow fell in March 1972. After demanding that

Israel return the "Occupied Territories" immediately, and after accusing the IAF of not training the Ugandan air force properly, President Amin ordered the Israeli military mission out of Uganda within four days. The Israeli colony in Kampala was in chaos. Homes and cars had to be disposed of in a hurry, and all baggage packed overnight. Amin refused to receive Bar Lev in audience and suggested that he should be the first to leave Uganda.

The Israeli construction contractors did manage to smuggle some of their heavy equipment across the frontier into Kenya, but a lot of expensive machinery was left standing in Uganda. The Israelis begged Amin for two more weeks in which to settle their affairs, but he was in no mood to listen. He expected the Israeli embassy to remove its personnel within ninety-six hours.

By the end of March 1972, not one Israeli was left in Uganda. Most of them left by night, arriving in Nairobi to request repatriation to Israel. No sooner were they out than Soviet-built MIGs, paid for by Libya, began to land at Entebbe military airfield.

A great deal of Israeli equipment remained in Uganda, including a Commodore executive jet belonging to Israel Aircraft Industries. Amin wanted it, but hadn't paid for it. In fact Uganda owed Israel tens of millions of pounds, but Field Marshal Idi Amin Dada rejected all demands. Amid a spate of anti-Israel declarations, he staged a large-scale military exercise purporting to show how the Golan Heights should or would be taken away from the Israelis. As if that was not enough, he opened the doors of the Ugandan air force academy to student pilots from the terrorist organizations.

Amin became a welcome visitor to the Arab countries, and occasionally offered advice to the terrorists. He sometimes compared himself with Hitler, yet chose an Israeli name—Sharon—for one of his daughters because, to the best of his knowledge, his wife had conceived while staying in the Sharon Hotel in Israel.

Shortly after his return to Israel, Colonel Bar Lev departed the ranks of the IDF, but Israel was not prepared to close the files on him: the police began to examine details of his behavior in Uganda. Aharon Chelouche, a senior officer with the Israeli police, was appointed to direct the investigation, yet he—like his military predecessor—did not find anything legally incriminating. Bar Lev went into private business and built himself a luxurious villa in a garden development near Tel Aviv. The army had no further interest in him.

All that remained of Israel and the vast aid program were piles of mechanical equipment, housing projects, airfields, and army camps. The home of Israeli ambassador Dan Leor, at 17 Mackinon Road, was now occupied by Haled el-Sid—who was as close to Idi Amin as the Israelis had ever been.

CHAPTER SEVEN

Idi Amin's
Private Nurse

Patricia Martel was awakened by the phone ringing in her hotel room at 5:30. Opening her eyes, she looked around for a moment, taking in the details of this strange place which she had arrived at through no choice of her own. She picked up the phone and Ahmad's voice greeted her. He told her he would pick her up in half an hour and get her to the airport in time for her flight to England.

On a short tour of Benghazi, before heading for the airport, Ahmad told her that Air France 139 had left the night before and had landed just before dawn at Entebbe, in Uganda.

"Uganda? I know the Ugandans. I was Idi Amin's nurse," Patricia murmured.

She had worked in Tel Hashomer Hospital with a South African internist, Dr. Bank. Because she spoke English, she had been chosen as private nurse for Idi Amin while he was hospitalized in Israel.

On her way to the Libyan Arab Airlines plane, equipped with a ticket and a Libyan visa, Patricia wondered how

Amin would have greeted her had she arrived at Entebbe. Would he have remembered her?

In the plane that left Benghazi and landed in Tripoli on its way to London, Patricia Martel was feeling something that was hard to define. Later she would call it "shame." The Libyans had showed a concern for her and her health, much more than she could have expected. Now she was ready to admit that apparently the Libyans were not as cruel and crude as the communications media painted them.

The British consul was waiting for her in Tripoli. He shook her hand, told her that he was "Her Majesty's representative," and departed. Now she became worried again. The plane was in no hurry to move on, and Patricia felt certain that her Israeli nationality had been discovered. Her mention of Israeli residence and lack of reaction the previous evening in Benghazi was small consolation. An hour passed and then finally a Libyan official arrived, handed her the British passport, and wished her "bon voyage." She put the passport in her bag, and once again breathed easily. Later she learned that while she waited at the airport, the Libyan officials had phoned England and tracked down the Manchester judge who authorized Patricia Martel's passport. The judge knew the Hyman family and confirmed the fact that Patricia Martel née Hyman was indeed a bona fide British citizen. As a neighbor of the family, she also volunteered the information that Patricia's mother had died, and the daughter was expected to join the family in mourning. Only after that call was the Libyan Boeing free to leave, with Patricia sitting in first class and eating a tasty breakfast. She was the only one of the Air France 139 passengers to escape the horrifying events which followed.

Nobody on board was asleep when the plane touched down at Entebbe Airport. Every passenger had new

theories and new questions. What will happen now? Is the
aerial adventure over? How will Idi Amin behave?

The guessing ended shortly after six in the morning,
when the familiar voice came on over the loudspeaker.
The terrorist was amazingly polite. He thanked the passengers for their cooperation and informed them that the
president of Uganda himself was coming to the airport
"to end the affair." Applause greeted the announcement.
The cold drinks handed out in the cabin could have been
champagne.

Sara Davidson could hardly drink for her nausea. The
stench from the toilets was disgusting after the twenty-
four hours on board, and it was impossible to keep any
semblance of cleanliness in the plane. Filth was accumulat-
ing under the seats and in the aisles. But Sara had to
admit to better spirits. Sitting in a grounded plane was
far more comfortable than the constant motion of flying.
Turning to Uzzi, she said quietly: "I'm afraid they're
going to separate us Israelis from the other passengers
while we're here. Then what will happen?"

No fresh supplies had been brought on board at
Benghazi, or now in Entebbe, so breakfast was a meager
offering. Each of the passengers received one roll and a
smiling *bon appétit* from the terrorist commander, who
added: "Enjoy your first breakfast in Uganda."

Sometime earlier, at 2 A.M., when the aircraft had passed
the "point of no return" and could no longer reach Ben-
Gurion Airport without refueling, the defense minister
and chief of staff ended their Lod vigil. They were wondering why the plane had not landed at Khartoum (the pilot
had never requested it). Much later, the prime minister
found out about the attempted coup d'état at Libya's
instigation which was taking place that same night. The
Sudanese refused the French Aerobus landing rights because they had caught a whiff of approaching revolution

from Libya and had closed down Khartoum Airport. General Numeiri, the ruler of the Sudan, was in Kenya at the time.

News of the landing in Entebbe caught up with Shimon Peres and General Gur as they were on their way to their north Tel Aviv homes. Prime Minister Rabin was only told in the morning. Rabin would need his sleep and, in any case, he could do nothing at this hour to influence the course of events.

Yitzhak Rabin was Israel's fifth prime minister, and had been for two and a half years. It was unlikely that the position gave him more satisfaction than it had any of his predecessors—David Ben-Gurion, Moshe Sharett, Levi Eshkol, and Golda Meir, who had all felt the wrath of Israel's three million citizens throughout their administrations.

In mid-1976, Yitzhak Rabin was having problems with his public image. From Golda Meir, his immediate predecessor, he had inherited the greatest hardships that Israel had ever faced: in security affairs, diplomacy, economics, and on the social scene. No Israeli government had ever been put to such severe tests—and at a time of low public morale following the failures of the first days of the Yom Kippur War. The Israelis were impatient and were demanding easy and fast solutions to difficult problems. When they were slow in coming, the government and the man who led it had to bear the full brunt of misguided public indignation.

Rabin had grown up in Tel Aviv and graduated from Kadouri Agricultural School—the source of many leaders in the defense of Israel. He took part in the Allied invasion of Syria, and in the liberation of illegal immigrants imprisoned by the British. When the British became aware of his underground activities, they locked him away for five months in Rafiah detention camp. When he came out, he was appointed a Palmach battalion commander. During the War of Independence, his main responsibility was for the food and ammunition convoys sent to besieged Jerusalem.

At the age of twenty-two, Yitzhak Rabin was a brigade commander—the youngest in the War of Independence army. His brigade fought the tough and bloody battles for the Jerusalem corridor and the life of the city itself. From Jerusalem Rabin moved to the southern front as deputy commander under Yigal Allon, who is now his deputy. Following that war Rabin took on his first semidiplomatic job: as a young lieutenant colonel he was a member of the Israeli delegation to the armistice talks with the Egyptians in Rhodes. Up to January 1964, when he was appointed chief of staff, he held a variety of senior positions in the IDF.

As chief of staff Rabin was the first to authorize the use of aircraft in localized incidents and flare-ups of terrorism. He was particularly sensitive about the situation of the settlements on the Syrian border, and made a point of punishing the Syrians at every opportunity. But he saw his main mission in thorough preparation of the IDF against the eventuality of war. His efforts paid off handsomely in the Six Day War. The victory over the armies of Jordan, Syria, and Egypt was greater than anyone had thought possible.

One year after the victory, Rabin traded his uniform for the formal attire of the Israeli ambassador to the United States of America. It was up to the ambassador to protect the achievements made by Israel when he was chief of staff. His term as Israel's senior representative in Washington marked a revolution in America's attitude to Israel, and his special relationship with the President and his advisors also helped to increase the IDF's military might.

Rabin returned to Israel in 1973. The outbreak of the Yom Kippur War caught him in transition from diplomacy to politics. He was a member of the Knesset, Israel's parliament, and then minister of labor in Golda Meir's government. Finally, amid the rubble of crumbling public faith in the Yom Kippur War leaders, Rabin was chosen to be prime minister. He had military and security expertise from his days as chief of staff, as well as a diplomatic background from his term as ambassador.

At 9:30 on the morning of Monday, June 28, the prime minister arrived at the Knesset building in Jerusalem to greet the coalition members of the Knesset Finance Committee who were waiting for him. The subject under discussion was the defense budget, and the session was well under way when Brigadier Poran received a phone call from London. Major General Zeevi wanted to know whether he should stay on in the British capital or should return home immediately.

"Stay there for the time being," the prime minister's advisor was told.

The telephones in the Prime Minister's office, the Ministry of Defense, the Transport Ministry, and the special bureau for the passengers' relatives never stopped ringing. From early Monday morning, the inventiveness and imagination of the Israeli public was evident in the thousands of ideas, at first offered hesitantly, and then with growing confidence, that began to pour in on how to get the captives out of Entebbe.

"I suggest that Israel should announce she is sending the requested terrorists from our prisons, and then I suggest a hijacking of that plane should be staged on the way to Entebbe." And then what? "Well, then Israel should send Archbishop Capucci, who will be on the plane, to Entebbe to negotiate the release of one set of hostages against the other. The plane that takes him to Entebbe should be full of soldiers, who will jump out and rescue the hostages."

Some of the suggestions were relayed to the prime minister, defense minister, chief of staff, or other senior officers. None were feasible—but the flood of phone calls did prove that the Israelis were in no mood to give in immediately. It was still possible that perhaps something could be done.

Yitzhak Rabin, like the other leaders of Israel, held very firm convictions about the terror operations against Israel. He knew nothing more, at this point, than the passengers' location at Entebbe, and he could really do nothing to effect any immediate change. The morning papers had speculated on this reversal of Arab terrorism. Gidon Gera, an expert on Middle East affairs and ex-senior officer, tried to guess why the terrorists had chosen to operate this way at this particular moment: "It seems that the Palestine question is no longer enjoying enthusiastic and growing support as it did a year or two ago when it peaked with Arafat's appearance at the UN. The war in Lebanon, the terrible slaughter, has damaged the Palestinian organizations' prestige, and detracted from their popularity even in the Arab world. The terror groups that thought up this hijacking wanted to prove one thing: the war against Israel continues! It is important to the terrorists to draw world attention away from events in Lebanon to the other front—the battle against Israel—as if to say that everything which harms the terror organizations in Lebanon helps Israel."

The guiding principle over the last two and a half years of Yitzhak Rabin's government had been that in any negotiation with terrorists, Israel must do everything possible to liberate hostages, by force if necessary, rather than give in to demands for the release of terrorists from the country's prisons. If the incident was within Israeli-controlled territory, the full responsibility lay with the government. In fact, during Rabin's premiership, the government had not entered negotiations with any terrorist group on anything that took place within Israel's boundaries.

When the locale of a terrorist strike was outside Israel, but in a country friendly to Israel, Rabin and his ministers believed that the responsibility for saving lives had to lie with the authorities of that country, and that it had to make all the efforts necessary. However, Israel was prepared to take military action beyond her frontiers.

Now, early on Monday evening, the prime minister, the defense and foreign ministers, and the others responsible knew that Israel was in deep trouble. Never before had so many Israelis been taken by force to a non-Arab country—and an unfriendly one at that.

The terrorists in the French Aerobus had an idea. Two of them asked the Air France stewards for their black ties, which they twisted together as a rope, and hung across the rear door of the plane. Then they opened the door, allowing fresh air to blow through the cabin, and equalizing temperatures between the cabin and the outside. The passengers were still nervous, but nevertheless the atmosphere was tranquil. From time to time, the terrorist chief chatted into the microphone. He told his captive audience that the hijacking was the work of the PFLP, and then repeated his accusations against France for helping Israel build an atom bomb and kill Palestinian "freedom fighters" in the streets of Paris. He told the passengers that they had no intention of killing them: "We only want to attract the world's attention."

Antonio Degas Bouviet stood on the ground and looked at the Aerobus. He had every reason to be satisfied: the hijacking was a success, and now—on the morning of June 28—he was taking command. Information that reached Israeli authorities indicated that, for a certain period, he had occupied a senior position in the terrorist network commanded by the man known as "Carlos." Bouviet was in command in London, but had escaped when the British uncovered the network.

Standing beside him on the tarmac was Faiz Abdul Rahim Jaaber. He had brought Bouviet to the airport in his white Mercedes. Within a few minutes they would be climbing aboard to take over responsibility from their four tired comrades.

The hijackers inside the plane were no longer insisting on closed curtains. Any passenger by a window or in a position to squint out the doorway could see two white men and a number of blacks, who were engaging the hijackers in conversation from the ground below. Among the group on the runway was a tall, bulky figure in camouflage uniform, liberally covered with medals and decorations. In less than a minute, all the passengers felt that their problems might soon be over: Idi Amin had arrived.

Half-jokingly, half-seriously, the terrorist up front in the cockpit now warned the passengers not to stand too near the improvised rope at the back doorway: "There are no steps. You might fall and hurt yourselves." His audience, who almost visibly snapped to attention whenever he spoke, in any case had no intention of walking to the back of the plane. The drawn revolvers and hand grenades were a very tangible warning not to move. An elegant figure, wearing a hat and clutching an envelope in his hand, now got out of the white Mercedes. He walked over to the front of the plane, and climbed up to talk to the terrorist commander.

Sara Davidson was hoping that the negotiations would be quickly over. The twenty-four hours of captivity had made her impatient. Perhaps they would separate the women and children from the men. Maybe they would send the women and children home? And Uzzi, her husband, would stay here alone. . . .

At midday the familiar German voice announced: "That's it! The drama is over. We are going by bus to the terminal building and getting off there." Almost all of the passengers were suddenly smiling. Some were hugging each other. A few Israelis even hugged the Palestinians. Sara Davidson shared the same elation that her husband, the boys, and all the others were feeling. The nightmare was over, finished! Flight 139 had landed and there was no more danger.

The nightmare was certainly over for one passenger

when the Libyan Arab Airlines Boeing landed at Heathrow, London. Patricia Martel had spent a good part of the flight in the cockpit, as a guest of the aircrew, who were charming and courteous.

All she had was what she was wearing. Her suitcase was still on board Air France 139. There were newspapermen and TV cameras waiting for her, but she was in a hurry to get to her parents' home in Manchester. But for the family tragedy, she might have been happy that she had succeeded in escaping from terrorists. But the circumstances were now completely different—and there were tears in her eyes.

No buses arrived by the hijacked plane. Instead, Michel Bacos started his engines, and taxied the Aerobus over to the old terminal building. As he killed the engines, steps were wheeled up to the plane. Slowly, the exhausted and cramped passengers lifted themselves out of their seats. Many of them carried their hand baggage with them. Others were asking about their suitcases.

"Come on, mother," Ilan Hartuv encouraged Dora.

Mrs. Bloch got to her feet with difficulty, and walked heavily to the door. Daylight dazzled her, just as it did the others. Almost all of them blinked hard for a few seconds before they could face the midday sun.

On the ground, the German commander of the hijacking team told Yosef Hadad: "It's all over. Everything's going to be alright." Yosef was already imagining a hotel, a warm bed, a cold shower, rest—and then the nonstop flight from Entebbe to Paris. He was sure it was all over.

But Lisette Hadad was suffering a sudden attack of fear. The plane was completely surrounded by Ugandan soldiers, their guns pointed at the passengers.

Sara Davidson also panicked. Like the others she had believed that the hijacking was a closed chapter, and that Entebbe was only a way station between Tel Aviv, Athens, Benghazi—and Paris and New York. The Ugandan rifles changed her mind. Something here was very wrong. There had to be a link between this threatening behavior of the Ugandan soldiers and the group of terrorists who were now standing by the plane. A few passengers who had started to wave goodbye to their captors quickly dropped their hands.

Faiz Jaaber and Antonio Degas Bouviet climbed out of the Mercedes that had brought them from the end of the runway. From now on it was their show.

Ugandan soldiers and civilians raced to the now empty plane, and started to collect anything that looked as though it might have belonged to the hijackers—apparently they wanted to destroy all traces of their identity. Meanwhile, the airport manager was explaining that he expected 260 passengers, and had prepared everything accordingly.

So he had been forewarned! What had he "prepared" and how long would they be detained were the questions in every passenger's mind.

CHAPTER EIGHT

"I, Field Marshal
Doctor Idi Amin Dada…"

"Surrender to terrorists is the worst thing that can happen
to the Jewish People. God alone knows, we preach to the
whole world about not giving in to them—we preached to
the Germans, the French, the Italians! Who haven't we
preached to? Can we give in?"

Minister Shimon Peres was speaking to his assistants.
His office in the Defense Ministry in Tel Aviv was
crowded with attentive listeners.

At noon on Monday, June 28, a temperature in the
mid-eighties was driving most Tel Avivans off the streets
and out of the terrace cafés. Many of the city's older
inhabitants headed for an afternoon nap in the coolness of
their apartments, while the younger clustered on the beach
or around the city's swimming pools. Heat and humidity
combined to make people irritable and nervous.

Heat didn't bother Kozo Okamoto, nor had it in his
three previous summers in an Israeli prison. In keeping
with standing regulations, the loudspeakers did not relay
radio programs during any incidents involving terrorists.
Aryeh Nir, the Commissioner of Prisons, had no interest
in exciting the inmates whenever hijackers demanded their

comrades' freedom in return for live hostages. But for some reason, Commissioner Nir decided to relax the rule at midday, and the broadcasts were resumed.

Even if Kozo was listening—which he wasn't—he would not have understood a word. For all his years outside Japan, he only spoke, read, and wrote Japanese—and was completely oblivious to his surroundings. He sat, day in and day out, filling stacks of notebooks with Japanese characters. Nobody knew what he was writing. Nobody even knew what he was thinking in his private cell.

The Israeli embassy switchboard in Paris was hard pressed to handle incoming calls from anxious relatives. The embassy spokesman could add nothing to the press, radio, and television reports. The building, not far from the Champs Elysées, had become a vast communications center. Security men blocked the entrance to all but embassy employees. Even the regulars among Israeli newspapermen in Paris couldn't enter. Traffic in and out was heavy: couriers rushed to and from the Quai d'Orsay, where the lights had burned right through the previous night.

Almost immediately after receiving news of the hijacking, the French Foreign Ministry set up a special staff to work around the clock. Jean Sauvignard, the minister, was beginning his second day without leaving his office. When the aircraft landed at Benghazi, he ordered an open line to Israeli ambassador Mordechai Gazit, to enable a constant two-way flow of information. President Valéry Giscard d'Estaing was demanding full reports on events at Entebbe, even if it meant disturbing the most important of his conferences during his visit to North America.

The Israeli evening papers carried banner headlines. But all they could really report was that the plane had landed in Entebbe, and that the passengers were in good health. Of course columns were given over to detailed descriptions and to surveys of airport security in the world in general, and at Lod and Athens in particular. Not to be outdone, the commentators wrote about the terrorist organizations, about Wadia Hadad, about the government and the way it was handling the hijacking. But news? There wasn't any!

Not a single serious word was written about the passengers. Their identity was a tightly kept secret. Transport Minister Gad Yaakobi appealed personally to editors and to the electronic media to give no names, no nationalities, no clues as to origins. There was a chance, however slim, that some of the passengers might be trying to bluff the terrorists, and any list could spoil that. To be doubly sure, Israeli censorship went to work with a will, deleting any inadvertent hint at identities.

In Uganda, Old Terminal was becoming stuffy and close. The disoriented passengers were packed in the long disused building; wherever they sat, clouds of dust rose. Though dressed for the summer they left only yesterday in Israel, and expected to find in Europe, most had rivulets of sweat trickling down faces, arms, and backs.

Some of the scores of Ugandan soldiers stationed around Entebbe Old Terminal were staring indifferently ahead. Others peered through windows into the building with obvious enjoyment. The passengers of Air France 139 were packed in, some sitting on the floor, some sprawled on armchairs, their scared children by their sides.

Exhausted, but still obstinate—as befitted the daughter of a pioneer family—Dora Bloch sat with dignity in a dusty armchair in the center of the hall. She was determined to remain calm as an example to her younger companions. After all, why give their captors the satisfaction of knowing they were terrified?

The first to be infected by Dora's tranquility were Ahuva and Eli Zeitani. The young couple from Beersheba had sat near Dora and her son on the plane. Long hours of tension and suppressed terror forged a friendship between them and the brave seventy-five-year-old from Jerusalem, Ahuva, a nurse by profession, was concerned about Dora, and spared no effort to make her comfortable—as far as was possible.

Sara Davidson had worked it out. The hallway was about three thousand square feet, so they had just over ten square feet per person. Even so, and despite the dust and stuffiness, Sara like many others was feeling somewhat easier. Sitting on solid, if uncomfortable, ground was safer than endless flying. Anyway, Ugandan soldiers were bringing in more chairs, apparently from a nearby hall. But the atmosphere was still gloomy.

The sight confronting Sara Davidson through a window that faced the runway was hardly designed to calm her apprehension. The Ugandan troops outside were all pointing weapons at the building. The last of her illusions was gone. When they disembarked, she had seen their four hijackers kissing Ugandan soldiers. When they walked to Old Terminal, it was between two lines of black troops. And now—the same faces and uniforms made up the cordon beyond the window. It seemed strange, though she did have a vague memory of a newspaper report about Idi Amin's support for the Palestinians.

Though the terrorist commander was using a portable bullhorn, the passengers had to strain to hear what he was saying. The German had accompanied them into Old Terminal. "We have arrived in Uganda, but you are in the hands of forces of the Popular Front for the Liberation of Palestine," he said. "We are already negotiating with your governments. We hope the affair will end in the best possible way. Now, listen carefully to our instructions— then no harm will befall you. . . ."

Negotiating? Negotiating! Like a magician's wand, the one word produced a sigh of relief and a tangible relaxation of tension. Many were willing to believe that liberation was imminent. Would they continue to Paris in the same plane? The same airline? Where, if not to France? In spite of their hopes for rescue, several passengers began stacking newspapers to make their seats on the floor more comfortable.

The German (Wilfried Böse, as they now knew him) and his three colleagues moved into a side room and flopped onto camp beds for a long-awaited rest. The passengers eyed them uneasily.

West German security police listed Böse as a German-born member of Baader-Meinhof, later known to have joined Wadia Hadad's faction of the Popular Front. He was the man who, in 1975, led an attack on an El Al plane at Orly Airport, Paris. With Johann Weinrich, another German anarchist, he loaded a bazooka into a Peugeot station wagon which he parked openly by the main building of the airport. As the El Al plane taxied out to a runway for takeoff, the two fired a rocket, which missed by inches, hitting a Yugoslav plane that was following the El Al Boeing.

Wilfried Böse and Johann Weinrich were caught by the French police but, for want of conclusive proof of their underground activities in France, they were handed over to the German authorities. The West German police made a great mistake by releasing them. Shortly thereafter Wilfried Böse was found to have connections with the terrorist known worldwide as "Carlos." As Carlos' collaborator, he was wanted for underground activities in a number of countries. This then was the character behind the courteous and cool facade.

After a late lunch of very fatty meat, rice, and curry, Sara Davidson was ready to show more interest in her surroundings. To one side of the room was a large stack of boxes. The relief terrorist team, who had joined the hijackers at Entebbe, curtly warned the passengers not to touch: "They contain explosives. Any jolt and. . . ." Both the fact and the voices were threatening. The boxes were evidently tea chests. But who could know for certain what they now contained? .

Newspapermen and a local television crew were allowed in to interview the hostages, and a Ugandan television camera was soon sweeping across a panorama of faces. Guided by an instinct that can only come from the Israeli experience, people were pushing into range of the camera lens. A telecast was both a life-insurance policy and a way of relaying greetings to worried relatives back home and abroad. This was something learned from Israeli prisoners of war in Arab hands after Yom Kippur, 1973: once you were seen on a TV screen, no one could deny your existence.

Shimon Peres was very tired. After his late night vigil at Ben-Gurion Airport, he only managed a few hours sleep before starting the new day. Now, on Monday afternoon, he sat in his Tel Aviv office, trying to guess whether or not Idi Amin was cooperating with the terrorists. His own inclination was to believe there was a direct link between the Ugandan president and the arch-terrorist Wadia Hadad. But the Israeli defense minister was hardly the type of man to force his views on his subordinates without adequate corroboration. This, as he told his assistants, was what he now wanted, adding: "If they are together in this, then it is the first time that a president, army, and state have cooperated with the terrorists in broad daylight. And if we give in to them, other African countries will also offer support for hijacking. No plane of ours will be able to fly to eastern or southern Africa."

"The troubles are only beginning," Yitzhak commented to Leah Rabin in their Jerusalem home. This was where the prime minister and his wife spent four days of each week, when government routine and Knesset sessions required his presence in Jerusalem. Basically an introvert, Rabin preferred to mull over his problems alone, taking advice from few men. Now, in the late afternoon, he was reviewing what promised to be a very unpleasant situation, and had already conceded that Israel had little choice but to negotiate. To save the hostages, Israel would have to release convicted prisoners.

Rabin knew it would not be easy. Particularly following the Yom Kippur War, the Israeli public was very sensitive to any exceptional government move—which surrender to terrorists would certainly be. Exchange of terrorists for innocent airline passengers could easily bring Israeli national morale crashing down—not that it had been noticeably high since the last war.

Previous governments had tried to hide unpleasant facts from the public. And when it was no longer possible to keep the lid on, the governments had dispensed minimal information and had tried to downgrade the importance of the event in question. Naturally, lacking data, the newspapers were left little choice but to expand on general knowledge.

The unpleasant facts were simple. In almost all cases where hijacked aircraft had been landed at Arab airports, Israel had been forced to pay the price. After the 1968 El Al hijacking to Algeria, Israel released fourteen terrorists; they were described as "small fish, invalids, and cripples" and the whole procedure was written off as "a humanitarian gesture." For two Israelis taken off a TWA plane at Damascus, Israel gave up fifty terrorists—and that fact hadn't been published at all.

Rabin was also reminded of the most painful incident of all. After the Yom Kippur War, the Egyptians announced that they were holding the bodies of thirty-nine Israeli soldiers. A saddened and hysterical Israel now proved more sensitive than ever before, and the Egyptians were well aware of it. In return for thirty-nine coffins, they got 130 live and healthy terrorists and spies straight out of Israeli penitentiaries. The names of the liberated convicts were never released. Nobody in government wanted to draw attention to this outrage.

Rabin voiced his thoughts: "Can the blood of Israelis in Entebbe be spilled just because I won't allow barter of terrorists for hostages?" He well knew that the country and government were in very serious trouble this time. The terrorists had been clever enough to bring the plane thousands of miles away from Israel. Rabin did not doubt for a moment what the terrorists would do if Israel did not release their comrades.

Idi Amin stood beaming in the doorway of Old Terminal, his white teeth shining. The passengers applauded him as he strode in, surrounded by his soldiers. This was the man who seemed able to solve the predicament, and if applause could flatter him. . . . For a moment Idi Amin looked as if his heart was softening. Certainly he was delighted at this reception.

"Shalom," he said.

The familiar word did the trick; some of the Israelis were now ready to believe everything Amin would say. A green commando beret on his head and IDF paratroop wings on his chest, the president looked pleased as he continued: "I think some of you know me. For those who don't, I am Field Marshal Doctor Idi Amin Dada, the man responsible for them allowing you off the plane to stay in Uganda. I did it for humanitarian reasons. I support the Popular Front for the Liberation of Palestine, and I think that Israel and Zionism is wrong. I know that you are innocent, but the guilty one is your government. I haven't slept since you arrived. I haven't yet received the demands of the Popular Front, but I promise you that I will do everything to protect your lives."

His words sent a chill through the audience, but most of them, even many of the Israelis, applauded the end of his speech. He departed, leaving them to argue whether he would actually help them.

Ugandan soldiers dragged in pots of meat, potatoes, green beans, and bananas. The food wasn't tasty, but everyone ate heartily. A Ugandan doctor circulated among them, handing out antimalaria tablets and lecturing on the dangers of the mosquito-borne disease, which was not very encouraging.

Night fell over Entebbe, the pleasant town originally created by the British—a place which boasted villas for the rich, a beach, luxurious resort hotels, a verdant botanical garden and, of course, the airport.

As darkness closed in, tens of thousands of mosquitoes and other bugs rose out of Lake Victoria's waters and moved inland. The exhausted travelers settled down on the floor and in armchairs, to wage a losing battle with the new invasion. Heat, stuffiness, and mosquitoes did nothing to alleviate their nervousness.

In Old Terminal, the lights burned all night.

CHAPTER NINE

The Ugandan
Chalk Circle

Yitzhak Rabin was used to getting up early, a habit acquired during his military career. At dawn on June 29, the third day, he glanced out of his office window, turning to acknowledge Froike Poran.

"Anything new?" Rabin asked him.

"For the time being, nothing from Entebbe," Brigadier Poran answered.

At this early hour, neither Jerusalem and Tel Aviv nor Paris knew anything about the terrorists, the aircraft, and its passengers—apart from the simple fact that they were in Entebbe—but London did. . . .

The night before, long after normal British working hours, Major General Rehavam Zeevi fought for urgent preliminary information on the hijacking. He spent the late evening in a room at the Israeli embassy in Palace Green. The prime minister's advisor on terrorism issued instructions to the appropriate Israelis in London and Paris to extract every bit of data.

"I have something," Froike Poran reported to Yitzhak Rabin, several hours later, based on Zeevi's first cable just in from London. "The hijackers, three men and one woman, are from the PFLP. They have pistols, hand grenades, and containers which they placed by the emergency exits of the plane."

Rabin listened carefully. This was more than they knew yesterday, but far too little to take any kind of action. In any case, neither Jerusalem nor Paris yet knew precisely what the hijackers wanted. He was shaking his head as he left his office.

Rabin climbed into one of his gray automobiles, and a small cavalcade raced across Jerusalem to the Knesset. A routine meeting of the Foreign Affairs and Security Committee was scheduled to begin at 8:30.

The Foreign Affairs and Security Committee is the most important of ten Knesset committees. The various parties appoint their most senior members to it, among them former army officers. In David Ben-Gurion's time as prime minister and defense minister, the committee enjoyed limited, almost nonexistent, influence. When Levi Eshkol became prime minister and defense minister, the government's attitude changed. More issues were brought before the committee, and fuller data on delicate subjects were submitted to their notice. Golda Meir as prime minister, with Dayan as her defense minister, kept up the practice, as did Yitzhak Rabin and Shimon Peres. The Foreign Affairs and Security Committee met behind closed doors, and its deliberations were never for publication.

Today's discussion began with a summary by Prime Minister Rabin. He reported, to the best of his knowledge at that moment, the details of the hijacking, and filled in for the committee members the decisions taken the day before by the ministerial team. In his diary for Tuesday, June 29, 1976, it was recorded that the prime minister would be spending the whole day in the Knesset. A final vote was scheduled on the state budget 1976/77 for later in the day. At 11:30 Yitzhak Rabin left the committee room and headed for his own office in the Knesset building.

"Shalom, Mr. Begin."

The leader of the opposition, at sixty-three, was many years older than the prime minister, and an experienced parliamentarian. For twenty-eight years, he had led the Herut party that had evolved from his underground Irgun Zvai Leumi organization, disbanded shortly after Israel won her independence. Menachem Begin was a brilliant orator, but even the best of his speeches had never brought him to the seat of ultimate power. He and his colleagues were the perennial opposition, sometimes aggressively opposed, but at other times ready to cooperate with the government.

Rabin had already sensed two days before that the hijacking was going to be one of the most critical problems Israel had ever faced in the war against terrorism. In matters of national security, the opposition in Israel considered itself an almost full partner with the government. There had been occasions in the past when prime ministers of Israel summoned opposition leaders to inform them of vital decisions concerning the country's defense. At the end of their meeting, the prime minister told the opposition leader: "Mr. Begin, I am of the opinion that this Entebbe business will be deadly serious and very difficult. If you have no objection, I would suggest that I keep you in the picture. . . ."

Begin thanked him. He was indeed interested in sharing in the deliberations on how to save so many lives. At the door of the office, the two parted with a handshake.

Hana Cohen had spent her first night in Entebbe Old Terminal half-asleep and half-dreaming—her repose troubled by anxiety for her children who lay at her side. The insects buzzing through the stuffy air, the engine noises from outside, the snoring and the rustling of newspapers that served as mattresses and, above all, the discomfort—none of it helped Hana sleep.

Hana stood out from the other hostages because she

could talk to the terrorists in their own language. She had arrived in Israel with two of her brothers under the auspices of an organization for youth immigration, and was trained as a seamstress. But she abandoned needle and thread to become a nurse and met her husband at Shaar Menashe Hospital where he served as an administrator. Like many other Israelis, Pasco Cohen, a tall, blond, and blue-eyed Jew, carried the scars of the Holocaust. Born in Focsani, a Rumanian wine-producing center, he moved to Bucharest as a youth. Weeks before his bar mitzvah, his father was killed by the invading German army and Pasco himself escaped with a scar from a Nazi's rifle butt. Trained as a hospital administrator in Rumania, he came to Israel and took over management of Shaar Menashe.

Shaar Menashe Hospital eventually closed down and the Cohens moved to Hadera with their two children. Hana gave up nursing and opened a clothing store. Pasco took over management of a local sick fund branch, winning respect as a loyal and conscientious worker. As a sideline, he had recently completed two research projects of his own—one on diabetes and the other on heart disease.

Pasco woke from a troubled sleep. He was still angry because the terrorists had taken his passport, driver's license, sick-fund card, camera, and movie camera.

"I have an idea," Hana told her husband and children.

She stood up and walked quickly over to the hijacker known as "Haled," who was standing in the doorway. This was the one who had told her, two days back, that he had "candies for her and dynamite for her kids."

"Perhaps we can take the children out to play in the sun?"

Haled was surprised by the question. It seemed impertinent. Nevertheless, he politely asked Hana to wait a moment while he went outside to ask his superior.

It was Hana's turn to be surprised: their captors agreed. Hastily, before they could change their minds, she took Yaakov, Zippy, and ten other children out to the courtyard next to Old Terminal. Armed Ugandan soldiers stared sternly, unsmiling, at Hana and the children. One of them, without a flicker of expression on his face, drew a white chalk circle, about twelve feet in diameter. Haled, who had joined the soldiers, put up a warning finger, and told Hana in Arabic: "You are forbidden to move out of the circle."

There was no real need for the warning. Hana ignored Haled and the Ugandans and set about organizing games: "catch," "hide and seek," "treasure hunt"—all inside the twelve-foot circle. After forty-five minutes, she suggested: "Let's dance a hora." The children formed a circle within the circle and began to move their feet. That was the end. Haled was furious. The singing and dancing—of all things an Israeli hora—reminded him of who and where they were.

"I don't agree to you dancing," he roared. "All inside!"

Uzzi Davidson was about ready to conclude that no salvation could come from Israel—2,187 miles away from Uganda. Through the windows of Old Terminal he could see the group of terrorists. Apart from the four on the plane, there were at least another three. Scores of Ugandan soldiers were stationed in two cordons around the building. One was quite close in, while the other was beyond the runway—and all the troops were armed.

Ron Davidson was the first member of the family to identify the soldiers' weapons: "Daddy, they've got Uzzis."

The "Uzzi" was an Israeli submachine gun named after its inventor, Major Uzzi Gal. Hundreds of thousands of them had been sold to armies and security services all over the world. Uganda was also a customer. Apart from the Uzzis, the terrorists carried their own arsenal, including grenades and Kalashnikov carbines.

Shortly before 5 P.M., the six ministers appointed to supervise handling of the hijack incident convened. Peres, Allon, Zadok, Galili, and Yaakobi arrived one by one in the prime minister's room in the Knesset, each accompanied by his senior assistants, and took their places around the rectangular table.

It was Yitzhak Rabin who insisted on General Gur's participation in this meeting. A while before the appointed hour, he suggested that Peres should summon the chief of staff immediately. Peres was not of the same opinion: "I doubt whether the chief of staff is needed at this stage. Mota went to watch an exercise in Sinai, or he's on his way there. . . ."

Rabin said, "We'll send a helicopter to get him."

The phone call caught Mota Gur at Dov Airport in north Tel Aviv, and he promptly abandoned his plans to watch the Sinai exercise. Jumping into his car, he ordered his driver to return through Tel Aviv. On the way to the Jerusalem road, he turned off for a moment at the General Staff building. Major General Yekutiel Adam, the head of General Staff Branch and virtually the "number two" man in the IDF, was in his office.

"Kuti," the chief of staff told him, "start thinking about plans for Entebbe. . . ."

That done, Gur's car raced up the inclines to Jerusalem. Gur took his place at the table at the very moment that the prime minister opened the meeting: "I have a question for the chief of staff."

The men in the room turned to look at the general.

Rabin's question was to the point: "Has the military a suggestion on how to extricate the passengers?"

Gur said, "Mr. Prime Minister, we have thought about it, and there isn't any military option at the moment—but we haven't given up."

The debate that followed was full of tension and surprises from all sides. General Gur explained that, the moment he received an urgent summons to Jerusalem, he understood immediately that, "They don't need me to replace the Foreign Ministry." So he had ordered his subordinates to make the necessary preparations. "There is a possibility of a military option," he concluded.

Rabin persisted: "What kind of an option do you mean?"

"If we want, we can get there, land a force to eliminate the terrorists, and get out. Then Idi Amin will have no choice but to release the hostages and the plane. . . ."

Rabin asked: "And how will the Ugandan army react?"

Gur smiled: "If they declare war, we'll win. . . ."

"I don't quite see it, but think about it, and prepare for it. . . ."

Defense Minister Shimon Peres asked for the floor: "I think that is neither the time nor the place for an operational discussion of military options. I also don't see us staging an operation to kill terrorists without liberating the hostages. Our job is to get them out; otherwise there's no room for any operation."

As a one-time chief of staff himself, Prime Minister Rabin was well aware that, given present circumstances, no general of any army could be expected to have a ready answer to the question he had posed to Mota Gur. In the past there had been serious differences of opinion between Rabin and Peres, but it now seemed that they were finding a common language.

A few minutes before the ministers convened in the prime minister's room, the phone rang in the office of Foreign Ministry Director General Shlomo Avineri. The callar was Mordechai Gazit, Israeli ambassador in Paris. He had just that moment received the list of demands submitted by the terrorists in Entebbe from the Quai d'Orsay. Professor Avineri hastily scribbled columns of names on a paper which he took with him to the ministerial meeting. A similar list came in to the defense minister's assistants at exactly the same time. Peres' military secretary, Brigadier Braun, and military aide-de-camp, Lieutenant Colonel Ilan Tehila, were getting their copies of the long list from the army report center and the press agencies.

Shlomo Avineri read out to the prime minister and his colleagues the names of forty terrorists in Israel they were required to release, and another list of prisoners whose release was demanded from Germany, Kenya, Switzerland, and France.

After he had read the list, the Head of the Institute for Intelligence and Special Duties reviewed everything that he knew about the hijacking operation, about the organization behind it, and about Dr. Wadia Hadad, who was commanding the operation from Mogadishu in Somalia.

"We will meet tomorrow," the prime minister said, "at a special session of the government, at eleven A.M. in Jerusalem."

Back in the hut compound of the Foreign Ministry, Shlomo Avineri ordered urgent cables to the embassies in Paris, Washington, Bonn, and Bern: "All vacations canceled, and stay on alert."

Sitting in his car as it raced down the road to Tel Aviv, Mordechai Gur was deep in thought. Though not surprised by the prime minister's question to him, the very idea of throwing the problem at the military was unexpected.

At forty-six, Mordechai Gur was the tenth chief of staff of the IDF. His military career began at an early age in the Haganah, where he attained junior command. After spending the War of Independence in a raider battalion on the southern front, Gur volunteered for the peacetime paratroops, rising to command and train a company which took part in many reprisal raids into Jordan, Egypt, and Syria.

In the 1956 Sinai Campaign, Mota Gur commanded a paratroop battalion that took part in a particularly bloody battle. After the war he was appointed head of Operations Department in the General Staff and, a little later, commandant of Command and Staff College. In 1966 he was given a reserve paratroop brigade, which he led in the 1967 Six Day War. The brigade was to have participated in the fighting on the Egyptian front, but was diverted to Jerusalem on the first day of the war. Gur's men took East Jerusalem, liberating the Western "Wailing" Wall and the Temple Mount—Judaism's most sacred sites. Overnight, Mota Gur became a nationally known figure.

After the war, he was appointed commander of IDF Forces in the Gaza Strip, and then commanding general of Northern Command. In 1972 he was posted to the Israeli embassy in Washington as military attaché, where he stayed through the Yom Kippur War. Gur was recalled from Washington to lead Israel's military delegation to the Geneva talks with Egypt in 1974, and then returned to Northern Command. In spite of his busy military career, he still found time to write books of stories for children.

When Lieutenant General David Elazar resigned following publication of the report of a committee of inquiry into the events of the Yom Kippur War, Mota Gur realized his dream and became chief of staff of the Israeli army.

Gur was always outspoken, ready to say aloud whatever he was thinking to himself. But Gur's self-confidence was dented by one simple fact: he hadn't been in Israel during the Yom Kippur War. He perceived the country's needs differently: he believed in the IDF and spoke of it in the terms used before the war. But the public wanted something new. The result was a flood of bitter criticism, particularly in the newspapers. None of his predecessors ever faced the epithets hurled at General Gur.

Mota Gur was a professional soldier, but not an advocate of aggression. He told, and tells, his intimate circle that, at the level of junior commanders, the principle should be to want contact with an enemy, and to want to destroy him. At the strategic level, victory must come from a minimum of battle—and the senior political-military echelon should win without all-out war.

Mota Gur will be recorded in public memory as the man who rehabilitated the IDF after the Yom Kippur War. In practice he built an almost completely new army. His disciples claim that there is practically no similarity between it and the pre-1973 IDF.

Gur maintained a very good working relationship with Defense Minister Peres. Gur actually benefited from the fact that his minister was not a military man. He respected Peres, enjoyed working with him, and in return, Peres gave Gur full backing. His relations with the prime minister were more complex. Rabin was a former chief of staff and, as such, would always compare his decisions to Gur's in any situation.

In the early evening, Gur came to Rabin's office. A number of senior officers were waiting in the anteroom. Before leaving Jerusalem, the general had phoned instructions to prepare a planning team for a military operation at Entebbe Airport.

CHAPTER TEN

Five Stones

In Jerusalem, early Tuesday evening, June 29, at the Foreign Ministry, a cable from the Israeli embassy, Paris, was handed to Haim Baron, the minister's personal assistant. He left his desk immediately and went to Yigal Allon's office.

The cable had arrived at the embassy by way of the French Ministère des Affaires Etrangères—the Quai d'Orsay. It contained the detailed conditions relayed from Entebbe, with a list of the terrorists to be released, confirming the one phoned through earlier to Director General Avineri.

"All fifty-three terrorists imprisoned in Israel and elsewhere to be brought to Entebbe Airport.

"A plane for the hijackers to be brought to Entebbe.

"Air France must arrange the flight to Entebbe of the terrorists imprisoned in Israel. The aircraft will carry the prisoners released by Israel, the aircrew, and no one else.

"The other countries requested to release prisoners must make their own arrangements to transport them to Entebbe.

"The ambassador of Somalia in Kampala, Hashi Abdulla, will represent the Popular Front for the Liberation of

Palestine in negotiations with the government of France, and the hijackers will recognize no one else as representing their interests.

"France will appoint a representative, who will handle negotiations with the Popular Front for the Liberation of Palestine."

Thursday, July 1, at 1 P.M. Israel time, was the deadline at which the Entebbe terrorists' ultimatum would expire. . . .

The defense minister of Israel sat behind drawn curtains, in the back seat of a car racing down the hills from Jerusalem to Tel Aviv. After several moments of silence, Shimon Peres' bodyguard had an inspiration. Turning in his seat by the driver, he said to the minister: "Shimon, I was once security officer of the Israeli mission in Kampala. I think it would be possible to exploit Idi Amin. He's a great admirer of Moshe Dayan, but absolutely crazy about Zonik [Colonel Zeev Shaham] and Burka [Colonel Baruch Bar Lev]. He's very sensitive about all the Israelis who did him favors. For all his madness, he doesn't forget them. I think we should do something along those lines. Perhaps it's worth a direct talk with Idi Amin, to try and influence him. . . ."

Peres reflected on the idea for a moment or two, then said: "Okay. Tomorrow, bring me Burka Bar Lev and two or three more officers who were in Kampala, and who know Idi Amin well. At this stage we have to try everything, including Amin."

Later that evening, Bar Lev and several other air force officers who had served in Uganda were summoned to an 8 A.M. meeting in the prime minister's office.

Earlier that day, in Entebbe, armchairs and couches were carried into the hall next door to the one in which the passengers of Air France 139 were being held. A terrorist and two or three Ugandans smashed a way through the plywood partition which separated the two rooms. A Ugandan soldier brought two planks to the gap, driving Jean Jacques Maimoni and his friend Thiery Sicker away to play their game—"five stones"—with the bottle caps that Jean Jacques had collected elsewhere.

With his dark complexion and "Afro"-style black hair, seventeen-year-old Jean Jacques Maimoni had already attracted the attention of all the other passengers. He was uncrowned king of the children. They followed him everywhere. For hours now he had been organizing games, with all the ease of someone used to working with young people. From time to time he left the children to prepare cups of coffee or tea for their elders. He was everywhere, never still for a moment. "The life and soul of Entebbe," they were calling him, trying to smile through the sadness that now marked all their faces.

Jean Jacques was a "child of their old age" for his parents, Lola and Robert Maimoni. The first boy, after five daughters, he had been truly spoiled by the family in their Tunis home. But the Maimonis did not stay in Tunisia long. They were driven out to France, and Jean Jacques grew up with his mother and sisters in a Paris suburb. His father, an investigations officer in the French police, was often away from home for long periods. At primary school Jean Jacques was an outstanding pupil. His dream was to follow in his father's footsteps: study criminology, then devote his life to rehabilitation of juvenile delinquents and street gangs.

Robert Maimoni had no desire to see his daughters married out of the faith, so he sent three of them to live in Israel. At sixty, when he became eligible for an early pension, Robert followed—with Jean Jacques and another of his sisters—to set up home in Natanya, a seaside resort north of Tel Aviv.

Jean Jacques went to an intensive Hebrew language course in Nirim, a kibbutz in the Negev; but did not feel at home there. Within eight months he was back with the family in Natanya. Accepted into a mechanical engineering school, he soon gave it up, deciding to learn draftsmanship. He had few Israeli friends, so eventually he gravitated to the French School in Jaffa, an institution run by the embassy of France in Israel in 1975. When he had completed part of the *baccalauréat* examinations, it was suggested to him that he should spend a year in France to fill in the remaining gaps. Meanwhile, he received his IDF draft papers. Conscription might well put an end to all his plans, so he applied for, and received, a year's deferment. He boarded Air France 139, together with his friend Thiery, on Sunday morning—on his way to make the most of the opportunity offered by that one-year reprieve.

Robert Maimoni, now a clerk in the French consulate in Tel Aviv, stood in Natanya post office writing a cable to Idi Amin: WE, THE PARENTS OF JEAN JACQUES MAIMONI AND THIERY SICKER, ARE PREPARED TO FLY TO UGANDA TO TAKE OUR CHILDREN'S PLACE AS HOSTAGES. Signing the cable form, Robert handed it over to the man on duty at the telegraph desk.

At almost the same moment a cable arrived in the office of the defense minister in Tel Aviv. Haim Yisraeli, the head of bureau, glanced at the signature and was reminded of something. As he read the message, his memory sharpened: I HAVE HEARD THAT THE TERRORISTS IN UGANDA HAVE INCLUDED THE NAME OF MY DAUGHTER ON THE LIST OF THOSE DEMANDED IN EXCHANGE FOR THE PLANE AND PASSENGERS. I ENTREAT YOU NOT TO PERMIT HER REMOVAL FROM ISRAEL. THANK YOU. ITZHAK HALASA.

The sender, an Arab, was the father of Theresa Halasa—sentenced to life imprisonment for her part in hijacking a Sabena airliner, and bringing it to Lod Airport, in 1972.

Twilight in Entebbe. The Belgian Jew who offered his phylacteries to others on the plane had just begun evening prayers. At first he was alone—then others joined in. As though by unspoken agreement, the corner of the room where they were praying fell silent—so as not to disturb the evening devotions. Sara Davidson stood aside, watching and gently rocking in time with the ancient chants.

"*Shema Yisrael, Adonai Elohainu, Adonai Echad. . . .* Hear O Israel, the Lord our God, the Lord is One. . . ."

Dora Bloch was serving as interpreter for the Libyan doctor sent by the Ugandans, since he knew only Arabic and a smattering of English. People were lining up to consult him, while Dora stood at his side, obviously proud to be of assistance. With an easy versatility she crossed the barriers between English and Russian, German, French, and Hebrew. The doctor thanked her effusively, made a list of drugs, and had them sent from a local hospital. For six-year-old Shai Gross, who was suffering from bronchitis, there was Penbritin. For others with more minor complaints, there were ample supplies of analgesics, and even tranquilizers.

"We've opened a branch of the sick fund," joked Dora Bloch, referring to the fact that the majority of Israelis get their medical aid from a labor union fund.

Outside Old Terminal, a cordon of Ugandan troops stood close in, while further out in the darkness another cordon could be faintly seen. There was no question in anybody's mind that the terrorists and the troops were on the same side.

Projectors floodlit the tarmac in front of the building.

Number eight, "Paratroopers Residences"—in Ramat Gan, at a wedding celebration, all the talk was of Entebbe. Many of the guests and the majority of Israelis were convinced that the terrorists had succeeded this time. After all, there wasn't really very much that anybody could do.

"I think we have no alternative. We'll have to give up some terrorists from prison." A burly paratrooper was speaking.

"It will be terrible," said the man's wife. "How will the public be able to accept surrender to terrorists?"

"They've got us by the short hairs," a veteran officer cut into the conversation. Tzuri Sagi was another pioneer of airborne troops, who had participated in dozens of operations across Israel's borders.

"The bastards. But listen," he suggested, "if it was possible to organize a Hercules, to fly to Entebbe and drop a few paratroops, then it could all be different. . . ."

"A Hercules can't reach that far," responded Tibi Shapira sadly. He was also a former paratroop officer. "Tell me, how far is it to Entebbe?"

"Twenty-five hundred miles," somebody volunteered.

"Then it wouldn't work," Tibi said with an air of finality.

The Head of the *Mossad*, also a guest at the gathering, had been listening closely to the conversation, and he commented: "What luck that we don't have to decide what's to be done. . . ."

The father of the bride was summoned to the phone, but quickly reappeared.

"Talik! It's for you!"

Deputy Defense Minister Yisrael Tal, until recently a major general on the active list, detached himself from a group in the corner of the garden. He returned briefly to shake hands with the bride and groom and their parents.

"I have to go. There's an urgent meeting. I'm sorry."

On his way out, Yisrael Tal muttered audibly: "It's about Entebbe, I'm sure. What else could be urgent at this time of night?"

CHAPTER ELEVEN

Selection

"Gentlemen . . . I was asked this afternoon by the prime minister if the IDF can rescue the hijacked passengers from Entebbe Airport. . . ."

To the right of the general's desk were direct telephones to the prime minister and defense minister, and a linkup to the central communications system through which Mota Gur could reach any unit of the IDF.

"Gentlemen," General Gur repeated, "what have you got to say?"

The highest ranking officer facing the chief of staff was the head of Staff Branch, Major General Yekutiel Adam, known as "Kuti." He was a field soldier—an infantry officer and a first-rate scout. Most of his service since 1948 had been passed in combat units, and he had been on the firing line in every one of Israel's wars.

Sitting by Adam's side was the commanding general, air force, Benny Peled, a member of a long-established pioneer family in Israel, who began his military career as an aircraft mechanic but eventually became one of Israel's first jet pilots. Peled, who had a degree in aeronautical engineering in addition to his other qualifications, was a tough character, inclined to be contemptuous of public opinion.

Across the table from Adam and Peled sat Major General Shlomo Gazit, head of Intelligence Branch in the General Staff. At fifty, Gazit could look back on a longer career than most other IDF officers, one which included service as head of bureau to Moshe Dayan, when he was chief of staff, in the mid-1950s. Quite apart from his seniority, Gazit enjoyed widespread respect for his intellect.

The fourth and youngest officer was Brigadier Avigdor Ben-Gal—a lanky thirty-eight-year-old known to one and all as "Yanosh." He had commanded an armored brigade on the Golan Heights during the Yom Kippur War, when his men and machines stopped the onslaught of Syrian armor. His brilliant management of the decisive battle on Golan, despite his incredible disadvantage in terms of numbers of troops, had made him one of the rising stars in the IDF firmament.

"Gentlemen," the chief of staff said, "I want to hear suggestions. . . ."

"I would propose landing an airborne force at Entebbe Airport. Once we have eliminated the terrorists who are guarding the hostages, Idi Amin will have no alternative but to let them go."

"To succeed in a military operation, we must have complete control over Entebbe and the neighborhood. It can be done by dropping a thousand paratroops. . . ."

"What about boats across Lake Victoria? Entebbe Airport is very close to the shore. . . ."

General Peled was well prepared for the meeting. When the chief of staff phoned his instructions through from Jerusalem to prepare a planning team, Benny hadn't wasted a moment. In the short time between that first call and this meeting, his proposal was in shape. Now he explained the logistics problems in getting to Entebbe and back. The necessary force could be flown, nonstop, to target. Peled in fact was the one who suggested taking control of the airport and surroundings. The chief of staff didn't yet agree, however.

Lights were still burning in the offices of the chief of staff and the defense minister. The plan submitted by Benny Peled had established a basic fact: if they wanted to, they could get to Entebbe.

General Staff planning teams checked and rechecked every detail that had arrived from the scene of the hijacking. Not much was known, but possibilities had to be measured against all available data.

It was late evening in Entebbe. A number of the passengers were quietly discussing the terrorists' demands, of which they had been informed during the afternoon. Now that they knew all the details, tension was growing, though the deadline was still two days off. Most of the discussion revolved around how the government of Israel might react. Would they capitulate to blackmail or not?

Suddenly, screams cut through the discussions and arguments, and shook the uninvolved from their torpor. A Frenchwoman in her fifties alternately shouted and laughed. While her fellow passengers remained frozen in astonishment, she stripped off her undergarments and urinated on her clothes. Michel Bacos, the first to approach her, was met with an apathetic, glassy stare.

Three terrorists heard the sounds and ran into the building. They were at first at a loss as to what to do and finally burst into laughter, making no move to help the unfortunate woman.

"She's gone mad." The whisper passed around Old Terminal.

The woman's behavior became even more pathological. Ignoring orders from their captors, she laughed in their faces and tried to push her way outside.

"It's an act to get out of here," someone ventured.

The Libyan doctor suggested that they all ignore her till she calmed down. He gave her an injection, but apparently it was too weak to be effective.

The mood now was even sadder. This woman's madness, whether real or faked, depressed everyone else.

"One possibility," Sara Davidson told Uzzi, her whispers barely audible even in the silence, "is that the terrorists will separate the Israelis and the Jews from the others."

She looked across at the men who had finished installing an opening into the next room. Earlier, a Ugandan soldier had nailed two planks over the opening in the shape of a "T." Only a few hours ago, Michel Coujaux had asked, in the name of all of them, for more space. Cramped and stuffy conditions were making for enormous discomfort. The open gap in the plywood partition and the chairs and couches which had been carried next door created the impression that their captors had accepted Michel's request. Soon there would be more room, as the passengers spread out over the second hallway.

Suddenly, there was more bustle inside Old Terminal. Wilfried Böse appeared, bullhorn in hand and a faint smile on his face. As always, his voice was relaxed and his words were almost reassuring: "I'm now going to read a list of the people who are here. When you hear your name, stand up and go into the next room. We have opened it up for your comfort, so you won't be so cramped. It has nothing to do with nationality. . . ."

The silence of death itself descended on Old Terminal.

"It has nothing to do with nationality. . . ."

Further explanation was unnecessary. A sudden cold shiver rippled through the captives.

"Hana Cohen," Böse read from the first blue passport.

Hana heard her name as if in a distant dream. She looked at them, her husband and children, then walked to the opening in the plywood partition. The "T" shaped planks left perhaps thirty inches of free space above the floor. Hana Cohen bent down almost to her knees and shuffled through, as the German girl watched with an evil smile on her face.

"Ezra Almog. . . ."

Wilfried Böse read another name from a blue Israeli passport. Very slowly, Ezra Almog, ex-member of Kibbutz Ein Dor, approached the low opening. Jeanette, his wife, watched incredulously, then—before he crawled through— burst into bitter tears. Ezra turned back for a moment to tell his wife: "I want you to swear not to follow me. Stay on this side!" Jeanette Almog held a French passport.

Dropping to his knees, Ezra crawled into the "T" and vanished into the other side. Jeanette sobbed. There was not a word from the others.

Dora Bloch was the first to master her own emotions and approach the sobbing woman. In a quiet voice, she explained to her that Ezra was right. It would be best for Jeanette to stay. But her soothing words didn't help.

"I can't live without him—and he told me not to follow him," Jeanette wept.

Next Böse named an American couple. By their dress, they seemed to be very religious Jews. The woman had on the wig worn by Orthodox wives in order not to appear attractive to men other than their husbands. The man was stunned—he wasn't an Israeli. He, like his wife, had been sure that he wouldn't be called. Suddenly the full implication sank in.

"I'm American," he shouted, "I'm not Israeli. I have no connections with the Israelis. I have an American passport! I'm not going through there!"

Wilfried Böse lifted a finger toward the opening. The man's protest ceased and the American couple walked as if in a daze over to the "T," bent down and crawled through. Right behind them were the Belgian couple. The man who had lifted the spirits of all with his phylacteries and invitation to prayer.

"Dora Bloch. . . ."

The elderly woman pulled herself up from an armchair

and walked slowly to the gap. Scores of eyes followed her slow march and proud posture. One of the terrorists suddenly softened. Taking her arm, he led her around to the door between the two halls. Dora Bloch was not obliged to crawl on her hands and knees.

Inside the other room, Mrs. Bloch turned immediately to Ezra Almog.

"You meant well—but you must take your wife with you. She won't be able to stand it without you. . . ."

"At least that way one of us will get out of here," Ezra defended himself. "There's no point in her being here with me. Perhaps they'll let her out. . . ."

"No," Dora repeated, "she must be with you."

Ezra listened, thought a moment, then walked over to the terrorist who was standing by the "T" and asked him to call his wife. Jeanette Almog bent over and crawled through to join her husband.

An ailing Jewish couple from Morocco also returned to the second hall. The terrorist had agreed to allow them back to the first hall, but without their twenty-year-old son. They opted to stay with him.

Yitzhak David stood still, next to his wife Hadassa, as though hypnotized by the sight of people crawling through the improvised doorway. His turn had not yet come. Slowly, the number of Israelis around him decreased, then the number of Jews. Yitzhak was thinking about his home in Kiriat Bialik, about his son and daughter who would be there at this hour.

"All my life," he pondered aloud, "I have been telling my children about the concentration camps in Germany, so they should know—as Jews and as Israelis—what was done to the Jewish people. But I always told them never to hate the entire German nation. Children shouldn't be made to pay the price of their parents' criminal behavior. . . . But now that German boy and girl—and they're very young—are doing exactly the same thing. . . ."

Selection.

Jews have lived more than thirty years with the shadow of the Nazi holocaust, through which six million of their brethren were slaughtered. Millions in Tel Aviv, New York, London, Paris and São Paulo who went through the Holocaust years in concentration camps, shelters, and bunkers—and in endless flight from death—can never forget it.

During World War II, there were millions of dead and tens of millions of wounded, there were gas chambers, mass graves, ovens, but perhaps worst of all was the Third Reich's concept of "selection."

"Selection" to the Jewish People was carried out by a handsome, erect German in an SS uniform with polished jackboots, a white glove on one hand: "the Angel of Death of Auschwitz," "the Doctor of Satan," he was called. Josef Mengele waited at the railhead for the torrent of Jews who flowed into Auschwitz. He watched the columns of miserable men, women, and children, marking the fate of each with his swagger stick or finger. If he pointed to the right, his victim followed the road from which there was no return—to the gas chambers, disguised as "showers." If he pointed to the left, a temporary reprieve: the victim went to forced labor, or to medical experimentation under the supervision of Mengele, the head doctor of Auschwitz.

No one objected then, and no one objected in Entebbe. As thousands of insects again rose from the waters of Lake Victoria and homed in, and the buzz of mosquitoes blended with the muted sobbing of women, the slow exodus continued. After five or six more names, there could be no more doubt that Wilfried Böse's selection was between Israeli citizens and Jews—and all the rest.

Michel Coujaux watched the Israelis crawl beyond the partition. He asked himself: "When will we reach the point at which it's permissible to fight and die here in Entebbe, rather than continue this passive and humiliating existence?"

In a corner of the new quarters, two terrorists sat examining passports and issuing the hostages a special passport of the Popular Front for the Liberation of Palestine as a substitute. Uzzi Davidson noticed that the ink on the PFLP document was still wet. He didn't doubt that it had been printed only hours ago, here in Uganda.

Rina Kipper sat beside her husband, Yerach, and laid her head on his shoulder. She had a premonition of imminent parting. Whether maliciously or not, the terrorists hadn't called the names of complete families and this added to the growing air of hysteria in Old Terminal. "I didn't want to part from my husband," Rina said later, "but suddenly they called my name. I felt as if being led to the slaughter. . . ."

In another corner of the new hall sat a terrorist emptying hand baggage onto the table. He put some items back, others he kept by him. Mostly he set aside documents, cameras, and watches and gave the passengers in return a slip of paper with some lines written in Arabic.

Moroccan-born Hana Cohen volunteered a translation. She began to read a poem—"Words on the Lips of Resistence"—by Suleiman el-Aissa, an otherwise unknown poet in the ranks of the terrorist organization:

> *In the Name of the Nation*
> I swear on the Arab flame
> That springs from among the soldiers
> We are the way
> *I Swear on the Brandished Sword*
> In your heat, mountains of anger
> The desert
> We are the way
> *I Swear by the Homeland*
> Ransacked
> Our revolution will continue to be
> Red

We Shall Lead Our Front
   To victory and our revolution
   Will remain red
In the Name of the Nation We Shall Enter the Depths
   Of the night to the birth of
   The banished to exile.
   Hoi, you words
   Vaunted of the revolution,
   Split asunder the soil,
   Revive the blow
   Revive the promise of the sun.

Yitzhak and Hadassa David passed through the "T" into the other hall. Yitzhak was still in a daze. The last few minutes in Entebbe Old Terminal had transported him thirty-two years back into the past.

Selection.

Who lives?

Who goes to the ovens?

"If you don't want to go to the gas chamber, tell them that you have a trade in building. . . ."

Father said he was a glazier.

Yitzhak said he was a plumber.

Selection.

Blue tattoo—left arm: 12346.

As though shaking himself free of a nightmare, Yitzhak turned to Hadassa and asked: "How long is it since we entertained those children?"

Kiriat Bialik, Yitzhak David's home town in northern Israel, had signed a twin-city agreement wtih Steglitz, a suburb of Berlin. Yitzhak David had been one of the leading opponents of union with a German town, but he finally gave in: "I was well aware that Israel didn't have many friends, and couldn't always choose the ones she wanted. Given our critical political and international situation, we need every friend, and that included Steglitz-

Berlin. On the other hand, it was difficult for me to realize that we were going to stand face to face with Germans as if all was forgotten."

In the spring of 1976, orphan children from Steglitz-Berlin visited Kiriat Bialik. Yitzhak, as deputy chairman of the local council, welcomed them. "I treated them, in all sincerity, like any other children who came to visit. I didn't think of them for a moment as Germans," he reminded himself and his wife.

At last, the selection was finished. Forty-nine men, women, and children remained in the first hall. All the others, including the aircrew, had made the debasing trip into the other hall. They were now more uncomfortable than before. One hundred and ninety-two hostages were crammed in to a room forty feet by eighty.

Sara Davidson peered through the partition at the group she had left behind. She could see the man in the satin dressing gown. Sara didn't know his name, but would always remember the man who treated Entebbe Old Terminal as if it were the "royal suite" of the Waldorf-Astoria. Each morning and evening, he put on his satin dressing gown to go to the washroom, toilet case in hand, to shave and brush his teeth. He went and came back as though this whole sordid business did not concern him. Again he was on his way to the washroom to brush his teeth before settling down for the night.

The toilets at night became the meeting place between the two groups of passengers. Each time that Sara headed to the washroom, a number of the women from the other side stood up and followed her. Among them was always an American with whom Sara had become friendly.

Once inside the washroom, the American woman whispered to her, "What can we do for you Israelis?"

Sara simply shrugged. There really was not much that could be done.

The lights stayed on in Old Terminal. Their captors would not allow them to be turned off, for fear of unpleasant surprises. Outside, aircraft engines thundered in the night sky.

The anguish of relatives and friends of the hostages was reaching its peak. They stormed the offices of Air France in Paris and Tel Aviv, trying to avoid the television cameras and reporters waiting to record yet another story of human misery. Some of the families turned to the Israeli embassy: "We are in favor of total capitulation to any conditions. The only thing that matters to us is to get our children and parents back as soon as possible," they begged.

"I would ask help from Satan himself, if I thought it would be of any use," a Moroccan Jewess told Edwin Eitah, an Israeli journalist in Paris.

"We are not going to sleep until we find a solution for the rescue of the hostages at Entebbe," Benny Peled informed his subordinates in his office in the General Staff building.

A steady flow of paper and data arrived in the offices of Peled's assistants: distances from Tel Aviv to Kampala, fueling possibilities, weather forecasts, airfields en route, radar stations from Tel Aviv to Entebbe, takeoff and landing strips at the Ugandan airport. . . .

During the night an aide phoned the homes of senior air force officers, past and present. Each of them had served, at one time or another, as flight instructors in Israel's program of assistance to the Ugandan air force.

The message was brief: "Tomorrow morning, at eight, in the general's office. . . ."

CHAPTER TWELVE

The Long Arm

Hana Cohen had been sitting in the new hall for two hours waiting for her husband, Pasco, and the children, Yaakov and Zippy. Now, with the selection almost completed, she suddenly saw them come crawling through the low "T" toward her and her face broke into a smile, although a while later she felt guilty for being so relieved to see the rest of her family leave the safe side for the unsafe.

The Ugandan soldiers began dragging in mattresses from next door. Dora Bloch received one and Ilan helped her place it near a wall before drawing up an armchair next to her. Though a mattress was far softer than the bare floor, the hostages could get no real comfort from them since both the Ugandans and the terrorists had insisted: "Don't remove the paper wrappers!" The result was that the slightest movement caused noise. With scores of people restlessly tossing and turning through the night, the paper-wrapped mattresses became a form of exquisite torture. Their captors hadn't thought of it, but they had added a maddening discomfort to the tension of Old Terminal.

By now it was late evening. More mattresses and armchairs were being brought in from the first hall, as well as banks of seats apparently torn from old aircraft. A Tel Aviv lawyer, Akiva Lakser, volunteered to distribute the furniture among his companions to prevent squabbling in front of the pistol barrels of the terrorists. He quietly began to perform his task with great tact, distributing the few mattresses among the older people, the women and children, and finally to the younger hostages.

The man from Hebron, Faiz Abdul Rahim Jaaber, made a sudden appearance in the doorway. Brandishing a pistol, he struck a brutal blow with its handle at Akiva Lakser's back. Akiva doubled over for a moment, then quickly moved away.

Just as suddenly, another visitor entered the room: it was President Field Marshal Doctor Idi Amin Dada.

"Shalom," he said.

As it had yesterday, the traditional Hebrew greeting again prompted involuntary applause from almost everyone, despite the hostages' previous argument about Amin. Even those who felt the man was insincere were now ready to pay any lip service to get out of this inferno.

Idi Amin's speech was brief: "I don't sleep at night. I am doing everything possible to achieve the release of the people, or at least part of them."

Amin smiled and continued: "You know that the hijackers suggested they release forty people, but I—Idi Amin Dada—convinced them to release forty-nine passengers."

His words confirmed the worst predictions of the pessimists. This was it then! Tonight, or maybe tomorrow, the people left in the first hall would be free. The victims of Böse's selection were to remain in Entebbe.

In the first hall, the passengers who were about to be released heard the applause, and were anxious to know what Amin had done to deserve it. But he wasn't finished with his Israeli audience: "I'm doing everything for you, but your government isn't doing anything. You are in the power of the terrorists but, if you return home, I hope you will work for peace."

Sara Davidson's attention focused on one word: "if." "What does that 'if' mean?" she asked Uzzi. "*If* you return home. . . ." They looked at each other and at their sons with solemn faces.

Amin left in his helicopter and in a few moments several Ugandan women came through the partition carrying new blankets, more mattresses, and clean towels.

It was late at night in Entebbe, but few settled down to sleep.

Jail el-Arja glanced at his watch. His tour of guard duty was about to end. In a few more minutes his relief would appear, and Jail would go to sleep in the side room allotted to the hijackers. Jail, thirty-four years of age, was born in Beit Jala, near Jerusalem. His parents in fact still lived there. He moved to Cairo in the early 1950s, then spent a few years in a Jordanian prison, sentenced for activities on behalf of the Arab Nationalist Party. In Cairo, he studied business management, continuing with a course in law. As an educated man he was an invaluable lecturer for the Palestinian cause in the outside world. Eventually he was appointed representative of George Habash's PFLP in South America, where he made contact with an international terrorist named Ramirez Sanchez—better known as Carlos. Jail was a man of words, not deeds. Guarding the Air France hostages was in fact his first field job.

He peered into the passenger hall. Despite the hour, many of the hostages were awake, though still sprawled on their mattresses and squirming uncomfortably. The noise of the paper wrappers was as disturbing as ever.

On the lot in front of Old Terminal stood a small fleet of cars belonging to the terrorists in Uganda: a white Mercedes, a gray Fiat, and a red Toyota.

A cable was on its way from Jerusalem to Paris: PLEASE BRING TO THE NOTICE OF THE HIJACKERS IN UGANDA THAT

NUMBER THIRTEEN ON THEIR LIST, MUZNA KEMAL NIKOLA,
HAS ALREADY BEEN RELEASED AND IS NOT IN ISRAEL. SHE IS
APPARENTLY IN LONDON. Muzna Nikola, a nurse by profession, spent a few years in London with her brother, a
doctor, before returning to Israel on a mission for the
Fatah terror organization. She was caught by Israeli security, served a few years of a prison sentence, and then
was released on condition that she left the country. Muzna
returned to London, but the terrorists apparently weren't
aware of it.

Another cable was on its way this morning from Paris
to Kampala: SYLVIA AMPALA MASMALA IS NOT IN FRANCE.
APPARENTLY SHE LEFT FOR COLOMBIA. Masmala, a beautiful twenty-five-year-old, worked as a secretary in the Paris
office of Lloyds. She was arrested in Carlos' apartment on
the left bank of the Seine—when French security closed in
on the "most-wanted terrorist" of the Western world, and
almost caught him. Carlos killed two detectives and a
police informer, then escaped alone. Accused of concealing
firearms, Sylvia gave her word not to leave France, but it
was suspected that she had gone home to Colombia.

"What can you tell me about Idi Amin?"

Shimon Peres' opening question was brief, but he expected a detailed answer. Facing him were the two air
force officers and Burka Bar Lev. Next to him sat his
military secretary, Brigadier Arye Braun. One of the airmen started his description. Bar Lev spoke next, followed
by the other airman. The conversation covered everything
from Idi Amin to the Ugandan army and Entebbe Airport, where the Israeli trio had spent days, nights, weeks—
even months and years.

Layer by layer they stripped off Amin's outer skin to
reveal his weaknesses. What did he like? Who did he hate?
How was one to talk to him? And what about?

"Perhaps Idi Amin won't want to talk to Israelis at all,"

one of them said. "Yet if he does, then only Burka can do it. . . ."

"Burka," said Shimon Peres, "this entire office, all the telephones, all the secretaries—are at your disposal. . . ." Time was growing short. The next day, at 1 P.M. Israel time, the terrorists' ultimatum was due to expire.

Brigadier Braun escorted Burka Bar Lev into a nearby room. Within seconds everything was under way to get the retired colonel his phone contact with Idi Amin's presidential palace in Kampala.

At the same time, Arye Braun was on the phone from the defense minister's office in Tel Aviv to the prime minister's military secretary in Jerusalem. Froike Poran listened carefully, then put through a call ordering Gandhi Zeevi to take the first flight out of London. Ten minutes later, he walked into Rabin's office to tell him about the call to Amin.

Ilan Kfir had dialed the number countless times. The London correspondent of *Yediot Aharonot*, a Tel Aviv evening paper, had been calling the international exchange in an attempt to get a call through to Idi Amin's office in Kampala. At last the operator had the Ugandan president's personal secretary on the line.

"Hello. Is it possible to talk to the general?"

"Sir," replied a somewhat annoyed voice, "His Highness is a field marshal—not a general!"

Kfir quickly corrected himself, in the hope that a polite amendment would appease the man.

"What do you want to talk to His Highness about?"

"I would like to hear particularly about Field Marshal Idi Amin's personal share in the negotiations."

There was no answer for a full minute, then the secretary returned to the other end of the line.

"The president talks only to heads of state. Not everybody can talk to him!"

*   *   *

All were now awake in Entebbe. Dora Bloch and Ilan Hartuv stretched cramped muscles, the woman on her mattress, her son in his armchair.

The first sight that morning through the windows of Old Terminal was hardly encouraging. Ugandan soldiers were laying wires in a crisscross pattern around the building.

"They're booby-trapping us ready for demolition," a passenger panicked.

"Those are electronic eavesdropping devices," ruled an expert.

Inside the two halls the tension rose, as hundreds of eyes followed the slow movements of the Ugandans—until they finally finished their job and left the area. As they went, a soldier came into the building and announced: "The wires outside are for you."

He was greeted by a moment of absolute silence.

"They are for your laundry. Anyone who wants to wash clothes may do so in the washrooms. You can hang them outside to dry. . . ."

The Ugandan couldn't understand the sudden sigh of relief. Permission to wash and hang clothes was a big step forward because it meant a chance to move around, even to go outside. Quick to exploit this unexpected gift, the women flowed through the doorway to hang wet garments and play "catch" with their children, while another group started a game of soccer, using a preserve can as football.

Wilfried Böse stood in the entrance to Old Terminal, a Scorpion submachine gun in one hand. The atmosphere was relaxed. It could actually have been a summer camp somewhere in Israel, rather than a detention area for Israelis who might be executed at 1 P.M. the next day.

Catching a faint smile from Böse, Sara Davidson walked over to him: "Perhaps we can take our bags out of the plane?"

"We wanted to bring them out," he answered politely,

"but they are in special containers, and this airport doesn't have suitable equipment to unload them."

Since she had already made the first move, Sara continued: "I don't understand you! How can you hold so many people without decent mattresses and blankets, in such terrible conditions?"

Böse dug into a pocket for a pencil and paper, and started to make a long list of Sara Davidson's requests: blankets, mattresses, soap, clean the toilets. . . .

When he had it all down, he warned her: "I want you to know that I am not in command here. I was only in command on the plane. They are the officers. . . ." He pointed in the direction of Antonio Degas Bouviet, Jail el-Arja, and Faiz Jaaber. "Now they're in charge."

Jean Jacques Maimoni didn't remain in the hall when the women and children were allowed out. He organized the games, chased the preserve-can "football" with the others, raced back and forth across the tarmac, despite the fact that, as an asthmatic, he didn't find it easy to compete with the youngsters.

The night before Jean Jacques had been near the end of his stay in Entebbe. Since he held only a French passport, he remained with the non-Israeli group. The pleasant perfume of freedom was already in his nostrils, as he contemplated the long route on to Paris. Then he heard a scream. The German girl discovered him among the French. She rebuked the Arab terrorist who had allowed Jean Jacques to stay put, and then ordered him into the other hall with the Israelis.

When Jean Jacques came through the "T," the others were sorry for him, yet they were happy to have him among them. He was a spark of life, keeping the children busy while remaining cheerful and attentive to the elders. This boy seemed, in many ways, much older than his years. The experience in Entebbe would undoubtedly add to his maturity.

*　　*　　*

The home of the head of Israel's Institute for Intelligence and Special Duties was in a typical garden suburb. This morning, the household was awake earlier than usual. The country's top secret service man was in his car on the way to his office well ahead of early morning traffic. He arrived before his assistants. Sitting at his desk, he pulled a square sheet of blank paper from a small box, and wrote across the top of it: "List of Essential Data."

Engrossed in thought, he recorded item after item of information that he still lacked on the Air France hijacking and on Entebbe Airport. And, at this early hour of morning on Wednesday, June 30, the list of missing data was a long one. One thing was certain: the main battle was against the hands of the clock. Thirty hours remained before the expiration of the Entebbe ultimatum.

The Jews' struggle to exist in Palestine, and later in Israel, was the motivating force in the development of the *Mossad*—as the Institute is known to all Israelis. In the early days of the modern Jewish settlement of Palestine, they were a tiny minority among a hostile Arab population. Simple guarding of the new colonies was no insurance against all their potential enemies. It was important to know what was happening in the adversary camp. For a very respectable fee, which was a considerable drain on the puny finances of the early settlers, local Arabs were only too willing to supply information on forthcoming attacks against the settlements.

World War I turned Palestine into a battleground. And it was in that war that the first Jewish espionage organization of modern times took shape, though without any of the supposedly essential structure or tools. A young agronomist named Aaron Aaronson and his beautiful sister Sarah headed a spy network that operated in Turkish Palestine on behalf of the British army, which stood at the southern gates of the country. The Turks caught most of the members of the spy ring, and Sarah Aaronson shot herself rather than betray her comrades under torture.

The Haganah's "Intelligence Service" took root as Arab activity against the settlements intensified. Over the years, it succeeded in penetrating Arab society and the highest echelons of the British administration. On the day that the state of Israel came into being, the service already had Israeli agents planted in the Arab countries and armies. In 1948, during the War of Independence, other agents crossed the frontiers disguised in the stream of refugees, and were swallowed up in the streets and alleys of Beirut, Damascus, Baghdad, Amman, and Cairo. In years to come, some of them reached prominent positions in the countries where they operated.

After the Six Day War in 1967, the Arabs attributed their crushing defeat to the long arm of Israeli intelligence. Their stories of its effectiveness were exaggerated out of all proportion. "Israeli intelligence broadcast messages to Arab pilots on operational flights," wrote the editor of Egypt's *Al Ahram*. "They even knew the names of our pilots, and the secret codes of our planes. They called the pilots by name, referred to actual members of their families, and persuaded them to abandon their aircraft."

The Israeli intelligence community is built from a number of sections, of which the most famous is the Institute for Intelligence and Special Duties. But "Institute" is a pale and inaccurate way of translating *Mossad*—and so the Hebrew name has come into common usage even abroad. The *Mossad* is in fact the central espionage agency for activities outside of Israel. It is responsible for clandestine operations, for collection of information on political, military, and security subjects—and for the special missions that fall within the classification of "intelligence warfare."

The *Mossad* has met with many successes: it kidnapped Nazi war criminal Adolf Eichmann and brought him to stand trial in Israel. It also removed five missile ships from their Cherbourg anchorage and spirited them out to sea after a French embargo prevented their delivery to the Israeli navy. According to the Arabs, the *Mossad* was the executioner of terrorist officers in Europe, and it provides security for Israeli representatives abroad.

Heads of the *Mossad* remain unnamed until they finish their tour of duty. The reason is that they personally take part in field operations. So far, three men have held the job at the top of the Institute for Intelligence and Special Duties: Isser Harel, Meir Amit, and Zvi Zamir. Foreign newspapers contend that "the current man" is Major General Yitzhak Hofi, until recently head of Staff Branch in the General Staff, and commanding general, Northern Command, in the Yom Kippur War.

The name is immaterial. What mattered on June 30, 1976, was that the head of the *Mossad* was issuing instructions to get him every piece of the vital information on what was happening at Entebbe Airport.

CHAPTER THIRTEEN

Paratroops on Entebbe

At the door of the prime minister's office in Jerusalem, Éli Mizrahi stood waiting for three visitors. They arrived exactly at 9:30, and Eli led them straight into Yitzhak Rabin's room.

"Shalom, Yitzhak."

"Shalom, Yitzhak."

Yitzhak Navon, chairman of the Knesset Foreign Affairs and Security Committee, was accompanied by two leaders of the main opposition party, Menachem Begin and Elimelech Rimalt.

Yitzhak Rabin summarized the little information available on events for his three visitors and added: "I have decided that it is most important to maintain national consensus on this subject. I must try to avoid unnecessary political arguments, and to achieve maximum cooperation and dialogue between us."

Begin responded: "Mr. Prime Minister, you can expect the full support of the opposition. The nation is united at a time like this."

After they left, Rabin thought for a moment, encouraged

to know that the opposition would support the government, and it seemed that he could rely on them even during negotiations with the terrorists—if there was no other alternative.

Shortly before eleven, the prime minister's cavalcade drove out from under the entrance pillars of the prime minister's office, and headed for the Knesset building, where all his ministers were already waiting in the Cabinet Room.

On the fourth day, with one more to go till expiration of the ultimatum, the governments of France and West Germany were holding a firm line. The general atmosphere in Paris was of anger and resolve not to submit to blackmail. Official word from the office of President Giscard d'Estaing was that he concurred completely with yesterday's Foreign Ministry statement that "France has no intention of surrendering to pressure and demands that she considers unbinding." Foreign Minister Jean Sauvignard's declaration was appreciated by the Foreign Ministry in Jerusalem, but both Foreign Minister Yigal Allon and his assistants knew that the toughest decision wouldn't be made in the Elysée Palace in Paris. In fact the French capital was waiting anxiously to hear what Yitzhak Rabin had to say. If the prime minister of Israel submitted to blackmail, then his French counterpart could follow in his footsteps without losing prestige.

According to that morning's impressions in Jerusalem, the West German government was also adamant in its opinion not to capitulate or be cowed by the approaching deadline. In the many phone calls between Jerusalem and Bonn, the Germans were insisting: "It is inconceivable, in principle, to give in to the humiliating demands of a gang of terrorist lawbreakers."

"France is asking you to help put an end to the affair," President Giscard d'Estaing told his Egyptian colleague Anwar Sadat and Syrian President Hafez Assad.

"France is asking you . . ." Foreign Minister Jean Sauvignard wrote in a personal message to terrorist leader Yasir Arafat, hoping against hope that it might be of some influence.

The atmosphere in the Cabinet Room of the Knesset in Jerusalem was relaxed. Only the clock hanging on the wall, its hands moving relentlessly forward, was a reminder. The afternoon headlines had proclaimed: "Terrorists Threatening Harsh Punishment for Hostages if Their Demands Are Rejected." More than one of the men in the room was thinking of the story of Joshua in the Bible where he made the sun stand still, but you just couldn't do things like that in the twentieth century.

"Gentlemen," the prime minister opened, "there is still no need to decide, but I foresee that we will have to meet again today, or tomorrow morning."

Benny Peled was in conference with his aides, but most of his time was spent with the men in charge of operations and intelligence. His office was at the receiving end of a steady flow of data needed to complete the still enormous gaps in their intelligence mosaic.

"The only danger is if they open fire on the planes," Peled decided. None of the other operational considerations worried him—not even the distance involved. "I think that the risks are reasonable. I don't believe that we are exaggerating. It's within normal range for a Hercules."

His self-confidence was infectious, even though few of the problems had actually been solved.

"There could be a problem of discovery by radar en route," one of the staff officers observed.

Peled shook his head: "The problem isn't radar, but rather what the enemy will do with the information he receives—if he receives it! Let's assume for a moment that we are picked up by radar in Uganda—or anywhere else on the way to Entebbe: What will they do? What will they think? The last thing that will come to mind is that these are Israeli planes on their way to rescue the hostages from Entebbe."

There was a note of caution in Peled's next remark: "But we must make sure that the chances of being discovered en route, and particularly in the target area, are reduced to the barest possible minimum. . . ."

Peled was not yet ready to drop his original suggestion, and so he repeated it to the chief of staff: "I still feel that we should take control of all of Entebbe."

"It won't work," Mota Gur replied.

By now, at 12:30 in the afternoon, the defense minister and the chief of staff were closeted with Prime Minister Rabin.

"I spent this morning consulting with people who have been in Uganda. There's a suggestion to take control of Entebbe with paratroops, but there's nothing firm yet."

Finding a military option before 2 P.M. tomorrow was not going to be easy.

They all knew that Israel would very shortly have to face the moment of truth. The impending decision might well be a precedent that would affect the future of the nation.

"Get me Motke Gazit in Paris," Foreign Minister Yigal Allon requested.

"Motke, my friend," said Allon when the ambassador came to the phone, "try to make an appointment with Sauvignard for eleven-thirty tomorrow morning. The government is meeting in Tel Aviv, and I guess we will have a decision, one way or another, by ten-thirty or eleven at the latest. I'll let you know the result immediately, and you will have to relay it to the French so they can tell Kampala before the ultimatum expires."

Mordechai Gazit understood perfectly well what Yigal Allon wasn't saying: the government of Israel was probably going to capitulate. He called the Quai d'Orsay and stated his request: "Yes, that's right. Tomorrow at eleven-thirty promptly. Thank you."

"Hello, international exchange? We want Kampala 2241. Government priority and urgent."

It took half an hour to connect the defense minister's office with Amin's palace. An officer stood ready to take notes alongside Burka Bar Lev, and a recorder was linked to the phone. Finally, four years after they had parted in anger, Amin and Bar Lev met again across the international telephone wires.

Bar Lev: "Mr. President?"

Amin: "Who's speaking?"

Bar Lev: "Colonel Bar Lev."

Amin: "How are you, my friend?"

Bar Lev: "How do you feel, Mr. President?"

Amin: "I'm very happy to hear your voice today."

Bar Lev: "I'm speaking from home. I heard what has happened. My friend, can I ask you for something?"

Amin: "I agree, because you are my good friend."

Bar Lev: "I know, sir . . . my friend, you have a great opportunity to go down in history as a great peacemaker. Since a lot of people across the seas, in England, in the United States, and in Europe, are writing bad things about you, you have an opportunity to show them that you are a great peacemaker, and if you liberate the people, you will go down in history as a very great man, and that will counter those who speak against you. I thought about that this morning, when I heard all those things on the radio."

Amin: "Now the Popular Front of Palestine has surrounded the remaining hostages completely. They say that if the Israeli government doesn't answer their demand, they will blow up the French plane and all the hostages at twelve noon their time tomorrow. So I suggest to you, my friend, that you report to Rabin—General Rabin, the prime minister, I know him, he is my friend—and to General Dayan. I know he is my friend, though he isn't in the government. Your government must do everything possible to release those hostages immediately—that's the Palestinian demand."

Bar Lev: "Mr. President, you are the ruler of your country. I think you have the power to liberate those people, and you will go down in history as a great man."

Amin: "I want you to know that you are my friend forever. I will be very happy to see you, because I know you well. I am prepared to make peace between Israel and the Arabs. And I want you to say that seriously to your government. Anything you want of me, let me know. Report to your government that they must send a declaration through the French, that I want to save the lives of the Israelis by their replying to the Palestinian demands."

Bar Lev: "Can you do anything to stop them killing?"

Amin: "I can stop them, if your government will accept their demand immediately. . . . Now they're calling me. At five they will publish their final decision, so you must act quickly, otherwise they will kill all the hostages. Your government must do everything possible."

Bar Lev: "Mr. President . . . do you remember your mother saying to you, before she died, that you should help the Israelis from the Holy Land? If you want to be a great and holy man, and to go into history, and perhaps even receive the Nobel Prize, then save those people. It's a great opportunity. It's given you by God, to show everyone that you are a great and good man."

Amin: "How are you, my friend? How is your wife?"

Bar Lev: "Everyone's fine. Do you want me to come to you?"

Amin: "I'll be happy to see you."

Bar Lev: "Can you stop them killing until I come to you?"

Amin: "Can you approach your government quickly, so that I will receive an answer?"

Bar Lev: "All right, Mr. President, I will be in touch with you later."

Lieutenant Colonel Jonathan Netaniahu, commander of the paratrooper raiding force at Entebbe International Airport,
July 3, 1976. (Credit: I.P.P.A., Ltd.)

Haled Haleileh

Ali el Meyari

Abd-el Razak el-Abed

Wilfried Böse

Jaïl el Arja

Halima

The
terrorists at
Entebbe

Faiz Jaaber

Yitzhak Rabin,
Prime Minister
of Israel. (Credit:
Israel Sun, Ltd.)

Defense Minister
Shimon Peres.
(Credit: Israel Sun,
Ltd.)

Foreign Minister
Yigal Allon.

Lieutenant General
Mordechai ("Mota") Gur.
(Credit: Israel Sun, Ltd.)

Major General Rehavam
("Gandhi") Zeevi.
(Credit: Israel Sun, Ltd.)

Minister-without-
Portfolio
Yisrael Galili.

Israeli paratroopers in training.
(Credit: Israel Sun, Ltd.)

Israeli paratroopers near airbase. (Credit: Israel Sun, Ltd.)

Minister of Justice Haim Zadok.
(Credit: Israel Sun, Ltd.)

Major General
Yekutiel Adam,
Chief of Operations.
(Credit: Israel Sun,
Ltd.)

Minister of Transport
Gad Yaakobi.

Major General Benny Peled, Israeli Air Force Commander.
(Credit: Israel Sun, Ltd.)

Photo of Entebbe Old Terminal used in planning operation.

Archbishop Hilarion Capucci, one of the terrorists demanded in exchange for the hostages. (Credit: Israel Sun, Ltd.)

Kozo Okamoto, member of the Japanese "Red Army" on loan to the "Popular Front." He was also demanded in exchange by the terrorists.

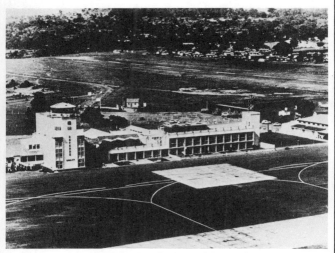

View of Old Terminal used in planning.

Israeli paratroopers in rehearsal on a Hercules plane.
(Credit: Israel Sun, Ltd.)

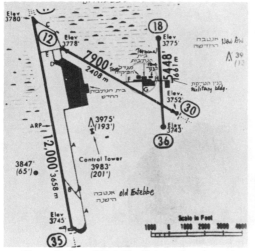

Ground plan of Entebbe International, used
for the operation.

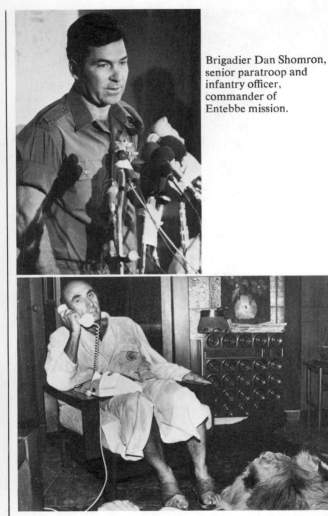

Brigadier Dan Shomron, senior paratroop and infantry officer, commander of Entebbe mission.

Colonel Baruch ("Burka") Bar Lev, former head of the Ugandan military mission. He was in phone contact with Idi Amin during the week of the hijacking.

The Mercedes "220 D" inside the Hercules aircraft.

Lieutenant General Mota Gur (chief of staff) and Defense Minister Shimon Peres (next to Gur) at press conference on the operation. (Credit: Israel Sun, Ltd.)

Yitzhak and Hadassa David, hostages in Entebbe Old Terminal, after their rescue.

All of Israel came to meet the 105 freed hostages at Ben-Gurion Airport. (Credit: *Stern* magazine)

The paratroopers rushed the wounded to a nearby hospital. (Credit: *Stern* magazine)

There was sorrow as well as rejoicing as relatives greeted one another. (Credit: *Stern* magazine)

But the world could once again believe that miracles were sometimes possible. (Credit: *Stern* magazine)

Lieutenant Colonel Jonathan Netaniahu, killed in action at Old Terminal, Entebbe International Airport.

Amin: "Phone me whenever you want. I'm waiting. . . . I'm speaking from the airport. I haven't slept for three days. I want to save the lives of those people."

Dora Bloch's behavior still amazed Yitzhak David. He watched how she straightened up to a posture typical of a Prussian martinet whenever Amin or the television crews came into Old Terminal. She wanted the world to see that no one was going to break the spirit and pride of an Israeli woman. She said so, in as many words, to Yitzhak, to his wife Hadassa, and to her own son Ilan.

Yitzhak was in a pessimistic mood this noon, but Dora was optimistic as ever: "Yitzhak, think what our nation has been through. Think what our generation has experienced! If we could survive all that, we will also survive this!"

"We are staying here with you till the last passenger is released," Captain Michel Bacos told the group standing around him. "I am not leaving even if they shoot me."

The remaining passengers of Air France 139 thanked him wordlessly. The dozen crew members of the Aerobus had proven themselves exemplary human beings. Apart from two stewardesses who were still in shock, the others had spared no efforts to help the passengers. Michel Bacos went through each day with an expression of relaxed composure on his face. He separated passengers who argued among themselves, placed himself between terrorists and hostages who were about to challenge them, and—with ever-present good humor—he tried to create the atmosphere of a holiday camp. Why not make the best of a bad situation?

Thunder rolled across Entebbe Airport as jet planes screamed overhead. The passengers in Old Terminal were startled, but they had heard the sounds earlier. They were not yet aware of the fact that the president of Uganda had ordered his air force to fly over Old Terminal from time to time to frighten the hostages and create the impression of tight and efficient guard. When Amin returned later in the day, he was accompanied by an even larger group of soldiers and guards.

"I am asking you not to forget your friends who remain here," he said. Dressed in full military regalia, complete with decorations, he faced the forty-nine passengers who had been split off from the main group last night. They would soon be boarding an Air France plane for Paris. "You are about to go free, but when you get to wherever you are going, please tell your governments to release the prisoners they are holding, those on the list that the Palestinians submitted. I think that their demands are very moderate. . . ."

With a broad smile on his face, Amin shook hands with each of the liberated passengers: "I am your friend. Happy landings! Have a good flight!"

A bus arrived in front of Old Terminal. A French nun hesitated, then asked to be allowed not to board it: "I want to stay here, and give my place to someone else who is old or ill," she said, but no one was listening. She was shoved into the bus, which promptly drove away in the direction of Kampala. French ambassador Pierre Renard was waiting at the consulate of France to greet the newly freed hostages. He smiled, shook hands, served glasses of orange juice. Then the bus took them back to Entebbe— but not to Old Terminal. They were led through New Terminal out to a waiting Air France plane. In nine hours time, they would land in Paris. Another group of non-Israelis would soon follow. For them the adventure which began on Sunday in Athens was over. They were free. . . .

CHAPTER FOURTEEN

"Sorry, No Military Answer..."

Faiz Abdul Rahim Jaaber looked at the wallets and hand-bags collected during last night's "selection." He spread the haul out on a table in the room allotted to the ter-rorists. Going through papers, money, and the other trivia belonging to the travelers, he noticed a batch of photos that were different: a youngster on a burned Syrian tank on the Golan Heights; the same boy holding a carbine, standing next to a rusted gun barrel in an abandoned bunker.

"Which of you is Nahum Dehaan?" the voice boomed through Old Terminal. "Come with us!"

Sara Davidson watched with anxious eyes as they took him out. An hour ago, Nahum had approached her.

"Didn't you buy those shoes a week ago in Ramat Hasharon?" he had asked her.

"That's right," Sara had answered.

"I'm the man who sold them to you."

"Well, this *is* a small world."

What on earth could the terrorists be wanting of a shoe salesman?

"You are a general in the Israeli army," Jaaber roared, his voice clearly audible in the main hall. "You are a spy. . . ."

"I have never been in the army. Those photos are from a tour of the Golan Heights," Nahum Dehaan tried to explain.

"You are a general, a spy!"

Nahum was ordered to write out his life story in French. He quickly did so, determined to prove that he had never served in the army, and that he was a bona fide dual national: French and Israeli.

As this interchange was taking place, the passengers were making preparations for yet another night. Mattresses were pushed up against the wall in long lines, one touching the next. Blankets were distributed to all who asked for them. Dora Bloch settled on a mattress next to Ida Borowitz, the immigrant from Russia who made history years earlier by writing to the president of the Supreme Soviet demanding her right to emigrate.

"What do you know of our history?"

Sara Davidson stood next to the terrorist and put her question hesitantly, half in a whisper. Wilfried Böse thought a moment before launching into a long answer. The captor and his captive were chatting as if in a Tel Aviv or Düsseldorf café.

Böse: "We must help the Palestinians. It can't go on this way. The Palestinians have rights. They deserve a state of their own. They're desperate."

Sara Davidson: "What are they to you?"

Böse: "I'm sensitive to the suffering of others. I can't stand aside and watch those miserable people. I must help them. I would do anything to help the Palestinians. . . ."

Sara Davidson: "Did you learn history? About what happened in 1948? You must have been a young child then, and you don't know anything about it. You should know that the United Nations partitioned Palestine between

Jews and Arabs. The Jews weren't happy with what they got, but they agreed to live with it. They really wanted peace with the neighboring Arab state. The Arabs didn't accept the UN decision. They started a war to destroy Israel."

Sara had Wilfried Böse's full attention. The German was obviously interested, though he occasionally glanced around to see where his companions were. He seemed very intelligent to Sara, well informed and anxious to answer to the point.

Sara Davidson: "You say that you can't watch the suffering of fellow man. Well—if you succeed in destroying Israel, and we have to disperse across the world, will you then hijack planes on behalf of the Jews?"

Böse: "You really need a state of your own. I'm in favor of the existence of Israel, but I'm also in favor of a Palestinian state alongside Israel, or a partnership between Israel and the Palestinians."

Sara Davidson: "But your organization isn't willing to recognize Israel's right to exist. The Popular Front wants to destroy us."

Böse: "I am not the spokesman of the Popular Front."

Sara Davidson: "Don't you think that the Jews need some corner of the world for themselves? We don't have another country."

Böse: "Madame, have you ever seen a Palestinian refugee camp?"

Sara decided that the time had come to find a way out of the conversation with this German anarchist.

"Captain," she said, using the title given him by the hijackers, "what did the Arab countries do with the Palestinian refugees? They didn't give them rights at all! They used them as a weapon in a political war. The Egyptians treated them like third-class citizens."

Böse: "Both the Egyptians and the Syrians are reactionaries. They don't care about the Palestinians."

Sara left it there. What good would it do her to argue with a man who was so completely committed to his way of thinking?

The Israel Law Association auditorium in Tel Aviv was only half full, but the audience this Wednesday afternoon was tense, red-eyed, and weeping.

The speaker's voice was firm: "We have to formulate a common line of action and, as necessary, pressure the responsible people to obtain the release of our dear ones."

This first meeting of relatives of the passengers on Air France 139 had convened on the initiative of Professor Yosef Gross, a lawyer whose brother, sister-in-law, and their children were in Entebbe.

"We demand the release of our families, no matter what price asked of the government," a woman screamed.

"Principles don't interest me. I want my family back, safe and well."

"If we don't use force, nothing will be done," a voice rose above all others. "Let's go to the prime minister's office in Jerusalem and demonstrate. . . ."

"We'll present an ultimatum to Rabin. If he doesn't see us straight away, we'll start a hunger strike."

Finally, one voice dominated: "All right, there is pain in our hearts, but we must use our heads. All these suggestions—they're exactly what the terrorists want us to do. Demonstrations will only work against us in the end. . . ."

The auditorium emptied, the angry and distraught relatives leaving behind overturned chairs and cigarette butts stamped out on the floor.

Foreign Minister Allon wanted to involve U.S. Secretary of State Henry Kissinger. Coming straight from the short Knesset debate where he had announced that Israel would continue to stand firm and take every possible step toward release of the hostages, he returned to his office.

He called in Director General Shlomo Avineri and his head of bureau, Haim Braun. After a short discussion, he dictated an urgent cable to Simcha Dinitz, ambassador of Israel in Washington, instructing him to get Kissinger to try "all possible directions" to pressure Idi Amin. Finally, Dinitz was asked to remind the Secretary that President Anwar Sadat of Egypt was known to have reservations about the use of terror and he had good connections to his Ugandan counterpart: SUGGEST YOU ALSO ASK KISSINGER TO ACTIVATE HIS FRIENDS AMONG AFRICAN LEADERS. THEY WILL MEET AMIN AT THE END OF THIS WEEK AT A CONFERENCE OF THE ORGANIZATION OF AFRICAN UNITY IN MAURITIUS. . . .

"I think we should also use Vivian," Shlomo Avineri suggested. "Vivian"—Haim Herzog, Israel's ambassador to the United Nations—was presently attending a conference in Jerusalem. "Tell him to bring pressure to bear on Amin. . . ."

Allon nodded his agreement. "What else can we do?" he asked his colleagues.

"What can we do?" asked Defense Minister Peres.

His small square office was filled with people. Facing him sat Chief of Staff Gur, Staff Branch Head Adam and his assistant, Brigadier Ben-Gal, Shlomo Gazit, Benny Peled, and others, mostly from Operations Branch and the General Staff intelligence departments.

"We are still short of a great deal of information," Gazit reported. "We must find out everything possible about the place where the hostages are being held. We must know how many men are guarding them; what they look like; where they are stationed, inside the building and outside. The size of the terminal building. The number of entrances to it. Understand, our problem isn't to capture an airfield. This is no war! We must reach the terminal in conditions of absolute surprise, and hit the terrorists before they can fire on the hostages, then get out of there! We also need aerial intelligence. It will take a lot of data to get planes from Israel to Entebbe. The pilots must be able to identify the airfield immediately and land without being detected. We also need to know the strength of Ugandan army formations in the area, and what force can reach the airport quickly. How much the Ugandans are capable of. . . ."

"Whatever happens, I believe that we can and must get them out of Entebbe. It must be done," Peled said.

The debate went on into the night. The minister did not allow any of the men the luxury of keeping silent. He was sure of these men—and proud of them.

Precisely at 7 P.M., the editors of Israel's daily papers seated themselves in the ministers' chairs at the long table in the Cabinet conference room. Rabin had summoned them for a briefing of the Entebbe hijacking.

The Newspaper Editors' Committee was perhaps the only institution of its kind in the world. It had been established to keep the editors up to date on current and secret information, most of it, of course, "off the record," because of Israel's unique security situation.

A somewhat tired and tense Yitzhak Rabin surveyed for the editors the moves and diplomatic activity from the moment the German hijacker entered Michel Bacos' cockpit through the landing at Entebbe. He said nothing of possible military activity, which on the evening of Wednesday, June 30, would in any case fall into the category of "remote possibilities."

"There is no way out of this crisis without some kind of trauma," Rabin ended his formal presentation. "If there is no concession, then we must expect a massacre of Israelis. We cannot prevent it, and must not blind ourselves to the possibility."

"Is it clear that they will put the passengers to death?"

"We are talking about Wadia Hadad's men. I wouldn't

like anyone to delude himself about the brutality of that group. They are not above any abomination."

"What position are other governments taking?"

"Well, at this stage, France and Germany are more or less holding firm, saying they will back us. I have no complaints on that count."

After the first barrage of questions, Prime Minister Rabin asked the editors to refrain from printing alarmist stories. "There is an attempt to organize on the part of the angry families. I know that some of the extremists among them have already made a direct approach to the French embassy. They sent me a telegram, asking: 'Do the dead bodies of army soldiers justify the release of terrorists, while the saving of lives of our relatives doesn't?' " No one needed reminding that the reference was to a deal made with Egypt long after the Yom Kippur War: live convicts in exchange for coffins.

The editors and reporters murmured their assent.

Yitzhak Rabin shook his head sadly: "It is complex, very difficult—and anything but pleasant—and that is the understatement of the year."

"Ladies and gentlemen," boomed a loudspeaker in the V.I.P. room of Orly Airport. "Ladies and gentlemen, please be quiet. . . ."

The hubbub of the released passengers and their relatives faded, to be replaced by the voice of an anonymous French government official: "Ladies and gentlemen, President Valéry Giscard d'Estaing has asked me to convey his congratulations. He shares in the rejoicing at your return from captivity. The president is happy that your suffering is at an end. He hopes, with all his heart, that the other hostages will soon also be free like you."

Jean Sauvignard, foreign minister of France, shook hands, stroked the heads of children, kissed toddlers, hugged a pretty young girl among the passengers.

"All our hearts are full of anxiety," Sauvignard told

reporters who had broken through the police cordon. "This is not the final solution to the affair. . . ."

Slowly, very slowly, the cries of joy died down. Not one of the hijacked passengers, their relatives, or the newsmen paid any attention to perhaps a dozen men in the crowd. They weren't laughing or crying. They weren't shaking hands or speaking a word. They listened—and noted down names and addresses.

It was nine o'clock in the evening. The six members of the ministerial team and their assistants now sat around the long table, its ashtrays still full of the debris of the Newspaper Editors' Committee. Rabin again opened the meeting with a question to General Gur.

"Mota, do we have a military option?"

With seventeen hours to go, the lives of scores of people in Old Terminal at Entebbe hung precariously in the balance.

"We'll know by tomorrow at two in the afternoon. Sorry, I do not now have a military answer," General Gur answered quietly, his matter-of-fact reply coming as no surprise.

"Under these circumstances, we must know that lack of a decision is in itself a decision. If we cannot rescue the hostages, we must assume that they will be put to death when the ultimatum expires."

From the silence in the room the prime minister concluded that his colleagues would accept negotiations with the terrorists through the French intermediaries. Even several right-wing Knesset members—usually strong opponents of the government's seeming weaknesses—were convinced that negotiation was unavoidable.

Dan Patir's report only served to heighten the feeling that capitulation would be necessary. The prime minister's advisor on media affairs told the gathering about his conversation with Professor Gross: "The families believe we must submit to the terrorists," Dan concluded.

"I think Gad and Amos should meet the families tonight, and try and calm them down," the prime minister suggested. The minister of transport and the director general of the Prime Minister's Office nodded their assent.

"Gandhi" Zeevi arrived in the Cabinet Room straight from his flight from London just as Gad Yaakobi was suggesting that an hour should be set for a full government session the next morning.

"If there is no military option, we should hear what has been done so far in the diplomatic field," another participant prompted.

Yigal Allon started his report with a summary of events on the French scene. He noted that "the French behavior so far has been satisfactory," and then told his colleagues about the cables to Ambassador Dinitz to enlist the aid of Henry Kissinger, and to Paris asking France to put pressure on the African countries within her sphere of influence. He finished with a report of his instruction to Haim Herzog to talk to Secretary General Waldheim of the United Nations.

"What about the Pope?" Yitzhak Rabin asked.

Rabin smiled faintly as he asked, but Allon answered seriously. "Gazit has been asked to get Catholic clergy to push the Pope into talking to Amin. After all, the Ugandan was recently received in audience in grand style—something which must have appealed to his ego. We should make good use of it."

Shimon Peres spoke up: "I suggest that somebody—perhaps Asher Ben-Natan—should go to Paris tomorrow to check the possibility of Israeli-French cooperation. I do have a plan. It might work. . . ." Asher Ben-Natan, now an advisor to the defense minister, had until recently been Israeli ambassador to France.

As the defense minister spelled out the details, Yitzhak Rabin did not appear convinced, though he said nothing. In his view, Peres' plan would result in severance of French relations with black Africa—a move he didn't believe Giscard d'Estaing would be prepared to contemplate.

The prime minister moved to close the proceedings: "We convene tomorrow at seven forty-five, here in Tel Aviv. The full Cabinet will convene at eight-thirty."

It was 10:20 P.M. when the six ministers went their separate ways. Fifteen hours still remained. . . .

The prime minister's advisor on intelligence and counterterrorism, Major General Rehavam Zeevi, went straight from the meeting to his own office. He had instructions from the prime minister to set up a special staff of senior intelligence agents.

Gandhi Zeevi wasted no time in outlining the objectives to his colleagues:

—Get data and distribute it to the competent authorities.

—Produce situation scenarios for the prime minister and the ministerial team.

—Keep the heads of secret services in the diplomatic and operational picture.

—Evaluate the possibilities of diplomatic and military action.

The lights in the prime minister's Tel Aviv headquarters burned through the night.

Shimon Peres usually worked a sixteen- to eighteen-hour day, then read late into the night in his north Tel Aviv home. Now it seemed as if exhaustion would defeat him. Nevertheless, he listened patiently to the flow of suggestions from his advisors. For each idea there was "insufficient data for precise planning." Yitzhak Rabin had rejected the notion of dropping paratroops on Entebbe: "It will be an Israeli 'Bay of Pigs,' " he said. Though he himself had not expressed such hopelessness, Shimon Peres also placed little faith in the chances of that plan, although it in no way reduced his respect for the senior officers' fund of inspiration. Still the fact remained that, at this eleventh hour, all the ideas seemed too imaginative and too little based on what could realistically be done—if anything was possible in the remaining time.

Despite the lateness of the hour, Israeli government emissaries were knocking on doors in Paris, disturbing family reunions. None were turned away once they had explained their business. They had a long list of questions to put to the hostages back from Uganda—questions later picked up by alert European reporters.

What does the building look like?

How are the terrorists dressed?

Can you describe the girl among them?

What kind of cars do they have?

Could you identify the weapons they carry?

How many Ugandan soldiers did you see around Old Terminal?

Where exactly are the hijacked passengers being held?

Traffic was still heavy at the defense minister's office. A constant flow of trays of coffee and sandwiches, and of slips of paper with information. One by one the details mounted up into a partial picture—and it seemed that a military solution was no nearer.

Yosef Hadad woke and heard the sobbing at his side. The lights of Old Terminal were still on and he could see his wife, tears pouring down her cheeks. He wrapped an arm around her, and said: "If we get out of here alive, we are going to offer a prayer of thanksgiving over the grave of our holy rabbi. . . ."

CHAPTER FIFTEEN

Roulette

The prime minister was listening to the 7 A.M. news when the doorbell rang. Leah Rabin brought the guest, a retired senior government official, into the living room. He had asked for "only three minutes" of Yitzhak Rabin's time—but he was obviously hesitant to begin. He sank into an armchair, tension and anxiety reflected on his face. Leah went to the kitchen to make coffee.

"Yitzhak," he said, raising his eyes, "do you know that my daughter is a hostage in Entebbe?"

The prime minister was silent, but the expression on his face changed almost imperceptibly.

"Nobody knows she's my daughter. She's married—and her husband's name appears on her passport now. Yitzhak," said the man, "I made a point of not joining the relatives' committee, so no one should know, but tell me Yitzhak, how long are you going to play roulette with the lives of our children?"

He turned to study the paintings on the wall, as if not expecting an answer. Rabin tried hard to ignore the man's personal involvement, and talked about the necessity of being firm, about the diplomatic options that were open, about the mounting pressures from other countries and international institutions: "The government is in no way going to abandon the hostages to their fate, but . . . only if we have no choice will we capitulate."

"Yitzhak, up to this week I thought just like you. Try and understand me! I don't want to give in to those bastards any more than you do, but I had to come and tell you—for the sake of my daughter's life. . . ."

As his visitor turned away, a deeply moved Rabin sat motionless. Six hours remained to the deadline.

Asher Ben-Natan, the defense minister's political advisor, had come in early this morning, as he had for the last two days, though he was barely involved in the Air France affair. He could recall a long service in the security establishment, much of it alongside Shimon Peres. In the mid-1960s Asher Ben-Natan transferred to the Foreign Ministry, to serve as Israel's first ambassador to Germany —hardly an easy diplomatic posting, but then he was a most undiplomatic ambassador. Ben-Natan went out of his way to remind his hosts of their past sins, and fought a hard battle against normalization of relationships between West Germany and Israel.

Even when he was posted to Paris, Ben-Natan continued to behave like the proverbial bull in the china shop. He had no qualms about attacking the unbalanced anti-Israeli policies of Presidents de Gaulle and Pompidou. The French authorities on occasion hinted that they would not be averse to a change of ambassador. Meanwhile, Ben-Natan was a favorite of the media because he was blunt and outspoken.

Returning to Israel after two full postings abroad, he was appointed political advisor to the defense minister. Shimon Peres and Asher Ben-Natan were very close associates and friends. Both were practical men of action, yet Ben-Natan had still been surprised at the defense minister's notion that he might go to Paris.

When Shimon Peres suggested the idea last night, he was thinking in terms of a meeting with French Interior Minister Poniatowski, to try and find grounds for cooperation—and not only in the diplomatic sphere. Prime Minister Rabin considered the idea foolish, even dangerous. Not only was there little chance of anything coming of it, but such a move would probably bring France into conflict with the African countries. However, he had no desire to aggravate his relationship with Shimon Peres. So, rather than a flat "no," and with the full cooperation and agreement of Foreign Minister Allon, Director General Avineri, and Ambassador-to-Paris Gazit, approval for Ben-Natan's trip was simply delayed.

At nine o'clock Yitzhak Rabin gave his assent to the trip, assuming that Ben-Natan could no longer catch the only plane that would deliver him to Paris before the ultimatum expired.

"Asher, get moving!"

The defense minister's political advisor was whisked into a car and driven to his Tel Aviv home. He threw a few things into a case and ran back to the waiting car. El Al 323 took off at 10:20.

The six ministers and their aides arrived promptly at 7:45 A.M. Though the atmosphere was tense, their discussion was brisk and fast-moving. As if to lighten the mood, Shimon Peres said: "I want you to know that there is a military option, and the officers say it has a chance of success."

"I think they're dreaming. I haven't yet seen any feasible plan. We're dealing with gangsters," the prime minister continued. "I wouldn't suggest that we dismiss their ultimatum. They're quite likely to kill a few passengers immediately, just to prove that they mean business.

"There is no possibility of delaying a decision. It's here and now." The wall clock read 8:40. The serious mood of the occasion seemed to hang in the air. Almost as a reflex action, the ministers kept glancing at their watches.

The Ugandan MIGs were still buzzing Old Terminal. Idi Amin's morning aerial greeting had also become routine. As the jets shrieked overhead, all conversation among the hostages came to a stop.

Children were booting a can around the lawn outside Old Terminal while the women hung laundry out to dry. Dora Bloch, who had washed clothes both for herself and for Ilan, was waiting for an appearance by Idi Amin: "The wind created by his helicopter dries them much faster," she told Yitzhak David. A Ugandan army armored car had recently been stationed some distance from the building, and its machine gun was pointing straight at them.

Sara Davidson told her husband: "You know, whenever I go to the toilet, there's a Ugandan soldier peering in the window."

"I'm not sure who we have to fear most—the terrorists or the Ugandans," he said.

The Davidsons mentioned their qualms to some of the others. The freedom with which the terrorist commander came and went, the now oppressive presence of Ugandan troops, the jets overhead and the armored car on the ground—all added up to only one conclusion: Ugandan cooperation with the terrorists was now far beyond the passive stage. This was full partnership.

Through the window they could see the white Mercedes of the PLO representative in Kampala. Alongside was another Mercedes—this one belonging to the Somalian ambassador to Uganda, who was talking with the terrorists out of earshot of their captives.

Uzzi Davidson made a headcount of the terrorists who had arrived in the last hour. There were ten of them, all armed. Apart from "Ali" and "Haled" from the hijack team, there were two more who seemed much younger than the others. The hostages learned later that these two were PLO flying cadets under training in the Ugandan air force.

Again the two MIGs swept low over Old Terminal.

"At this stage," Colonel Avner Ram—as we shall call him—opened the morning's discussion with his team, "our most urgent question is whether Uganda was coincidence or a part of the terrorist plan."

Ram was one of the most brilliant young officers in the Intelligence Branch. An intellectual and a talented writer, he was an expert in "intelligence warfare" both at staff level and in the field. He told his colleagues that, in his own opinion, the Ugandans must be cooperating with the hijackers, but there was still no hard proof. Colonel Ram asked for more data as quickly as possible. He knew there was no time to mount a military operation.

The intelligence officers left that meeting in a hurry. One of them raced to the office of an engineering firm that had built Entebbe Airport with this request: "Give me everything you have on that airport, please. . . ." He received maps, photographs, and a wealth of other material. The problem here was that the maps and photos dated back to 1972. Certainly there must have been changes since then, and knowledge of those alterations might be critical.

Another officer went to a Tel Aviv travel agent to procure the manual of scheduled international airline services. Other members of the IDF team used their creative intelligence to ferret out facts known to very few. They had to beat the opponent with cunning if not with force.

"I must state that there is no chance of a military operation," the prime minister opened the Cabinet discussion. "The necessary steps have been taken to examine all military options."

The eighteen ministers knew at once that Rabin had not convened the meeting to discuss half-baked army plans. In fact, General Gur—a regular participant in sessions of the ministerial team—was not present at this Cabinet meeting. The prime minister had made sure that the chief of staff would not be invited. It was his way of protecting him from any suggestion that the lack of a military option was his fault.

Nine o'clock. The brief summary of diplomatic moves during the last twenty-four hours was over.

"Gentlemen," the prime minister said, "we must decide. The deadline is very close, and a lack of decision will be tantamount to abandoning the hostages. Under the existing conditions, I propose that the government of Israel resolves to negotiate with the terrorists, through the good offices of France, for the release of the hostages in exchange for Israel's willingness to free prisoners held in this country."

Perhaps to put off the unpleasant finalization, Prime Minister Rabin observed: "I have requested a session of the Knesset Foreign Affairs and Security Committee at nine-thirty, in order to report the government's decision. I will listen to their opinions, but I informed them that I can only accept their viewpoint as a consultant recommendation—no more than that. . . ."

He then yielded the floor to Yigal Allon. "As of now," said Allon, "we have no alternative. We must decide in principle to negotiate with the terrorists, via France. But, it's important to remember that a positive decision will give us some time to see what will happen. . . ."

Some of the ministers nodded their agreement with Foreign Minister Allon. Nobody thought to comment on the incongruity of any idea to gain time.

Shimon Peres took the podium, and in a controlled and quiet voice, he began with an almost immediate rebuttal of Rabin's statements. "I don't say that we shouldn't negotiate, an act which will inevitably be interpreted as submission to blackmail, but I want to stress that if we surrender, we are inviting trouble in the future. The terrorists will repeat the exercise, and who knows what they will want then. . . ."

Rabin reminded him, "Shimon, what we need now is a decision—not speeches!"

Peres insisted, "We'll decide! But at least we can delay publication of the fact."

The hands of the clock had passed 9:30. Despite the pressure of time, the prime minister was not ready to report to the Knesset members. Turning to General Zeevi, Amos Aran, and Shlomo Avineri, he ordered them: "Go over to the Defense Ministry and hold them with information briefings until I arrive."

The majority of ministers felt that, sadly but inevitably, Rabin's viewpoint was the correct one. Meanwhile, one of the prime minister's secretaries brought a note to Eli Mizrahi: "Chief Rabbi Goren is on the phone." Eli went to talk to the spiritual leader.

"Eli, my dear boy, I want the prime minister to know that the *Halacha* [a compendium of legal precedents in Jewish religious tradition] allows the exchange of terrorists for hostages. . . ."

Eli Mizrahi listened carefully as the chief rabbi began to quote chapter and verse.

"The Rambam [Rabbi Moses Maimonides, 1135–1204] writes in his book *The Strong Hand*: 'The redemption of prisoners takes precedence over ministering to the wants of the poor, and there is no greater commandment than the redemption of prisoners, for the prisoner is among the community of the hungry, thirsty, and naked and is in danger of his life, and he who turns his eyes away from redemption transgresses against "thou shalt not harden thine heart, nor shut thine hand from thy poor brother . . ." (Deuteronomy 15:7) for there is no commandment greater than redemption of prisoners.' "

At almost the same moment, the Sephardi Chief Rabbi of Israel, Ovadia Yosef, was phoning his message to the government, in much the same vein as that of his Ashkenazi colleague. It was rare indeed for the leaders of the two great Jewish religious communities to agree with each other. . . .

Eli Mizrahi scrawled the news on a note which he handed to Yitzhak Rabin.

The prime minister rose from his seat and apologized to the ministers; though the debate was still actively going on, he had to attend the Knesset Foreign Affairs Committee. Defense Minister Peres asked him to tell the committee about the reservations held by himself and other ministers.

"I will make a point of it," said the prime minister. He left the Cabinet Room and walked quickly down the pathway to the nearby Defense Ministry building. It was still conceivable that he could save the hostages and save face for Israel.

CHAPTER SIXTEEN

"Bloody Hands"

Four more hours.

Sara Davidson went outside to hang laundry and nodded to Wilfried Böse who stood in the covered passageway out of Old Terminal. He smiled at Sara as if they were old friends. She finished hanging her clothing, then turned to talk to him. He was the most dangerous of the lot— Sara was sure of that. His aura of tranquility, his smile and good manners, had led many of the hostages into believing that he was what he seemed. Now Sara also thought of the Holocaust which had engulfed the Jews of Europe. Being Israeli-born herself, she had never quite understood why the Jews didn't take up arms against their Nazi oppressors. It took Entebbe and Wilfried Böse to give her the insight that had so long eluded her.

"Tell me, please," she opened tentatively.

The German smiled.

"How do you feel facing women and children with a loaded submachine gun? Why don't you fight our soldiers?"

"Believe me," Wilfried Böse answered, "I have a very

bad feeling indeed having to face your children and the others. . . ."

Sara Davidson looked around. Twenty-odd children were racing after an empty can on the grass in front of the building—putting heart and soul into their make-believe soccer game, completely oblivious to their surroundings. In less than four hours, these children might be dead.

"Tell me, what you will do when the Middle East war is over?"

Wilfried Böse blushed, as though too shy to answer: "I know that I will end my life with a bullet in the head, or a long term in prison. I have a feeling that it will happen soon, but I am German. I love my Germany—but not the one that exists today. I want a different Germany. . . ."

The Knesset Foreign Affairs and Security Committee had put aside its internal political wars. The twenty-one senior Knesset members sat grave and tense facing the eighteen ministers.

The prime minister came directly to the point: "Gentlemen, there is no possibility of delaying this affair further. We favor negotiation through the agency of France. The text of the decision, even if it isn't final, will shortly be submitted to the vote in the government. . . ."

The tension rose tangibly. Some of the committee members held pencils or pens ready to record as the prime minister began to read the text: " 'The government empowers the small ministerial team to express willingness to open immediate negotiations to save the hostages, while willing to release detainees. . .' "

"I would be grateful for your opinions of the draft government resolution," Rabin told the members of the committee when he had finished reading. Almost all of them were amazed that the prime minister should ask for opinions when 2 P.M. was not so far away, and they appreciated his gesture—though it could make no difference.

"I must emphasize," the prime minister observed while

waiting for someone to begin, "that a number of ministers, including the minister of defense, put it on record that they are voting for negotiation in order to gain time."

The head of the opposition in the Knesset chose this moment to ask for a ten-minute recess to allow a short consultation among the members of his party. When they returned, Menachem Begin pointed out that there was no other choice—the terrorists' demands had to be satisfied.

"It is our duty," Menachem Begin informed the prime minister, "to do everything to save our brethren from mortal danger."

For a moment the tension dropped. The prime minister wanted, and indeed needed, national unity at this tragic and dramatic moment. Both he and the members of the coalition parties were relieved by Begin's announcement.

"It's appropriate to adopt a national viewpoint in this case," Begin continued. "I would propose to the prime minister that no reservations be added to the conditions of a positive announcement on willingness to begin negotiations for the rescue of the hostages, on the assumption of preparedness to release convicts. Reservations can only cause lack of clarity and confusion. We should say what we have to in positive and direct terms, for who knows what may happen and whether we won't be compelled to concede those reservations that we might now stipulate."

This was an additional surprise for Yitzhak Rabin. He could now proceed with the negotiations.

The main gate of the General Staff compound swung closed and its bolts shot home. Scores of angry civilians were demanding access to the prime minister's office, which was in the compound, "before it was too late. . . ."

The families of the hostages had spent a sleepless night. Like the ministers and committee members, they were also clock-watching this morning. Behind the crowd were a number of foreign network TV cameramen. Angry relatives assaulting a locked gate was first-rate material for satellite relay. The cameras were rolling, and some of the cameramen were shoving demonstrators aside to get their close-ups. Beyond the gate stood a number of military police, torn between their duty to protect the General Staff compound and their sympathy for the people outside. The television crews were delighted: screaming men and women facing supposedly tough policemen with tears in their eyes makes wonderful newsreel footage.

The telephone lines to the prime minister's Tel Aviv office were jammed. From Paris and Bonn, the ambassadors of Israel were holding open lines, ready to receive the complete text of any government decision.

"There's no time," Mordechai Gazit prodded from Paris.

"Have all your clocks stopped?" asked Yohanan Meroz, the ambassador to Germany.

"I'm prepared to see a delegation from the families at eleven," Rabin scrawled on the back of a note handed to the committee session. The other side read: "The families have broken into the General Staff, and are waiting for you."

The distraught relatives were no longer willing to listen to the instructions of military policemen. Encouraged by the foreign television crews, they broke into the compound and raced down the road to the Prime Minister's office. The police stood aside. Their hearts weren't in this task. They ran after the demonstrators, but made no attempt to stop them. The relatives of the Entebbe hostages settled down on the lawn across from the office waiting impatiently for Yitzhak Rabin.

Less than four hours now remained. The time had come to decide. Yisrael Galili, the expert at drafting tricky resolutions, polished the wording of the proposed decision and Yitzhak Rabin read the draft to his ministers.

"Gentlemen," said Rabin, "we shall vote. . . ."

Rabin insisted that every minister should vote for or

against, in order to prevent the possibility of either position remaining vague: no man could duck his responsibility by abstaining. On a show of hands, there was no opposition, though the reservations of Shimon Peres and Shlomo Hillel were recorded in the minutes at their request.

The ministers rose from their chairs and slowly left the room—without any of the customary animated chatter. Israel had submitted—had surrendered! Some of them were already contemplating a bleak future as the terrorists moved to exploit the precedent. Finance Minister Yehoshua Rabinowitz mumbled, half to himself: "We have let ourselves in for a very dangerous example, very dangerous! Did we have any other choice?"

Yigal Allon rushed to a nearby room and picked up the open line to Mordechai Gazit in Paris: "Motke," the foreign minister said, "get a pen and write. . . .

"The government of Israel . . . expressed willingness . . . to release prisoners detained in Israel. . . . Pay attention," Allon warned, "to the wording 'prisoners detained in Israel' and not simply 'the prisoners.' It's up to you to translate that fuzzily. We are not concerned with prisoners in Germany, France, Switzerland, or Kenya. . . ."

In the prime minister's office, voices were lowered, hushed by the gravity of the occasion. Thick carpets absorbed the footfalls of men pacing up and down the passageway cum anteroom. A few were sitting in the Cabinet Room, others waited on a hard bench outside.

In the prime minister's own room were his closest aides: Amos Aran, Froike Poran, Eli Mizrahi, and Dan Patir. There were mixed feelings, partly of relief and partly of nervousness, as Rabin began to speak: "I think we are trapped in a situation which is certainly not good, but what will be worse? I'm not interested in the argument over terrorists in our jails. And I don't allow myself the dishonest luxury of talk about tactics and stratagems. We have decided on negotiation, and I bear the full responsibility for it—and that is that!

"What time is it?" he demanded suddenly. Then, before anyone could answer, he went on: "Get me Yigal."

Allon had just arrived in his temporary Tel Aviv office when Rabin's call came through. In his restlessness the prime minister wanted to be told again whether adequate steps had been taken to relay the government's decision to the French authorities: "Time is pressing," he said, "and the news of our willingness to negotiate has to reach Kampala."

"Don't worry," Allon reassured him, "I asked Gazit last night to make an eleven-thirty appointment with the French foreign minister. Right now the embassy is translating our message into French, and Gazit will take it personally to Jean Sauvignard at the Quai d'Orsay. You've got nothing to worry about, Yitzhak."

"Yigal, keep me informed! Let me know immediately when the decision is relayed to the French."

"In another few minutes you will be receiving the decision of the Israeli government," a senior embassy official told someone at the French Foreign Office.

"The decision of the government of Israel is already on its way over to you," the embassy in Bonn informed the West German Emergency Committee.

"How much longer to two o'clock?" Yitzhak Rabin wanted to know.

An hour had never before seemed so long.

Late last night, Wednesday, Shimon Peres had spent a long time on the phone. It was a strange call. Peres had not said a single word, nor had Brigadier Braun who was also listening on an extension. A few yards away in another room, Burka Bar Lev was making his second call of the day to President Idi Amin. Now, late Thursday morning, Shimon Peres found a handwritten transcript waiting for him on his desk.

Peres skimmed through the document, marking a few key remarks by Amin with red lines. "It's worth paying some attention to those items," he instructed his military secretary.

Amin: "If you come here, you'll feel at home . . . because you're my good friend. Nobody will harm you."

Bar Lev: "I can trust you and God, nobody else."

Amin: "My daughter, Sharon, asks after you."

Bar Lev: "Thank you, Your Excellency. Till I find opportunity to come, will you be able to take all the necessary steps and see to it that nothing happens to the hostages?"

Amin: ". . . I am now with the leader of the Palestinian Popular Front, who has only just arrived. This is the man who decides. . . . He's only just come. The man I negotiated with up to now was number two in the chain of command. Now the right man is here. About forty minutes ago, he told me that he will not change the decision, unless he has some answer by ten tomorrow, Ugandan time. . . ."

Bar Lev: "Your Excellency, I'm doing my best to come and see you. Perhaps I will also be of some help to you. . . . When I heard the news on the radio, I said: now Idi Amin Dada, my friend, has his great opportunity—his great chance to do something very great. Everyone will be speaking about you. Please, stop all the bloodshed. I'll try to come to you and find another solution."

Amin: "But they have now moved all the Jews in together, and they said that they will surround them with explosives, and so there has to be an answer immediately."

Bar Lev: "I am a private individual. . . . If you remember, I always gave you good advice, and never misled you. Right? It's your country and you are the president and the power. If something happens, they'll blame you. If you save people—you will be a holy man. What is the situation, Your Excellency?"

Amin: "They refused, and said that the last deadline is tomorrow at twelve noon. They won't wait for me. They said that they even brought on their bodies a load of TNT and they will all commit suicide with all the hostages. They have already prepared everything to press a button and blow it up themselves."

Bar Lev: "Where are the people? In a hotel or a plane? Where do they sleep?"

Amin: "They are in the old airport of Entebbe. . . . We have built a modern airport. . . . The old airport is just a building, and that's where they are holding all the hostages. There's no plane there. They asked to have all the planes taken away. All the air force men are now out of Entebbe. . . . There are two rows of explosives, inside and out. They came with them on the plane, in crates. I think that certain people, perhaps in Athens, agreed not to check the boxes. . . . And they're ready to blow up. If you can help me tell your government to release those men, whom you call criminals. . . . It's better to save the lives of people. . . . They said they'll start by demolishing the plane, and then immediately kill everyone with the explosives. They said that, if any plane comes over Uganda—they'll automatically blow up everything immediately. . . . They want to bargain through France. . . . I told them that I have a number of friends in Israel—such as you, General Dayan, or even the prime minister—with whom I can bargain, but they told me that they want the French government."

Bar Lev: "Remember, sir, you have a great opportunity, given to you by God. . . ."

Amin: "Tell your government that I want to see you in a very important post."

"Amin isn't the idiot they make of him," Peres remarked as he finished reading the transcript. Nevertheless, the defense minister was grateful for the important information that the president of Uganda let drop in the phone conversation. But for the lateness of the hour, the details could have been used for the purposes of planning a military operation. However. . . . It was too late now!

"Its not too late," the prime minister told the delegation of relatives, who were now in his office. "Don't panic!" Rabin spoke quietly, though he couldn't conceal his own tension. He told the delegation of the government's decision to negotiate with the terrorists and his audience sighed with relief.

"But I must ask you to keep the contents of this conversation between us until the decision is published. That will be after we are informed that France has received it and relayed it to Uganda."

They nodded their agreement. The news was too good to spoil by leaking to reporters.

Major General Rehavam Zeevi turned into his office in the prime minister's Tel Aviv suite. Although he was depressed, he did not doubt that the government's decision was both courageous and correct—there was no choice. He began to collate data on the prisoners requested by their comrades in Entebbe, then called in his assistants to run through the list of names with them.

"Anyone with blood on his hands," Gandhi Zeevi told his companions, "will not leave Israel, even if he is on the list that they submitted."

"Bloody hands!" General Zeevi repeated the criterion. Anyone whose action had resulted in the death or injury of Jews in Israel was not going to leave. . . .

The events of the last few days were far from Lieutenant Colonel Yonatan (Jonathan) Netaniahu's mind— about as far as his physical distance from Tel Aviv. "Yoni" Netaniahu was in a training base in the south of the country, preparing intensive exercises for his unit. And he was sparing no effort, in keeping with the excellence of the men under his command. As far as Yoni was concerned, every little detail deserved his attention.

Now, with only minutes to go to the expiration of the Entebbe ultimatum, Yoni Netaniahu found time to phone his own headquarters.

"What's new?"

"Nothing new," Yossi Yaar answered.

"Anything happening?"

"Not a thing."

"Where are the guys?" Yoni wanted to know.

CHAPTER SEVENTEEN

"The Guys"

The Israeli Defense Forces' most important training manual is not a classified document; indeed countless millions of copies have been sold, distributed, or simply given away in dozens of languages. Its name—the Bible.

Israel's "Book of Books" holds the answer to every problem—be it political, military, religious, or social. Yet, from the hundreds of chapters and thousands of verses, the IDF has chosen these words: ". . . by wise counsel thou shalt make thy war" (Proverbs, 24:6), and a verse to reinforce their case: "Where no counsel is, the people fall" (Proverbs, 11:14).

The Bible was also the trustworthy companion of a non-Jewish British army officer—Captain Orde Charles Wingate. He was anything but the model of a spit-and-polish British soldier. He constantly chewed onions, some said as a deliberate tactic to scare away those whose company was not to his liking. His dress was sloppy and untidy, and he was known for his frequent use of the less polite terms of the English language. But his copy of the Bible went with him everywhere, crammed into a back pocket of his uniform pants.

Wingate the eccentric, specialist in guerrilla warfare and "special operations," was one of the first to distinguish the special talents of Israeli soldiers. He was posted to Palestine in 1936—the first year of a new wave of bloody clashes between Arab and Jew. Both sides were sustaining heavy losses, and an atmosphere of hostility pervaded both camps.

The Haganah—the defense organization of the Jewish community in Palestine—received Wingate with considerable suspicion. First there was his strange behavior. He had a foul temper and doubtful manners. But he did love the Bible, from which he frequently quoted. Before long he became an enthusiastic friend of the Jews of Palestine. To his cousin, Sir Reginald Wingate, the British High Commissioner in Egypt, he wrote: "I have seen the Jews of Palestine, and I tell you that they will produce better military men than ours. They only need to be trained."

Wingate was persistent. He pestered his superiors and inundated them with letters and cables, demanding permission to raise "special operations" teams from among the Jews. He never intended it to be a job for others. He would train them and, of course, lead them. Finally, the captain's persistence paid off, and Palestine got its first Jewish commando units.

Orde Wingate revolutionized Jewish concepts of warfare. There was no more waiting at home to fight off Arab attackers. Wingate's men, dressed in blue shirts and broad-brimmed Australian hats, went out by night on surprise forays into hostile Arab territory. As Wingate put it in talking to his men: "They think the night belongs only to them. We Jews will teach them to fear the night."

He took the models for his lectures from the Bible. A favorite in his talks with the members of the Special Night Squads (SNS) was Joshua's conquest of Canaan. Wingate greatly admired the man who took fortified towns and cities without frontal assaults. He taught his men Joshua's values of psychological diversion, of the consistently unexpected, and of the indirect approach. The result was that Wingate's SNS provided the turning point in the 1936–39 disturbances.

But Wingate's great success was also his downfall. The British Mandate authorities detested the man, his opinions, and his projects. Their urgent dispatches from the office of the High Commissioner in Jerusalem begged the Colonial Office in London: "Take him away!"

One bright morning, Wingate packed his belongings and left Palestine. On the eve of his departure he told his men of the SNS: "Your force has been disbanded, but that doesn't mean the end of the dream, which I hope will only be postponed for a while. I pray that the vision of a free people of Israel in their homeland will soon materialize."

The man who wanted to be a latter-day Gideon, going out to beat the Midianite hosts with only 300 men, looked around for the last time at his Jewish friends, and said: "I promise you I shall come back, and if I cannot do it the regular way, I shall return as an illegal refugee."

Major General Orde Charles Wingate did not return to Palestine. Early in 1944, after two brilliant military campaigns, he was buried by the wreckage of his crashed plane near Bishenpur, India, in the jungle where he fought his last battle.

Four years later, during Israel's War of Independence, his widow dropped a small package from a light plane circling over besieged Yemin Orde—a settlement named for her husband. Wingate's Bible had returned to complete the circle and the promise.

Yigal Allon, Moshe Dayan, and Yitzhak Rabin were all either his students or disciples; all three were among the first commanders of the Palmach, and all three took part in World War II intelligence missions into Vichy-controlled Lebanon and Syria. The Palmach, the elite arm of the Haganah, was heir to Wingate's Special Night Squads, which were disbanded when he left. The Palmach established many of the principles and set many of the standards that would later be absorbed by all units of the army. First and foremost, the Palmach demanded of its men "purity of arms"—in other words, they were never to harm innocent noncombatants. They also maintained a unique comradeship and brotherhood. They demanded for themselves the toughest, most complicated, and dangerous missions.

The Jews never deluded themselves. In any clash or confrontation, they would always be inferior numerically. On the face of it, a nation of three million can have no chance of holding out in endless war against one hundred million neighbors. And in Israel's twenty-eight years of existence, the Arab armies have always had more men, more tanks, more planes, more ships. The implication: in the face of massive enemy numbers, the army has been obliged to use imagination, cunning, wisdom, and originality. This bent for special operations, combat subterfuge, and surprise is deeply stamped in the character of the Israeli soldier from the General Staff down to the lowliest private.

In the early 1950s, Israel's situation was anything but easy. Arab marauders were roaming at will, operating in Jerusalem suburbs and Tel Aviv outskirts. In 1952 alone, there were some 3,000 cases of infiltration, robbery, and murder. The army was helpless. There was no way to stop the marauders, and the situation seemed desperate.

A young law student in the Hebrew University named Ariel ("Arik") Sharon had the answer. He was a twenty-five-year-old recently released soldier, recalled with the rank of major to organize a commando force. Sharon scoured the villages and towns of Israel to find his old comrades. They brought others with them, and together created a force that would achieve fame as "101."

Sharon made it a rule that no one was to return from any mission until it had been completed according to plan.

He would not accept any excuse for nonperformance. Next, he insisted on precise data about the target area before staging any strike and insisted that no comrade, wounded or dead, was to be abandoned in enemy territory: everyone came back—alive or dead.

Like Wingate and many of his own successors, Sharon personally handpicked his men. He talked with them to learn their motives and trained them personally. Unit 101 never numbered more than forty-five men. In the five brief months of its existence, the unit staged many operations in Arab territory, including deep-penetration raids. They were difficult missions, but the performance was always perfect. Moreover, Unit 101 struck the spark needed to revive the failing army.

Army morale was then at its lowest ebb. In fact, 101 was more like a partisan group than a part of a modern disciplined army. Rank was meaningless. Men were commissioned as officers, if necessary, without any formal course or command schooling. Its members were mostly farmers from the kibbutzim. Normal military discipline was nonexistent, but operational discipline could not have been better.

The army did not like Unit 101. Its very existence revived an old argument as to whether there should be special formations. The opponents claimed that the best men should be distributed throughout the ranks in order to improve the quality of the entire army. Eventually the debate was resolved by a decision to merge Sharon's forty-five "wild men" with the paratroop units. Arik Sharon was given command of the new merged unit, and he led the paratroops in many missions across the borders, setting new standards by which the whole army would function.

Moshe Dayan, who was then chief of staff, borrowed one of Arik's principles: "Any commander who returns from a mission without having carried it out, and who has sustained less than fifty percent losses, will be removed

from his command!" The message was obvious. Now, they
no longer returned from unfinished work—and they knew,
again thanks to Sharon, that they would not be abandoned
on the field of battle. This principle cost the paratroops a
great many dead, but it was of profound influence in
forging brotherhood and willingness for sacrifice.

One thing was clear from the beginning: the commander's place is not in a command bunker. An officer
leads his men, no matter how great the danger. While
other armies used "charge!" or "forward!" as routine battle commands, Israeli officers were brought up to use
"follow me!" This principle is almost unique to the Israeli
army, and has cost the lives of many officers. One-quarter
of the Yom Kippur War losses were officers. But an officer who leads his men can impart a combat spirit and,
moreover, is better equipped to know what is possible and
what is beyond attainment. He has the opportunity to read
the battle as it develops, rather than having to wait for reports before issuing his orders.

When the paratroops took upon themselves the staging
of all missions in enemy territory, another argument began
in the IDF. There had always been special operations units
made up of the best men, concentrated in elite formations.
There were officers who wanted to devote special attention
to picked echelons and to give them the best of their available weapons. However, there was always a fear that elite
units might damage the morale of the rest of the army.
Those in favor countered with the argument that elite units
were the best way to raise the general level: "They can
serve as models, set high standards of combat and performance—and of dedication to purpose." Nothing was
resolved on this score for many years.

In 1976, there are no commando units in the army.
After "Operation Jonathan" in Entebbe, a great many papers around the world printed stories about special commando formations. One could gain the impression from
headlines that the boys concerned were the heirs of James

Bond. There were actually only volunteer elite units in the IDF, and it was these men who did the job in Entebbe.

The volunteer formations are not specifically trained for the war against terrorism. These units can and do fight terrorists and saboteurs, but they are also capable of fighting against regular, conventional armies—in fact, they can all perform any role required of them.

The volunteer echelons do not advertise in the daily press for recruits, though they are often written about by journalists and columnists. Generally, the commanders go out to look for the men they want. A few months in advance of draft dates, officers visit the secondary, trade, and agricultural schools to lecture on the army and its volunteer units. They usually talk about some of the missions and the men in the units and answer questions. Usually the youngsters have already heard something from their classmates who have already volunteered. In many places, joining one of these units has become a kind of social status symbol. The very secrecy itself is attractive. Many of the youngsters devote time before enlistment to improving their physical condition. They can be seen running through the streets at night, hiking in the deserts, and scaling Israel's few "mountains" in order to pass the rigorous standards for entry when the time comes.

For many youngsters, any means of gaining acceptance is fair, including use of family influence and social connections. The pressure to get in is particularly strong among young kibbutzniks. Entire school classes from the kibbutzim volunteer en masse for specific units.

There is no shortage of volunteers. Moshe Dayan in fact revealed after Entebbe that two members of his family belong to one of the elite units—and the son of a cabinet minister was in the rescue force that went to Uganda. In some cases, there are ten times as many volunteers as the units can absorb. The IDF's problem is to select the best and most suitable. For this purpose, the army has built a thorough selection process in addition to the special tests applied to candidates for each individual unit. Quite naturally, the elite units put particular emphasis on motivation. Psychological interviews are used to try and eliminate those who wish to join because of lust for adventure rather than because of pride and love for Israel. The candidate's social tendencies are reviewed, as are his attitude to his comrades, and his ability to cope with crises, difficulties, and critical situations. The naval commando, for example, uses a fast 93-mile march along Israel's coastline, with a military psychologist in attendance on the marches. But not all of those who reach the finish line are accepted, nor are all those who drop out necessarily rejected. The psychologist keeps his eye on how the candidates react to given situations. For example, a group of ten men is given eight ration packs to see what they will do. Any man who does not consider his fellows is welcome to march an extra 93 miles, but he will not be accepted into the unit.

Within the unit, the tests are tougher. Soldiers are asked, in sociometric tests, to grade their comrades as soldiers, as commanders, as leaders, and as friends. Anyone who is not acceptable to his fellows in the unit is quietly but quickly shipped out. Officers and psychologists have uniformly agreed that a group composed entirely of the highest caliber of men is not necessarily the best fighting unit. The objective, therefore, is to find a balance.

"Commando" is not a word commonly used in the IDF's elite formations. The young officers and men prefer the term "reconnaissance unit." Some of the units were formed over the years to deal with terrorist activities. After the Six Day War, when the terror organizations stepped up operations from Jordan and Lebanon, special small reconnaissance groups were formed. The groups, which began on each of Israel's frontiers, grew in an atmosphere of constant competition, each group trying to prove that it was better than the others. Officers in the General Staff Adjutant's Department complained that these crack units were swallowing up the best candidates for commissions, and then holding on to them at the rank of private.

The elite formations have no special badges or insignia other than small lapel pins, which usually are meaningless both to Israelis and foreigners. The paratroops wear red berets, but there is no way of knowing who belongs to the elite unit and who doesn't.

The men of these units are of regular conscript age—between eighteen and twenty-one. Difficult as it may be to believe, their officers are only two or three years older than the men. Jonathan Netaniahu, the break-in force commander who led the rescue mission at Entebbe, was only thirty.

The commanders of these elite units may be young, but they are not lacking in experience. Usually they serve no more than two to three years in these positions. Rotation guarantees freshness of command approach, and career advancement for the younger officers.

The Entebbe rescue was not the first operation undertaken by IDF elite units. The least publicized of recent operations was the first of the series. It took place on the night of October 31, 1968—following a heavy Egyptian bombardment and commando raid on Israeli positions by the Suez Canal. In retaliation, and in order to disrupt President Nasser's war-of-attrition plans, a small unit of paratroops probed 250 miles into Egyptian territory. This force of fourteen men was carried by Super-Perlon helicopter to a transformer station at Naja Hamadi in Upper Egypt. The entire operation involved only two copters, one of which dropped its load of paratroops and returned to Israel empty. The second craft flew out, empty, after the operation to collect the men and bring them home. Landing close to the substation with its power lines from Aswan to Cairo, Alexandria, and Port Said, the fourteen approached on foot, laid demolition charges by nine oil tanks—each of which contained fifty tons—and blew them up. That same night, there were disruptions to the electric system all over Egypt.

The entire world wanted to know how the Israelis could venture so deep into Egypt and return safely to their home base. The depth of penetration revealed Egypt's vulnerability; following this operation, the Egyptians were compelled to divert their attention to guaranteeing the security of hundreds of strategic targets. The war of attrition was delayed by four months.

Another surprise army strike took place on April 10, 1973. The night before, men of an elite unit boarded missile ships headed for the coast near Beirut. They crossed the last strip of water in rubber boats, and climbed into six rented cars that were waiting above the beach. The automobiles had been rented—so said the foreign press—by operatives of the *Mossad*, Israel's Central Institution for Intelligence and Special Services. The paratroops raced through Beirut to an apartment house in the city's luxurious Verdun district. They raced up the stairs and executed three of the residents: Muhamad Najar—Yasir Arafat's deputy and the operations officer of Black September; Kemal Adwan—responsible for sabotage and terror inside Israel; and Kemal Nasser—spokesman of Fatah. Another force operated that same night against the headquarters of the Popular Democratic Front for the Liberation of Palestine in the heart of Beirut. Some forty terrorists were killed and the building was demolished.

All the IDF elite units' missions are characterized by imagination in the choice of method, coupled with boldness in performance. The motivating force behind the operations generated by the command echelon has been known to influence the political decision-makers. It is this pressure that allows Israel's political leadership to choose between military and other options when the need arises. There have been occasions, and Entebbe was one of them, when the operational plans have been ready in precise detail before the government has convened to discuss the military option. At least four plans for the rescue of the Entebbe hostages were submitted, and the rejection of one plan in no way reduced the team's willingness to prepare another.

The force that went to Entebbe was composed of men from at least three elite units. Their names and pictures will never be seen in the newspapers, because Israel is still at war against Arab and international terrorism. The soldiers live and fight under a screen of secrecy. There is no point or need to endanger those whose exploits speak for themselves.

Still, it is possible to sketch the Israeli soldier who landed at Entebbe and released the hostages. He is usually Israeli-born, most probably from an agricultural commune or cooperative—though some do come from the big cities. He is likely to be between eighteen and twenty-five, and he volunteered because of his deep patriotic motivation. He is in first-rate physical condition, dislikes publicity, knows precisely how and when to use his weapons, is highly trained, and generally does not see his future in wartime involvement. When the time comes to end his tour of regular service, he will return to civilian life to become an engineer, doctor, farmer, or businessman—but one phone call will bring him back on the run to his uniform and gun. But he was never a James Bond in the past—nor will he be in the future.

CHAPTER EIGHTEEN

"Any Answer
from Paris?"

"Any answer from Paris?" Allon asked his aides. The answer was still "no."

"Come on then, let's eat something," he suggested to Shlomo Avineri and Haim Braun. The three adjourned to a modest restaurant which served traditional Jewish food, at the corner of Ibn Gvirol and Kaplan streets, not far from the government complex in Tel Aviv. No sooner were they seated than the awaited call from the ambassador to Paris came into Allon's office. The foreign minister's duty secretary in Tel Aviv rerouted Mordechai Gazit's call to the restaurant.

Amid the clatter of cutlery, watched by all the customers, Allon tried to lower his voice, but the din wouldn't allow him to.

"Hello," Mordechai Gazit opened the conversation, totally unaware that his minister was in such a public place. "I gave the message to Sauvignard. He is satisfied with the wording. With President Giscard d'Estaing's blessing, he told me that France takes on herself the full responsibility for handling the negotiation. . . ."

Allon was growing impatient. He wanted to know the important things—the things that Gazit wasn't saying.

"The content of our message has already been passed on to the French ambassador in Kampala," Gazit reported.

Yigal Allon suddenly relaxed. He glanced at his watch: the time was 12:30. With ninety minutes to go, he felt sure the message would reach its final destination.

"Motke," Allon asked, in a very loud voice, "can we be sure that they are not soft-soaping us?"

"Yigal, I'm certain of it."

Convinced that the conversation was at an end, Yigal Allon was about to replace the receiver but Ambassador Gazit wasn't finished: "Sauvignard told me that he intends to call you personally."

"What does he want of me?"

The foreign minister was almost shouting in a desperate attempt to drown out the clatter of the restaurant.

"To talk with you directly," Gazit screamed into the other end.

"*Tfahdal*," Allon shouted back, using an Arabic word for "okay by me." "Motke, make sure he has my number. . . ."

He threaded his way through the tables, and sat down to gulp down a bowl of soup with kreplach. He quickly dictated a series of cables to Haim Braun, bringing other ambassadors in Europe and the United States up to date on the recent developments.

Dan Patir, the advisor on media affairs, knew that the entire nation, perhaps the entire world, was waiting for a word from the prime minister's office in Tel Aviv. Three million Jews were waiting and listening for a government communiqué. Nevertheless, it just wasn't possible to release an official text of the decision until it had reached the terrorists in Entebbe. As a partial solution, Dan enlisted the aid of Yisrael Galili and, together, they drafted a bulletin for the midday news, without it being "official." Minutes later, their text was being dictated over the phone to

Radio Israel's political reporter. Sixty seconds before the time signal for a news bulletin, the message was transmitted. A newsreader announced to the waiting world: "Our diplomatic correspondent reports that according to an informed source...."

"I have been informed that the government of Israel is being obstinate," President Amin of Uganda announced.

He faced the Israelis in Entebbe, dressed in combat fatigues, his Israeli paratroop wings glittering proudly on his chest. His young son was with him. He spoke slowly, enjoying every minute: "Though your government is being obstinate, I have succeeded in obtaining a delay of the ultimatum from these men. The ultimatum will now expire on Sunday, at eleven A.M. Ugandan time...."

His audience was astonished. Even though they knew nothing of the details of negotiation between Israel, France, the Somalian ambassador, and the president of Uganda, they had hoped that the whole affair would end in the next few hours. Now, Amin was telling them that the end was further away than ever.

"I am talking to the Israeli government, through the agency of Colonel 'Burka' Bar Lev—a good friend of mine...."

Idi Amin left in his helicopter. Inside the building there was absolute silence. There was no reason for conversation. Each individual sank back into his or her own privacy. The only noise to disturb them was that of the children playing outside. It was almost 2 P.M., Israel time.

Shimon Peres again skimmed through the transcript of Bar Lev's third phone conversation with Idi Amin, and again he muttered, "Amin is not the big idiot he's made out to be." The Ugandan had neatly sidestepped the trap laid for him by the Israelis, giving them no information.

Amin: "Inform your government officially that an announcement by the Popular Front for the Liberation of

Palestine will be broadcast at eleven A.M. [Ugandan time;
2 P.M. in Israel] It's the only answer I can give you. Those
are the instructions that I received from the Popular Front.
Okay? We had some very difficult discussions up to now.
It's best you should wait for the announcement. . . ."

Bar Lev: "Can you tell me what's happening? What are
the main points?"

Amin: "You know that what I tell you is no secret, because my voice was recorded on the Voice of America."

Bar Lev: "Can you prevent the Front from taking action until I reach you? I'm coming with very interesting
proposals."

Amin: "Phone me after you hear the announcement."

Bar Lev: "Sir, how did it happen that more Popular
Front people arrived in Uganda? There were only four on
the plane—and now there are twenty or more. How did
they get in?"

Amin: "They were on the plane. There weren't only
four, but some thirty from all over the world. For your
information, I tried to put all the hostages on a bus and
take them in a different direction, but the hijackers wanted
to bring them to Old Terminal. I did everything I could,
but I think that your government is responsible for the
fate of all the passengers."

Bar Lev: "My government is trying to help by sending
me to you with a number of good ideas. . . . I repeat that
you have an opportunity given by God to do a great deed,
and you will be recorded in history. Don't be influenced
by the Popular Front people just because they are sitting
next to you telling all sorts of stories."

Amin: "I am not influenced by the liberation movement. I decide my own decisions, and I try to do everything I can to save the lives of the Israelis and of the other
passengers.

"I want to tell you that, if I hadn't done everything I
could, all the hostages, including the aircrew, wouldn't
have stayed alive till now. . . . You must consider my

status. You mustn't insult me, as you did now, when you say that I cooperated with hijackers who aren't clean people. But my position is very difficult, and you must know that. Everyone in the world must know that."

Bar Lev: "I know three things about you: that you are a great soldier, a great Ugandan, and a man with faith only in God. In this case—I think that you can prevent massacre and bloodshed. Nobody can give you orders. You do what is best for your countrymen and on God's instructions. The Popular Front people don't have the right to do things in the territory of your country."

"That God-fearing gentile didn't reveal a thing about the terrorists' intentions," Shimon Peres complimented Idi Amin.

The hour hand of the clock reached two.

General Zeevi was now the practical one among the big group in the prime minister's office. Before the meeting, he had already prepared a first draft of the list of terrorists to be exchanged for the hostages.

"I suggest," the prime minister said, "that Gandhi should submit a detailed proposal on the technique of exchange. He can bring it to the ministerial team meeting tonight. . . ."

It was after 2 P.M., and nothing had happened.

"It's possible the terrorists extended their deadline because of the African Unity Conference due to convene in Mauritius on Saturday. The team will meet again at five this afternoon," the prime minister announced. The ministers departed quietly, but in a much better mood than they had arrived.

Michael Golan's logbook recorded 18,000 hours of flying time. Michael—not his real name—was one of the Israeli air force's first pilots. He had flown the first Israeli Dakota to drop paratroops over the Mitla Pass in the 1956 Sinai War. To the youngsters of his squadron, Michael was "the old man," though he was only forty-four.

Michael Golan had spent the previous night at a friend's home with his wife. As in many other Israeli homes, the conversation sooner or later got around to the Entebbe hijacking. "Can a Hercules get there?" his host asked Michael. The pilot made some quick calculations before answering. It seemed to him that a Hercules could fly from Israel to Entebbe, but it would mean using every last drop of fuel.

"Do you think there will be a military operation?" his friend persisted. Golan didn't know but was willing to volunteer an opinion: "If they were to ask me, I would conquer the whole of Entebbe in order to rescue the hostages!"

CHAPTER NINETEEN

"The Devil's Own Idea"

Early the next morning, stories began circulating in the corridors of the Ministry of Defense in Tel Aviv and the Knesset in Jerusalem. People whispered to each other, volunteering fragments of information and gratefully accepting tidbits in return. Rumor grew like a snowball rolling downhill.

"Moshe Dayan is going to Uganda. . . ."

Yitzhak Rabin was against the idea. The adversary relationship between Rabin and Dayan was no secret in Israel. The prime minister did not hide his feelings: "I don't believe in Moshe Dayan's magic powers, and I certainly don't need a prestigious hostage in Uganda. I don't trust Amin, and I don't need to send Dayan so that Amin can make him crawl on the floor. [As Amin had actually done to a British general sent to plead for the release of a fellow countryman.] And then it could end far more tragically, and people will say: 'Rabin wanted to be rid of Dayan.'

"If we send Dayan to Uganda, we must remove from

the agenda any idea of a military operation. Who will stage a mission at Entebbe while Dayan is in Amin's palace as a guest of the Ugandan regime? And if Dayan gets there— how will we talk to him? The telephone system is wide open and the whole world is listening. We don't need Entebbe to employ Dayan as a telephone operator. . . ."

There was no problem, because Dayan resolved it himself: "I won't go to negotiate with pirates." So saying, he ended the matter for the government.

Colonel Avner Ram was the one who had pushed, as early as Monday and Tuesday, "to do something." Now, as head of the intelligence team, he was the one who first noticed the discrepancy between the debriefings that arrived from Paris and the maps turned over to his men by the company that built Entebbe Airport.

"It doesn't make sense," he told his assistants. "And no operation is possible at Entebbe if we don't get all the data on the airport, the terrorists, and the Ugandan army."

On an interoffice phone, Avner Ram reported the problems that were still not completely solved to the head of Intelligence Branch, General Gazit. The general, a quiet man who rarely lost his temper, commanded the senior body in the intelligence community—the agency responsible militarily for maintenance of the IDF's data pool and field security systems, for the development of these systems and for supplying situation appraisals and data to the General Staff. Up to October 1973, when the Intelligence Branch had received a lot of blame for the early-warning failure of the Yom Kippur War, the department even enjoyed exclusivity in the submission of national situation appraisals to the government. The branch had a great many departments, including collation, research, field security, combat intelligence, and air and naval intelligence. Gazit still enjoyed considerable influence in the design of military and political moves.

*   *   *

As senior paratroop and infantry officer of the Israel Defense Forces since the end of the Yom Kippur War, Dan Shomron was of the new generation of senior officers. Now thirty-nine, he enlisted in the paratroops in the mid-1950s straight from a Jordan Valley kibbutz. He participated, both as a private and later as a junior officer, in reprisal raids across the frontier and in the 1956 Sinai Campaign.

After the 1967 Six Day War, Dan returned for a while to the paratroops, then moved on to command an armored brigade. At noon on October 6, 1973, Dan Shomron was in his command tank at a military base many miles from the Suez Canal. He ordered his tanks to move toward the waterline, following notice of imminent war between Israel and Egypt. While making their final preparations to move, two enemy MIG aircraft swept over their brigade laager. Dan didn't wait for any further orders. Egyptian bombs were just as good as any formal declaration of war. He ordered his Pattons forward into the hell that was the Suez Canal line on the afternoon of Yom Kippur—the Day of Atonement—1973. His brigade tried to stop the deluge of Egyptians from crossing the canal. Many of his tanks went up in flames, and many of his men were killed or wounded. Dan later led his tanks across the Suez Canal to become the brigade that completed the noose of encirclement around the Egyptian Third Army.

Shomron was a tank soldier, but he remained a paratrooper at heart. Thus, it was only natural for him to return to the red beret after the war.

Now, he sat in his command post in Tel Aviv and looked up at his secretary who had just entered the room. "Dan," she told him, "they want you immediately at Operations in the General Staff. . . ."

"What's going on?" Dan Shomron asked the head of Staff Branch as he was ushered into the defense minister's office. Lieutenant General Gur, Major Generals Peled and

Gazit, Brigadier Ben-Gal, and a few other officers were already there. They were not used to the idea of surrendering to terrorists—and certainly not so quickly.

"Gentlemen," Peres announced, "the government made a decision today. . . ."

In spite of his mood, he was speaking with his usual vigor: "I am not happy with the decision, neither am I at all certain that it will be possible to secure the release of the hostages from Entebbe. I want to hear your ideas, no matter how crazy they may be. . . ."

The defense minister's invitation was unexpected.

"Doesn't that mean that we are now discussing something contrary to the government's decision?" General Gur asked.

"Why? I am perfectly well aware of the decision, and a discussion of an alternative is not a violation of it. Now, if we can go on with the discussion. . . ."

With all their experience in spur-of-the-moment planning, none of the senior officers had any operational schemes ready, so Peres decided to prod them along: "Benny Peled suggested dropping a large number of paratroops on Entebbe. . . ."

No reaction. The officers already familiar with Peled's project were not impressed. Determined to get an exchange of views, Peres tried Peled directly: "Benny, what have you got to say?"

"I'm a hundred percent in favor of it."

"I'm not," someone else remarked. "An operation of that sort can arouse whatever remains of the rest of Africa against us." He was concerned with the fact that very few African countries maintained diplomatic relations with Israel. After years of receiving considerable technical assistance from the various nations, most of the new African states gave in to Arab pressures after the Six Day War.

The other men present estimated that the feasibility of such a plan ranged from 70 percent to 90 percent, and that only on condition there were no leaks.

Major General Yekutiel Adam interjected: "I suggest we get down to precise planning. After all, we all agree that something must be tried."

The men were tired, and ideas were not immediately forthcoming. The nervous tension this afternoon had taken its toll.

Peres again intervened: "I want each of you to write on a piece of paper the percentage of probability that you give the plan that has been offered. . . ."

It was a surprising request, but they did as they were asked. Shimon Peres collected up the slips of paper. As the officers filed out, on their way to the General Staff wing of the building, he thumbed through them. Only one of them really caught his attention: "one hundred percent." It belonged to Brigadier Dan Shomron, who was now on his way to the chief of staff's suite, with the other officers.

Peres was absolutely certain that a military answer had to be found to the problem of Entebbe, but on the afternoon of Thursday, July 1, it still seemed a remote dream.

"Keep working," Yitzhak Rabin ordered when Peres came to see him, "and bring something that can be done!"

In the prime minister's office, the phones didn't stop ringing. Ordinary citizens and former army officers of all ranks wanted to suggest their own plans to Rabin to rescue the Entebbe hostages.

"I'm going straightaway to phone Asher Ben-Natan in Paris," Peres told Rabin. "I must tell him not to mention cooperation with France in his meeting with Poniatowski tomorrow."

"That's no problem," Rabin responded, "you know it wasn't my idea to send him. . . ."

Peres raced out to find a free line.

"So then what do I talk about if I can't discuss cooperation?" asked the astonished political advisor when Peres gave him the instructions.

"Get him to tell you how reliable France will be in the whole business, and what he thinks about the negotiation that's coming up."

Asher Ben-Natan didn't have the faintest idea about what was going on in Tel Aviv. All he could do was guess at the reasons for the sudden change of instructions. He simply agreed, then hung up.

"You're moving," Wilfried Böse said to the group of hostages that stood by the doorway of Old Terminal.

"Where to?"

The Israelis were guided back into the larger hall, where they had been until the "selection." Everything remained as the French hostages had left it two hours before. As the 105 Israeli passengers and crew members settled down, Sara Davidson noted with an amused eye the flirtations in progress between unattached male and female hostages.

"There's nothing more to say," Sara told her husband, "we're going to be here longer. . . ."

Whatever she was about to say was cut short by a sudden uproar. Pierre Renard, the ambassador of France in Uganda, ran out of the twilight towards Old Terminal. Not allowed to approach the building, he shouted: "Israel is willing to negotiate!" Faiz Abdul Rahim Jaaber jumped up with a shout. Jacques Lemoine, the flight engineer of Air France 139, asked what he was so happy about: "Israel has surrendered! Israel has surrendered," Jaaber roared.

Jacques then told Captain Michel Bacos, who promptly relayed the glad tidings to the others. People leaped up from mattresses and out of armchairs. They hugged and kissed one another. Some wept, others laughed.

"Tomorrow! Tomorrow we go home!"

"You know," one of them confided to Michel Bacos, "I'm happy that I'm about to be released—but I'm certainly not happy that my government is giving in. . . ."

*   *   *

"I understand that the government is capitulating," transport pilot Michael Golan said to his wife when he came home. He was upset. "It means that we can expect more attacks on civil aircraft." Since his job kept him long hours in the air, and often took him abroad, Michael was only too well aware of the dangers that this precedent could spawn.

Before his wife could respond, the phone rang.

"Michael? Where will you be in the next few hours?"

He recognized the voice: it was the operations clerk of his squadron. "Something's happening," he told his wife. The woman hadn't even greeted him with her usual "Shalom" or asked "how are you?" So evidently she didn't have time to chat.

"Perhaps they are going to do something," he wondered aloud.

"Even if they do, they won't take you. You're too old," his wife reminded him.

Michael Golan, aged forty-four, a veteran of 18,000 hours flying time and twenty-three years air force service, grinned from ear to ear.

Lieutenant Colonel Jonathan Netaniahu was back at the telephone in the training base in southern Israel. He asked the operator to put him through to his deputy: "Make it fast!"

"Yossi, what's going on?" Yoni asked impatiently.

"Get your ass up to the General Staff immediately!"

The white fiberglass mini-Carmel flashed past long convoys on the road from the south to Tel Aviv. As darkness settled over Israel, the roads were packed, but Yoni Netaniahu was a fast driver.

CHAPTER TWENTY

And His Name
Was Yoni

Bent over maps, sketches, and photos of Entebbe Old
Terminal, Yoni Netaniahu seemed to the men around him
in the General Staff to welcome a task that would have
frightened others away. Though staggering from the fatigue of a week's intensive exercises in the south, the new
project revived his spirit. Nothing else interested him now.
Everything he was, and everything he had, was devoted to
the creation of a plan to rescue hostages from this two-
dimensional Ugandan airport on the photos spread out
beneath him.

In 1940, Ben-Zion Netaniahu, a young Zionist, packed
his bags and went on a mission for the Israeli Revisionist
party to New York. The United States was to be his new
battleground in war over Palestine. Ben-Zion traveled from
town to town, state to state, across America—talking,
making speeches, trying to persuade people of the need for
a Jewish state.

Quite apart from an arena of political activity, America
was for Ben-Zion Netaniahu an academic haven to finish
what he had begun at the Hebrew University. He started

a major research project in Jewish history of the Middle
Ages, and continued his studies even after he married Zila
Segal-Marcus, a friend from his university days, and
daughter of a pioneer family that came to Palestine in the
late nineteenth century. In 1946, their first child, a boy
named Yonatan (or Jonathan), was born in New York,
but the Netaniahus returned to Jerusalem two years later,
while the young state of Israel was fighting for its very
existence.

Jonathan basked in the cultural and political atmosphere
of a home where every wall was lined with books, and
where discussions of the problems of state and society
were a daily event. Yoni's young life revolved around the
Bible, twentieth century culture, and Zionism. The pathway of his life led from school to home and on to the
residences of the great men in Israeli science and politics.

In 1963, the family again packed their bags to go to
America, partly to allow Professor Netaniahu an opportunity to widen his research. Yoni was then over sixteen,
and the draft board wouldn't let him leave Israel that close
to conscription age. Professor Ben-Zion Dinur, a past
minister of education in the Israeli government, came to
the family's aid. In a letter to then Deputy Defense Minister Shimon Peres, he asked that Jonathan Netaniahu be
allowed to go to the United States, because, without any
doubt, he would return. And the man was right. In letters
to his friends back home he invariably asked about the
troops and training. He was really quite homesick, although he hid it from his immediate family.

Yoni had problems with Cheltenham, his new school.
He battled against an alien environment and a language
he barely knew. In the Jerusalem Gymnasia Ivrit, Yoni
had been an outstanding scholar. He had also been an
admired and popular troop leader in the scouts. Now he
suddenly found himself alone and foreign.

However, he had inherited some exceptional abilities
from his mother and father. In an astonishingly short time,

Yoni took an exam in English and passed with grades which would have done credit to a boy from Houston or Chicago. At home after school, he would often disappear to sit in the attic and write poetry and record his random thoughts.

The year 1964 was by far the best for Yoni Netaniahu. He arrived back at Lod Airport, exactly as Professor Dinur had promised Shimon Peres. He found an attic room with friends of the family in Jerusalem, but the army was his life.

> "He had a book of Plato. He was in the middle of reading it like a thriller. In the line for induction, he opened it and began to read," remembered a comrade in the same army intake group. "Of course the boys thought he was showing off. They couldn't stand the idea of a guy standing in line with a mess tin in one hand and a book by Plato in the other. . . ."

Yoni chose the paratroops, and his service records consistently read: outstanding. Every document, every fitness rating said the same thing: outstanding. He excelled in every course, including officer school, at the end of which he received his graduate pin from Chief of Staff Yitzhak Rabin. Jonathan Netaniahu was posted to a paratrooper battalion, where he gained many admirers among officers and men, but not particularly for courtesy and consideration. Second Lieutenant Yoni was tough, demanding, uncompromising, but undoubtedly a model officer, as the IDF understood the word. In the Israeli army, officers are expected to set an example, to be out front.

> "My first thought was: how did I fall into the hands of such a tough commander?" said a soldier in his platoon. "I think our greatest fear of Yoni was when he ordered us to run. I can remember one occasion. The gap between us and him opened up. He used to

run, get to some point, stand and wait, make a remark to us, then widen the gap again. He was proud
of his fitness. Used to push himself to the very limit.
. . . Men used to drop out, but never Yoni. He wasn't
a martinet. He was a super-martinet. But, if he made
us jump into the water, he jumped into the water. If
he sent us on a run, he ran with us. And when we
had to run with stretchers, he ran with stretchers."

"You know," Yoni wrote to his girl friend, Theresa, "I once told you that I help the boys on runs
and route marches. But, when it comes down to it, I
don't like doing it. For me it's unjust reward. I can't
see someone make an effort, and then fall, without
picking him up. If he doesn't make an effort, then he
doesn't deserve help. . . ."

Yoni was on his way to Harvard University to study
mathematics, physics, and philosophy when the Six Day
War broke out. He canceled his trip to the United States,
reported for duty, and fought with the paratroops in a
bloody battle for Um-Qatef in Sinai.

". . . The battle is over, and I am safe and sound," he
wrote in a letter to Theresa. "We left behind sand
expanses full of burned dead bodies covered in
smoke. I'm anxious about you. Tonight we will shoot
again, and men will be wounded and die. I will be all
right, but it's a pity for the others. I have been
through so much that if something happens now, it
will be a bad joke of fate. . . ."

From the sands of Sinai, Yoni's paratroops moved on to
the Golan Heights to face the Syrian army. Four hours
before the end of the war, one of Yoni's men was shot in
the neck. Yoni bent down to help him and was hit in the
elbow. The bullet hit a nerve junction, causing terrible
pain. Yoni crawled to the rear, across scorched terrain and

under enemy fire, then walked to a casualty receiving station. When he reached a doctor and the medical orderlies, Yoni passed out on the floor.

He recovered from the wound but lost the full use of his left arm. After the war, he married Theresa, and his choice of the wedding site was typically extraordinary: the amphitheater of the Hebrew University on Mount Scopus in Jerusalem. The amphitheater faced a magnificent desert landscape, dropping away to the Jordan Valley and the Dead Sea. Enemy territory for nineteen years, Mount Scopus had only been liberated days before during the Six Day War. Its emotional significance was enormous to the Israeli people.

Yoni and his new bride went to the United States, and true to form, his marks were way up at the top of the list. To keep up his physical fitness, Yoni took to running up the stairs of a twenty-story building every day. He stayed in America for a year, but his heart was in Israel. Exchanges of fire on the frontiers and, particularly, terrorist strikes both in Israel and abroad left him restless to return.

"... Each terror operation in Israel," he wrote to his brother Edo, "increases my recognition that the sooner I come back the better. . . . I know I must. If Fatah can come to fight, then my responsibility is many times greater. One thing is certain: I am a better soldier than any of them, and my national conscience is stronger than theirs. If they want war—we have no choice but to fight for our existence."

At the end of a year at Harvard, Yoni was back in Jerusalem. He studied at the Hebrew University, and worked at a variety of jobs, including gardening and porterage.

"... He found work and made lots of money," recalled a friend. "He moved pianos, refrigerators, and

washing machines and enjoyed it tremendously, for
it was both a physical challenge and a skilled trade."

Yoni was utterly devoted to his studies, yet he was
aware that Israel's security needs were increasing. He
wanted to join the army, but feared that they wouldn't
accept him for combat service because of his disability.

". . . I believe with all my heart," he wrote his wife,
"how important I can be to the army now. Anyone
who can contribute anything should do so. I believe
that the question of Jewish existence depends on us,
our abilities and our spirit. It's enough to read the
war slogans of the tens of millions of our neighbors—
all that hatred and destruction and ambition to kill—
to get an added motivation to be in the army. . . ."

Binyamin Netaniahu, himself a combat officer, talked
about his brother to Uzzi Yairi, a senior paratroop officer.
Uzzi asked for Yoni's service records, took one look, and
was smitten: "Get him for me! Immediately!"

Jonathan Netaniahu served in a reconnaissance unit,
chasing terrorists on the Jordanian and Lebanese borders.
He was good no matter what job he was doing. He led his
men on the long runs and tough route marches, but also
went with them to sick calls, to see they were properly
treated.

"I remember there were incidents with the Arabs,"
Yoni wrote in a letter. "In one of them I killed a man.
It was the first time at close range. Half a yard. I
emptied a whole magazine into him until he died.
That was difficult. To kill at close range is not like
firing a rifle hundreds of yards away—I've being doing that since I was a boy. But since then I've learned
to kill close up. It adds to a man's sorrow—not the

sorrow of a moment, but something that settles inside."

In one of his last postings, Yoni Netaniahu was deputy commander of a crack volunteer unit that was frequently in action. Service here, for Yoni as well as the others, demanded a great deal of courage and initiative. He saw death often, but never grew accustomed to it.

". . . He liked to read *All Quiet on the Western Front*," one of his comrades remembered. "It's the personal story of a simple soldier in World War I. That war meant something to Yoni. Men rotting for year after year in trenches and mud—the kind of things that degrade a human being. This whole business of killing, all the filth of war, the destruction— he hated it. Yoni hated wars."

In a letter, Yoni himself wrote:

". . . what sort of a mad world do we live in? In the twentieth century, they got to the moon, Hitler murdered, and there was World War I—the worst of all. A whole nation was eliminated in Biafra, and it doesn't shame anyone. This sick world doesn't do anything. Everyone is steeped in his own wars, including Israel, including Israel, including me. And me? I feel that I can thrust away the end as far as Israel is concerned. How do I do it? By learning war!"

In 1972 he took a leave to return to Harvard as a student of Professor Karl Deutsch in a seminar on international relations. Yoni had abandoned mathematics in favor of political administration and the history of Middle Eastern government. In two months, he went through three courses in political administration in a tremendous drive towards a bachelor's degree. On all three, he received the highest marks. But he was always more than a hard-working student, and his classmates took note of that.

"This place does attract some pretty unusual people," wrote the *Harvard Crimson*. "So it is not a big deal to say you have come across somebody who is going to be a future senator or a bigwig in national or international life. But there are few people that you do meet whom you generally feel add to you as a person, and really make being here and being associated with them in some way, a fuller development of your own life. . . . Netaniahu was a person who lived a kind of exemplary personal life without being schmaltzy about it, that made you kind of feel warm when you were with him. A conversation with him always made you think about your own life in a way you wouldn't have thought about it if he hadn't dropped in to see you."

Yoni Netaniahu came home in the fall of 1973. Within weeks, Israel was fighting. In the Yom Kippur War, Yoni led a force that eliminated a Syrian commando detachment on the Golan Heights. An officer remembers:

"We got word that we were virtually the last force defending Golan. We stood on the road and looked for the enemy, and then we saw Syrian commandos landing, and they opened fire while they were under cover and we were exposed. At that point, somebody simply had to start giving clear orders, otherwise it could have been very messy. I remember that it was the moment when I began to be scared. Very scared. What I saw then, I will remember for the rest of my life. Yoni lifted himself up very quietly, as if we weren't under fire. He waved the men to get up together with him. They were all lying behind shelter and he began to advance as if he were playing in a firing exercise. He walked upright, throwing orders right and left. I remember my thoughts as one of his men: 'Hell, if the commander does that—then I'm not going to pass it by myself!' I got to my feet and began to fight."

Yoni Netaniahu raced with his men across the Golan Heights, then into the bulge driven deep in Syrian territory. Suddenly he picked up cries for help on his radio. He recognized the voice. It was Yossi Ben-Hanan—commander of an armored battalion. Yossi was trapped in an inferno of Syrian fire on one of the inert volcanoes that dominate the Golan landscape.

"We were hit and part of my force withdrew. My driver and I remained alone in the field," said Yossi Ben-Hanan. "I was in a not-very-encouraging situation and had lost a lot of blood. The brigade commander radioed: 'Yossi, hold on! I'm sending Yoni!' He took a big enough risk coming deep into an area held by the Syrians. His rescue was very decisive as far as I was concerned personally. I owe my life to Yoni."

After the Yom Kippur War, Yoni was assigned to rehabilitate an armored battalion that was almost beyond repair. He had no trouble at all with the transfer to armor, becoming first a company commander, then taking over a battalion in the war of attrition that followed Yom Kippur on the Golan Heights. Yoni, a paratrooper by nature and inclination, nevertheless became a successful tank soldier. But his service as a battalion commander in the armored corps was temporary—to develop his military knowledge before getting shifted back to paratroops and up the ladder of rank and responsibility:

"In the war of attrition, thirteen months ago, I got command of the battalion," Yoni opened his farewell speech to the armored corps. "The battalion was just taking shape. Four months earlier it hadn't even existed, and it only began to gain its skeleton framework under shellfire. A battalion is not created in one day, or by one man. A battalion is the sum total of the hundreds of soldiers of which it is composed, of the degree of their willingness, their adherence to mission, methodical training, recognition of the correct order of priorities of jobs they must do, their obstinacy in doing those jobs and—above all—their understanding of our objectives as soldiers, and the importance of our standing here in the face of so many who hate us.

"In the short time since the war, we have got a great deal done. You all participated in the enterprise of building the battalion, and you created something—but this is not the end of the road, rather only the beginning. We have built a framework, and it is firm. Now you must add the entire structure, and there is a lot of work to do. The basic assumption in our work was also the battalion's main mission—and that is to prepare for war in the best possible fashion, in order to stand quietly on the day of judgment, when it comes, in the knowledge that we did everything we could in the time that we had. I believe in a number of things which, in my opinion, are essential for the maintenance of any framework, and I want to leave them with you:

—I believe first of all in common sense, which should guide everything we do.

—I believe in the responsibility of commanders: a good commander is one who feels a sense of full responsibility for everything done under his command.

—I believe that the buck should not be passed to someone else.

—I believe in going into details. Anyone who doesn't do it, and who tries to save himself work, will miss the main objective of preparing the unit for war.

—I believe that there can be no compromise with results. Never compromise with results that are less than the best possible—and even then look for improvements.

—I believe that the danger in the life of a unit is in personal satisfaction. I want the men of the battalion always to be slightly worried—in case perhaps there is something else we could do, we could improve, and we haven't done it.

—I believe that all the efforts of the battalion must be committed to the main objective—victory in war.

—I believe, with absolute faith, in our ability to carry out any military task entrusted to us, and I believe in you.

—I believe in Israel and in the general sense of responsibility that must accompany every man who fights for the future of his homeland.

"I leave with the feeling that much still remains to be done, and I admit that it is difficult to leave. But I also know that I am leaving the battalion in good hands, who know what must be done, and how it must be done.

"I would like you to know that I believe in you— the officers and men of this battalion. With a battalion like this, a man could go to war."

At the end of 1975, Jonathan Netaniahu took command of one of the elite units of the IDF and became a prominent figure among the new generation of commanders. He was that rare mixture: a fine military man and a philosopher. A young Israeli, who by force of circumstances was compelled to hold a submachine gun and shoot at other men, instead of teaching history or physics in a university.

"Yoni very much loved life," said a brother officer.
"You mustn't think of him as a man of force and
violence. The record that he played more than any
other was of cello and harpsichord sonatas. . . . It was
strange to see an army commander, after night exercises, settle down by a lamp with a book in English
and a pipe between his teeth."

As commander of a crack unit, Yoni was as tough and
uncompromising as ever. In every exercise and operation,
he went into every little detail. Nothing escaped his eyes.
Bent over maps, sketches, and photos of Entebbe Old
Terminal, Yoni Netaniahu seemed to the men around him
in the General Staff to be taking on his own shoulders the
fate of the entire Jewish people. . . .

CHAPTER TWENTY-ONE

Thunderball

Yitzhak Rabin showed the other members of the team out, then returned to his desk to face his remaining visitor—a man he had known for many years. In fact, Rabin had appointed him head of the *Mossad*. There was a long pause, during which Israel's top secret agent had already guessed what the prime minister wanted to say. When Rabin did speak, his voice was somber.

"We're relying on you. Remember, nothing will happen if we don't get from you the information we lack. And we're missing a lot!"

The head of the *Mossad* replied: "You'll have it."

"Germany wants an answer by tomorrow morning," Ambassador Meroz cabled Yigal Allon from Bonn. "They want to know the Israeli position vis-à-vis the demand for release of terrorists imprisoned in Germany."

"Under no condition whatsoever are you to put pressure on Germany," Allon cabled, following the guidelines established by the ministerial team. "The German government should not view Israel's willingness to negotiate and release convicts as a recommendation to Germany to do likewise. Certainly not!"

What will be in tomorrow's papers? The question bothered both Dan Patir and Naftali Lavi. Each sat at his own desk, one in the Prime Minister's Office, the other in the Defense Ministry, trying to answer scores of newspapermen who were inundating them with phone calls. Behind all the routine formula phrases—"no alternative," "helpless"—lay one simple truth obvious to all. Israel had given up. The evening *New York Post* summed it up in a banner headline: "Israel Surrenders."

"France will be the only pipeline for negotiation with the terrorists," Rabin ordered. "And the negotiation must be based on the lowest possible price." Then he greeted his first visitors of the evening: Menachem Begin, his opposition colleague, Elimelech Rimalt, and Knesset Foreign Affairs Committee Chairman Yitzhak Navon. Rabin brought them up to date, concluding: "There is no military option, and we have no alternative."

A phone rang in the headquarters of the chief medical officer, IDF. Brigadier Dan Michaeli raced out on his way to the General Staff.

Another summons took Brigadier Yisrael Zamir, chief communications and electronics officer, from his desk.

In the General Staff building, and some of the smaller edifices around it, the lights burned all night. At air force headquarters, the teams were hard at work seeking solutions to flight, landing, and fueling problems. In Staff Branch, Yekutiel Adam, Avigdor Ben-Gal, and Dan Shomron were poring over maps and aerial photographs. A great many senior officers were rushing around obtaining the details needed for the plan of ground operation. Dr. Dan Michaeli was calling in some of his assistants from the medical corps to form a team of their own.

Brigadier Zamir studied a chart of the Red Sea, Gulf of Suez, and Indian Ocean regions, trying to solve communications problems for a distance of 2,264 miles—no easy matter even with the technology available in 1976.

Colonel Ram called in his aides for yet another discussion. "Gentlemen," he said, "according to the information we now have, the choice of Uganda was no coincidence. The Ugandans are cooperating fully with the terrorists."

While Avner Ram was opening the intelligence team colloquium, a cable from Paris arrived on the desks of the prime minister and the defense minister: SOMALIAN AMBASSADOR, SERVING AS MEDIATOR, INFORMS THAT THERE CAN BE NO TALK OF NEGOTIATION, ONLY RESPONSE TO DEMANDS.

An instruction was forwarded to IDF Computer Center from the General Staff building: "We need a code name for an operation." In the past, IDF officers chose their own code names, in many cases those of their wives or girl friends. To prevent misunderstandings and eliminate dangerous duplication, the selection of code titles for operations had been transferred to the computers.

The first name to come back wasn't to Dan Shomron's liking. The computer offered another: "Thunderball."

"Very good," said Shomron, forgetting for the moment that it was also the name of one of Ian Fleming's "James Bond" novels.

"I still think the plan isn't good," Mota Gur contributed to a discussion that now seemed interminable. "It smacks too much of gimmickry."

The defense minister said nothing. The maneuver now before him was different from the one presented in the afternoon to the prime minister. It was only a skeleton—but the planning team was going in the right direction.

Yekutiel Adam: "I propose to start calling in the forces that we need to train on a model. We shouldn't forget that we are fighting the clock!"

None of the notes and memos flowing into the chief of

staff's office particularly aroused General Gur's enthusiasm. "The assumption is that hundreds of Ugandan soldiers are at the airport," read one. "How do you overcome such a large force, so far from your own home base?" How indeed.

"At the airport there are apparently sixty to a hundred troops," read a later correction. The men were relieved.

"And how many terrorists?" asked Mota Gur.

"Eight."

"Eleven."

"Perhaps twelve."

The data continued to pour in from different sources, some open, others covert.

"We must assess all the possible reactions," Colonel Ram instructed his aides. What he needed now was some informed guesses about Idi Amin. What would the field marshal do, and how would his soldiers behave?

Different teams were working in different places. By this hour of the evening, scores of men were party to the big secret: the IDF was preparing to rescue the hostages from Entebbe.

"Nobody who isn't connected with this mission is to know about it. Not even the slightest hint," the chief of staff ordered. Nothing was to be said over the phone. Not a word was to be typed. Everything was to be on a "need-to-know" basis. And no one was even to inform the staff generals who weren't already involved.

It was well after nightfall when Jonathan Netaniahu parked his car in the General Staff lot and turned, tired and dusty from the long drive, to run up the steps to Kuti Adam's office, then down again to the "pit"—as the General Staff command bunker was known, to find his deputy, Yossi Yaar.

"What's it about?"

"Planning. . . ."

"Where are the guys?"

"Spread out."

"You had better call them in to base by one tonight. . . ."

Yossi Yaar guessed that the Ugandans wouldn't fire on white men. Yossi had been an instructor in the Ugandan army, and recalled: "The black man thinks a number of times before he starts shooting. . . ." It was just one of many details that he and Yoni were considering, but they didn't have a plan yet.

"Be prepared for a sleepless night," Yoni warned Yossi, "there's a lot to be done."

"Nothing is firm yet, but. . . ."

Shimon Peres stood facing Moshe Dayan at a table at the Capriccio Restaurant in Tel Aviv. The time was about 9 P.M. on Thursday, July 1. "Moshe, I must talk to you in private. Please come over to another table for a few moments."

In a few succinct sentences, Peres described the situation. "Nothing is firm yet, but. . . ." He described the rejected plan to take the whole of Entebbe, and revealed that the General Staff was, at that very moment, working on improvements to the plan. He went on to tell Dayan of Rabin and Gur's reactions to it.

Dayan, Israel's former defense minister, nodded vigorously: "Shimon, I am one hundred and fifty percent with you! There has to be a military operation! If the General Staff submits a plan that does make sense, even if it is dangerous, accept it!"

Thanking Dayan, Shimon Peres departed back to his desk.

"Get me Gad!"

In less than half an hour, Transport Minister Gad Yaakobi was in Peres' office. Yaakobi and Peres were members of the same faction of the Labor party—both confidants of Moshe Dayan. Peres briefed his colleague about the situation in general, and about the conversation with Dayan.

"Shimon," said Yaakobi, "I'm with you."

In the elegant embassy of Israel in Paris, camp beds were being moved into the offices of the ambassador and his senior assistants.

The prime minister's duty secretary in Tel Aviv closed the door on the six ministers and their entourages. Again Peres, Allon, Yaakobi, Zadok, and Galili took their places at the rectangular table. The prime minister opened the session: "We will now discuss the arrangements of the negotiation that begins tomorrow through the good offices of the French government."

The room of very tired men made a conscious effort to listen as General Zeevi picked up a sheaf of papers and said: "I suggest the following stages. . . ." Gandhi Zeevi had spent most of the day poring over the list submitted from Entebbe, classifying the terrorists into different categories.

"Our operative stages will be as follows:

"A. To submit our proposal to the French.

"B. To get their reactions, and those of Idi Amin and Wadia Hadad.

"C. Discuss the gap between positions, and reach agreement.

"D. To submit list of terrorists, and receive lists of the passengers at Entebbe.

"E. To carry out the exchange."

"France will never agree to Paris as the site for exchange," Peres commented. "In my opinion, we should try to convince the French to make the exchange in Djibouti, which is territory under their supervision."

Justice Minister Zadok agreed.

Peres continued: "I can foresee problems in Paris. I think we should send General Zeevi to France to handle the negotiation alongside Ambassador Gazit."

Allon: "I'm in favor."

From the prime minister's bureau, Yigal Allon phoned Ambassador Gazit in Paris. At two in the morning, Gazit phoned Allon in Tel Aviv: "On the French side, it's okay. They have appointed to the negotiating team the deputy director general for African affairs in the Foreign Ministry, M. Georget."

At 2:30 A.M. on Friday, July 2, Yitzhak Rabin summoned General Zeevi to his office.

"Gandhi, you're going in the morning."

Long after midnight in the General Staff, officers bent over plans—operations officers, intelligence experts, airmen, paratroops, signals officers, military doctors—piecing together the thousands of details that would make up "Operation Thunderball": flight, landing, fueling, rescue of the hostages, the way home. . . .

Perhaps half an hour after midnight, the minister of defense invited the chief of staff over to his home: "Mota, I don't intend to suggest a plan against the judgment of the chief of staff, but I want you to understand that in my opinion, the future of the country and the nation is in the balance. This is the time for boldness. You can have nothing without sacrifices. And I'm not deluding myself—there are likely to be some along the way. Failure will mean that I have to draw some personal conclusions. But if we give in to terrorists, not even the faintest memory of us will remain."

They talked for two hours or more, but at the end the general wasn't yet ready to concede that the plan was feasible.

"I agree to them setting up a model of Entebbe, based on the data that we have," Mota Gur said—and that was already a big step forwards.

Shimon Peres went to bed at 2:30. In his diary for Thursday, July 1, 1976, he wrote: "I spoke to Mota with all my powers of persuasion. . . . Today was the hardest of my life. . . ."

CHAPTER TWENTY-TWO

A Ray of Light

The first rays of light penetrated the windows of the General Staff building in Tel Aviv, but the men in the "pit" weren't aware of it. They were still working over their maps and outdated aerial photos, and contemplating the same plans that Colonel Avner Ram had discussed the previous day with Yossi.

"There are ideas for an operation in Uganda," the colonel had said. "For the time being all of them are crazy. They all deal with hitting the terrorists in Entebbe *without* evacuating the hostages."

From that point on, Yossi devoted himself single-mindedly to planning the details. He was everywhere—in the intelligence team, among the combat officers, with the air force and medical corps—asking, questioning, probing, and suggesting his own solutions.

As evening approached, it was clear that the air force had found answers to all its problems except for refueling for the way home. The ground-operation team also had a few hunches but hadn't yet checked them out properly. The basic outline was beginning to make sense, and Yossi was thinking about its overall design when General Adam burst into the room where Yossi was working with the Operations Branch officers.

"Tell me," Kuti Adam demanded, "can you present most of the plan to the prime minister right now?"

The men nodded their assent.

He strode out, followed by a file of officers. Yossi stayed where he was. "Let Dan Shomron talk," Yossi said as he turned back to the details, agonizing over the amount of missing data.

Like his superior, Dan Shomron, Yossi was convinced that the whole thing depended on surprise—the first minutes were going to determine success or failure. "Everything has to be done to arrive unexpectedly and operate— but how?" he asked aloud. None of the other officers in the room knew the answer.

Unlike Shomron, Yossi thought it would be a mistake to send in ten Hercules aircraft and a great many vehicles. "I have been in Uganda," he told his companions, "and I know that army. In my opinion, a couple of shots would be enough to start them running all the way to Kenya." Yossi thought four planes would be enough, and that too many vehicles "would clog up the whole business." On the other hand, a lot of infantry would be needed to hit the terrorists, set up blocks, and evacuate the hostages. He didn't doubt for a moment that his unit, under Yoni Netaniahu, should be the one to perform the rescue—but who would the others be?

"Prepare me a company of paratroops and a company of Golani," the senior paratroop and infantry officer phoned instructions to his headquarters. He also told his staff that they were not to take leave or be absent until further notice.

For a good many years now there had been stiff competition between the paratroops and the Golani Brigade. Back in the 1950s, the paratroop units carried out most of the combat missions. After all, these were volunteer elite squads of highly skilled and motivated soldiers. Nobody volunteered for Golani, where the operational level was far from good in the 1950s and even in the early 1960s. However, intensive and methodical training slowly raised the level of the brigade. Soldiers from Golani took part in missions and acquired operational experience. Though they were not the cream of Israeli youth, they were beginning to show first-class capabilty. Their performance in the 1973 war and in routine security and counter-terror duties was so good that Dan Shomron decided to use them at Entebbe.

Late Thursday evening, Dan Shomron, Yoni Netaniahu, and Yossi were hard at work on plans that Yossi still considered "primitive."

"Yoni," Dan said, "get over to your unit and concentrate on the ground planning."

Yoni left in a hurry, fully aware of the time problem. Minutes after his arrival at his camp, all the officers of his unit convened in his office. As he waited for them to assemble, he concentrated on the quote from the Long Range Desert Force of the British Eighth Army which hung on his wall—"He who dares, wins!"

He briefed the men on their coming operation, dividing missions between detachments, ordering mobilization of reservists, assigning men to the task of checking serviceability of weapons and equipment, assigning others to liaison with the General Staff departments that could supply additional information, and entrusting others with data analysis and detailed planning of a ground operation that seemed reasonable.

When most of the men had left the office, Yoni held a small planning session with several of his best officers. At 3 A.M., Yossi proposed a recess for a few hours sleep, although he himself spent the remaining hours till dawn checking things over. He sat alone preparing lists for each detachment: missions, equipment, aircraft.

Characteristically, Yoni had assigned himself the hardest part. His force would be the first on the ground, and would have to race straight out of the plane to Old Terminal, eliminate the terrorists, and release the hostages. He told his officers and men to remember to keep checking the various possibilities of opposition on the ground at Entebbe Airport: "We must assume the worst possible situation, and every opening for encounter—no matter how absurd it may seem." He went on to list the probabilities:

"A. Fire on the plane while still in the air ("that is the worst case of all").

"B. Fire at the moment of landing.

"C. Fire while the plane is on the runway and moving.

"D. Fire the moment the plane brakes to a stop.

"E. Fire when. . . ."

"It's like a needle plunging into a body," said Yoni, "and we are the needle!"

Later on in the session, Yoni Netaniahu said almost in an aside: "I can't understand these Ugandans. We have nothing to do with them. Why do they hate us?"

"I don't hate you," said Idi Amin. This time he really surprised the remaining 105 hostages. "I don't understand why the papers write that I hate Israel. You will be the proof that I don't hate you. . . ."

Everyone felt that, at last, the affair was about to end. It seemed that this would be their last encounter with Idi Amin, and so the audiences were less inclined to take his remarks seriously. Thus the shock was greater when the president of Uganda said, almost in passing: "I want to tell you that Israel has not so far accepted the demands, and your situation is very critical. The men who brought you here have mined the building and, if their demands aren't met, will demolish it!"

This was the last thing they expected on the morning of Friday, July 2.

One of the women passengers in the circle around Amin whispered something to him. "When we return to Israel," she said softly, "a public announcement will be made about the fact that you treated us nicely."

Antonio Degas Bouviet was standing close enough to hear her and he quickly made a suggestion to Amin. The Ugandan president nodded: "I have an idea. You write a letter to the government of Israel, and if you pass it on to us before one o'clock, I'll have it read over Uganda Radio. It will help you."

Only the previous day, there had been a debate between two opposing factions among the hostages. The subject—whether applauding Idi Amin could make any difference in their chances for decent treatment and release. The outcome had been a typical Jewish compromise: clap for him when he brings good news. The opposing camp felt that any sign of appreciation of Amin offended their own pride, but at least they had agreed that all the hostages would greet his bluster and ill tidings with absolute silence. There was no applause this time. Amin swept out of the room, barely noticing the scene going on in a corner of Old Terminal.

This morning, Jean Jacques Maimoni had not awakened with his usual cheerfulness. He discovered when he woke after a night of severe abdominal pains that he could not even raise himself off his mattress. He was suffering from food poisoning. Pale and quiet, he allowed Yaakov Cohen, Benny and Ron Davidson, and the other children to tend his needs. For the first time, Jean Jacques was receiving aid rather than giving. The adults looked over at the boy, feeling almost as badly for him as they now did for themselves.

Sadly, they began to compose the letter Amin had demanded, which none of them wanted to write: "We are grateful to Idi Amin for his good attitude to us and for his frequent visits. Idi Amin told us about his efforts to secure our release. In the light of that, we ask the Israeli government to respond positively to his efforts, and to try and bring about the release of all the people who are still here."

Ilan Hartuv made sure to insert "all the people," as a way of telling everyone back home in Israel that all the Israelis were still in Entebbe.

In Paris, the general feeling was: "Israel is behaving intelligently." Senior officials of the French government were satisfied with the Israelis: "There couldn't be any other decision. This isn't surrender—it's wisdom."

The Friday morning press in Israel reported that "Government circles in Bonn were surprised by Israel's agreement to negotiate with terrorists," and through the mediation of France at that. The last-minute decision, they said, was contrary to the previous Israeli attitude: "If Israel submits to an ultimatum, then we can no longer speak of a united front of the countries involved in the Air France hijacking."

London reacted differently. "We are relieved that President Amin secured the release of some of the prisoners, among them three British citizens," said the Foreign Office spokesman. "We hope that the efforts to release the other hostages will be crowned with success, and we welcome the steps that lead in that direction."

In Cairo, President Anwar Sadat ordered a special plane put at the disposal of Hani el-Hasan, Yasir Arafat's political advisor, to fly him to Entebbe: "So he can join the efforts to release the hostages, to prevent a tragedy which can only be to the detriment of the Palestinian cause."

Shimon Peres phoned Yitzhak Rabin at 8 A.M. on Friday morning. The call was intended as a progress report on the military information that had come in during the night, and on his conversation with General Gur. Peres told the prime minister that Gur now inclined towards recommendation of a workable rescue plan.

Rabin was cautious. "Let's wait and see," he said, but immediately agreed to a session with the defense minister and chief of staff at 10:30 in his office.

"I assume," said Peres, "that the chief will be able to present his operational plan at the meeting."

Peres went straight to his Tel Aviv office, where he was informed by General Gazit that the cost of preparations so far had exceeded one million pounds ($120,000). Peres merely shrugged, but as he sat alone at his desk, he considered the situation.

He suspected that three of the six ministers in the team were likely to support a military rescue operation at this stage, no matter what the cost or the risk: i.e., Transport Minister Yaakobi and Foreign Minister Allon would go along with him. That left them one shy of a majority vote, one more minister to be convinced—and Shimon Peres chose Haim Zadok, the minister of justice since Golda Meir's administration.

Haim Zadok was not a member of Shimon Peres' political camp. Shimon Peres was a "hawk," Zadok wasn't, but the two men maintained a good working relationship. The prime minister, too, relied on Zadok's judgment and unhesitatingly consulted him on matters in and beyond his legal jurisdiction. Peres was careful not to wield his ministerial seniority over Zadok, and perhaps this was why he could now approach the justice minister without any loss of prestige.

Peres sat in Zadok's office and told him: "If we don't rescue the hostages from Entebbe, Zionism and the concept of a sovereign state of Israel become pointless. Submission to terrorist demands, when we have no guarantee that they will release the hostages unharmed, will be a hard blow to the nation and the army."

"The question isn't what Zionism and our sovereignty can expect if we don't rescue the hostages," Zadok answered. "The question is whether there is a plan for a military rescue—one with a high probability of success?"

Peres paused only slightly before answering.

"Yes, there is a plan!"

Zadok was surprised. Though he had been present at the ministerial team session and had followed everything with close attention, he wasn't aware that a plan had been formulated overnight. Peres quickly filled in the gaps, then added: "It will be discussed today in the team, and the decision must be taken today, or at latest tomorrow. . . ."

The justice minister nodded. He did not promise to support the plan, yet he did allow the defense minister to believe that he was inclining that way. Shimon Peres departed secure in the feeling that there would be no argument between him and Haim Zadok.

"All the Israelis are still in Entebbe, and our problem is to bring them out alive," he told an audience composed of all the staff officers, the commander of the Golani Brigade detachment, and the paratroop unit commanders. Yoni was also there. "In a normal military operation, we have to take a given area. In this one, there is no point to taking the place and bringing back 105 bodies to Israel. We must do a spotless operation. We have to get them out and bring them home, and that's what makes this different from anything else we have done.

"Our first problem is to achieve surprise on arrival.

"Our second problem is to get to the terminal building at high speed.

"Our third problem is to eliminate the terrorists and neutralize the Ugandans.

"Our fourth problem is to create conditions of relative quiet in the entire area, and get this large number of people to the plane in comparative safety.

"Our last problem: our transportation from Israel to Uganda is by plane. We must guarantee that the new runway, the new terminal, and the entire area will be under our control, so the flights in and out can be made without interference.

"Otherwise, gentlemen, we shall be remaining in Uganda. . . ."

High above the waters of Lake Victoria, two twin-engined planes were circling—so *Der Spiegel* later reported. They had come from Wilson Airport, outside Nairobi, after filing a flight plan with the control tower that specified their destination as Kisumu. The young men in the rented planes had a magnificent view of Uganda, but their cameras were aimed at only one spot: Entebbe International Airport. Their photographic equipment wasn't the most modern, but under the circumstances it would do. Satisfied that they had shot enough film, the pilots descended for a short stopover at Kisumu, on the Kenyan shore, then flew back to Nairobi, landing at Ambakasi International. No one noticed who met the men nor knew what they had been doing over Lake Victoria.

Radio Israel was saying absolutely nothing new this morning. The commentators gave rehashed versions of the stories told by the second group of freed hostages, mentioned the meeting of the Foreign Affairs Committee and the forthcoming session of the ministerial team and, of course, repeated the assertion that Israel, having beyond a doubt surrendered, would be opening negotiations any minute now. The daily papers were more explicit: they had photos of the released hostages in Paris, and a lot of terrifying headlines: "More Terrorists Join Entebbe Hijackers," "Hijackers Threatening to Demolish Building," and "Hijackers Brought Crate of Dynamite." A few editorials were warning the government against traps in the negotiating process. The mood of the entire country was one of depression.

"The chances of you getting out of Entebbe alive are negligible," the one known as Haled told Hana Cohen. He sneered at her and walked away.

Threading her way through the hall, Hana reported the conversation to Captain Michel Bacos, adding in furious tones: "If that's the case, and our chances really are zero—then there's no point in sending the letter to Idi Amin." The aircrew, together with the dual nationals, had formed the main camp in favor of writing the letter, while Hana's husband was against. Armed with the reason donated by Haled, Pasco Cohen returned to the fray; anything to stop that message being broadcast over Uganda Radio! He didn't know that the French aircrew had already agreed to write, but their first letter was rejected— because it did not contain a direct plea to the French government.

The news from Paris made Shimon Peres anxious. It was clear that the negotiations would only move ponderously, through no fault of the French Foreign Ministry. Technical difficulties of communication between Paris and Kampala, and too many middlemen between France and the terror organization were slowing the exchange of conditions and viewpoints. Apparently, the terrorist spokesmen in Kampala were being obstinate. They had told Ambassador Renard that they would agree to an exchange only in Entebbe itself: the freed convicts had to be brought there before the hostages would be released.

"This is the moment I was afraid of," Peres muttered. "Once Israel capitulates, the extortion really begins." Under conditions like these, it would be extremely difficult, if not impossible, to negotiate. Because of this, Peres was even more convinced that a military solution was essential.

Shimon Peres had carried responsibility for security of Israel on his shoulders since the 1956 Sinai Campaign. Protecting such a small country with few inhabitants from the surrounding multitudes who sought their extermination had never been and would never be easy. In 1959, he was appointed deputy minister of defense, a position which he held for six years.

When Ben-Gurion retired from the government in 1965, Shimon Peres went with him. With Ben-Gurion, he founded a new party, becoming a member of the Knesset on its slate. His next nine years of government service led up to his decision to seek the position of prime minister. In 1974, he offered his own name in nomination and contested the Labor party election against Yitzhak Rabin, who won by a small margin. Peres took over as defense minister, and set about the task of rehabilitating the IDF after the trauma of the Yom Kippur War.

In what passes for normal times in Israel, Peres is described by some as a civilian sandwiched between two chiefs of staff—the incumbent Mota Gur and the veteran Yitzhak Rabin. On Friday, July 2, 1976, this definition was truer than ever. Rabin was still applying brakes to the plans for an army mission. Mota Gur was submitting plans and immediately discrediting them, weakening Peres' hand. Both as a citizen of Israel and as minister of defense, Peres was utterly convinced that it was now up to the Israel Defense Forces to get the hostages out of Entebbe. Otherwise, their chances of coming out alive were slim indeed.

CHAPTER TWENTY-THREE

120 Seconds

Yoni Netaniahu returned to his unit in the late morning to supervise the progress of training and preparation. In front of the huts, at various spots around the camp, soldiers were drilling all the possible permutations of the rescue plan. They raced along in vehicles, tumbled out on the move, charged towards a simulated target building, firing as they ran.

Yoni told Yossi as they watched: "Up to the point that the aircraft lands and reaches its braking station, we have nothing to do and cannot control the situation. But from the moment the plane comes to a halt, *everything* must be under our absolute control. That will be the critical moment. We must cut down the time it takes to get out of the plane and to hit the terrorists by driving in a straight line from the plane door to the building—and by deceiving and surprising anyone on the way there," he added.

They were all exhausted. Drivers and infantrymen had been exercising the landing stage from first light this morning, using different types of vehicles. Less than two minutes, less than 120 seconds! That was what the journey took from the white paint mark that served as a Hercules, to the white paint mark that denoted Old Terminal.

Yoni Netaniahu wasn't satisfied: "It's possible in less. . . ."

Late in the afternoon, Yossi had a brilliant idea of a way to further confuse and paralyze the Ugandan troops and the terrorists.

"Everyone in the Ugandan army has a Mercedes," he crowed to Yoni, jumping from his seat. "I remember from my service in Uganda." Not waiting to explain, he reached for a phone.

Asher Ben-Natan returned to the embassy of Israel in Paris and phoned the defense minister in Tel Aviv to report on his conversation with Interior Minister Michel Poniatowski. Since he had been instructed not to raise the possibility of Franco-Israeli cooperation, Ben-Natan had talked to the Frenchman about a subject close to his heart: a regional election system. Poniatowski, a friend of Israel, was known to have strong views about electoral reform, and willingly played the game—though both men were aware that Ben-Natan had not come to Paris for this conversation. They did discuss the details of the hijacking, and Peres' special emissary could now report: "Poniatowski advises us strongly to do everything but rely on the terrorists and the negotiations. He also believes that it isn't negotiation but extortion."

By now, it was clear in Tel Aviv that the terrorists weren't interested in negotiating for the release of the hostages, but rather in humiliating Israel in the eyes of the world. Reports from Entebbe indicated that they intended to add more demands, without freeing all their prisoners. As Pierre Renard, the French ambassador in Uganda, reported to his colleagues in Paris, "this business will never end."

Cooperation with France was important for the success

of a rescue operation at Entebbe; however, Paris would have to be kept in the dark on the alternative plan. On the afternoon of Friday, July 2, the success or failure of the mission in fact depended on a nation that knew absolutely nothing about the plans of the General Staff in Tel Aviv.

There had already been a discussion in the government and the General Staff on whether to inform Kenya, with whom Israel had an excellent relationship and Uganda a terrible one, about the operation. Some wanted to force on them the refueling of Hercules aircraft on their way back to Israel from Entebbe. One camp argued that Kenya must have been a party to the hijacking from the very beginning.

"No question of it," said the prime minister, "and anyone who asks permission to speak to them will be refused."

The prime minister believed that any approach to the Kenyan government in Nairobi would be dangerous. During the time they would have to think it over, they would undoubtedly decide against aiding Israel because of the dangers they themselves might attract, both in the area of African unity and, more importantly, in their already bad relationship with Idi Amin.

"And the biggest danger of all," Rabin added, "is the possibility of a leak, which would jeopardize everyone concerned."

The prime minister presented his final argument: "I believe that, if we reach a position where we have to tell the Kenyans that there are wounded on board the planes, they will not deny us landing rights at Nairobi."

Even before the ministers convened for their morning session in the Prime Minister's Office, the first report came in: the Kenyans knew nothing and suspected nothing, but there was a good chance they would cooperate, even without the heads of the country knowing exactly what it was about. Everyone was relieved. Rabin actually agreed to consider setting up a refueling base and a medical station in Kenya. There was even a possibility of a secondary rescue base if something went seriously wrong.

The morning session in the prime minister's office found Rabin, Peres, Allon, and the others in a much more optimistic mood. After last night's talk with the chief of staff, Peres was certain that General Gur would recommend the operational plan he favored.

The prime minister conceded that he did not see much hope in an official approach to Kenya, but the "signals" coming in from the Israelis in Nairobi did allow a more extensive base for operation.

Mordechai Gur spread out a map on the prime minister's desk, then placed a detailed sketch of Entebbe International Airport next to it. He began to describe an operation based on flying paratroops in Hercules aircraft to Entebbe and back.

Inscribed on the map and the sketch was the legend: "Top Secret. Operation Thunderball."

The debate moved into military technicalities. Rabin put a lot of questions to General Gur, but he was still not ready to make up his mind one way or the other. There just weren't sufficient data on the airport and on the disposition of the Ugandan troops. A number of logistic and technical problems still remained to be solved before any final approval could be accorded: "I intend tonight to take part in an exercise on a model, in real time," Gur stated. "I will also make a flight in a Hercules, at night, in order to get a close look at the problems of landing and takeoff in conditions similar to the ones we can expect in Entebbe. In my opinion," he summed up, "the plan that I have now described can be carried out."

Yitzhak Rabin closed the session with a cautious analysis of the dangers, and a summary of the critical implications of an operation that did not go according to plan. The first plane to land would be the crucial one, and the entire success of the mission would depend on it.

Peres told the meeting: "Benny Peled claims that he can land on Entebbe runway without them noticing."

Rabin nodded. "I suggest that the defense minister and chief of staff present to this team a full and official version of the plan later today."

By now the ashtrays were full and the air was smoky, but the atmosphere in the prime minister's room was certainly easier.

Pasco Cohen approached Wilfried Böse. He looked extremely anxious. "My wife has fainted," he told the German. "I beg you to bring a doctor."

As usual, Böse was courteous and went off to call the Arab physician. Hana Cohen was stretched out on the floor of Old Terminal, apparently suffering from food poisoning, contracted from the Ugandan meat. Since the second part of thirty-seven non-Israelis had been released, conditions had grown much worse. The Arab bent over and asked Hana a few questions, then gave her morphine tablets to deaden the pain.

A short while later, she passed out again, undoubtedly because the morphine dose was excessive. Pasco was worried and insisted another opinion was necessary, but the terrorists ignored him.

Towards noon, Hana's condition deteriorated. It seemed as if she was not going to leave Old Terminal alive. Pasco tried once again.

"Perhaps you could transfer my wife to hospital to get better treatment?" he asked the terrorists.

"Daddy, are you mad?" his young son interrupted. "You would give Mommy to those men?"

Pasco Cohen thought it over a minute, then gave up the idea. He turned back to make a cup of tea for his prostrated wife, and noticed Jean Jacques still lying on his mattress, surrounded by the children. Would help ever reach them in time?

* * *

El Al 323 landed at Charles de Gaulle Airport at 11:25. The same black Citröen that had picked up Asher Ben-Natan yesterday was now waiting for the prime minister's advisor on intelligence and counter-terror. General Zeevi ran down the steps, jumped into the car, and was sped away to the Israeli embassy where Mordechai Gazit was waiting for him. Within a few minutes of his arrival, the two men were back in the Citröen, on their way to the Quai d'Orsay. Gazit skimmed through the "working paper" that Gandhi had prepared on the plane. The title read: "Guidelines for the Exchange of Terrorists and Hostages."

—All terrorists and hostages will be exchanged simultaneously.

—Arrangements will be made against the event of reconsideration or deception by either party.

—The place of exchange will be acceptable to the three parties: Israel, France, and the terrorists.

—The negotiation will be short, but not hasty.

—The parties agree to a total news blackout on the details of negotiation.

At the Quai d'Orsay, the French Foreign Ministry officials as well as representatives of the various security agencies were already in their places at an oval table. Mordechai Gazit introduced General Zeevi.

"I'm sorry," apologized the general, "for screwing up your weekend, but we don't have any choice."

The Frenchmen smiled, and they got down to work.

At 10:15 the defense minister's room was packed with officers in uniform.

"It can be done," said General Gur, "but we need more work on the intelligence aspects."

He skimmed quickly through the plan timetable and the forces that would participate.

"Zero hour is 11:05 tomorrow night," he concluded.

The men were already getting up to leave for the meeting with Rabin when Gur added: "The risks we are taking are greater than ever before."

At 10:45, the chief of staff and his aides were closeted with the prime minister. Shimon Peres made no attempt to hide his satisfaction with the plan as he pressed to have it approved.

Mota Gur was still cautious in his recommendation: "This operation can be performed as it is now, but we need more precise intelligence. What we have is up to date as of the day before yesterday."

The prime minister glanced at his watch. It was 11:15. Turning to Eli Mizrahi and Froike Poran, he ordered: "Get hold of Haim Zadok and Yisrael Galili. The ministerial team will convene here at 12:15."

Shortly after 10 A.M. the phone rang in the foreign minister's Tel Aviv office. The call was from the Quai d'Orsay and confirmed that France was accepting full responsibility for the negotiation, according to the guidelines laid down by Israel.

Yigal Allon and Jean Sauvignard were old friends, and even now there was complete accord between the two men.

"We will do the utmost," Sauvignard said, "and you can rely on us." This was reassuring, since it had already been suggested in the Israeli Foreign Ministry that France might try to bring the United Nations in as mediator, a problem that Allon now felt safe in raising.

"I do have a request to make of you. Please don't turn to the UN. It would only complicate matters."

"Nobody in France is even thinking of it."

Sauvignard went out of his way to explain the technical difficulties involved in contacts with the terrorists. Every message coming from Israel was being sent straight on to the ambassador of France in Uganda, who gave it to the local authorities, who in turn passed it on to the Somali ambassador. Only then did it reach the terrorist representative in Kampala.

Anxious to get all the details settled, Allon changed the subject: "We have sent you one of our best generals," he told Sauvignard.

"I know. We're waiting for him. We have already set up a team under the deputy director general, who is an expert on security and logistics."

At the close of the conversation, Sauvignard softened his tone a bit: "I want you to know—the president is showing special interest in the Israelis in Entebbe, and wants me to guarantee to you that France will not surrender."

Yigal Allon was delighted with the call. Pausing only to give a brief report to his director general, Shlomo Avineri, he rushed out to his car in order to attend the team session in the prime minister's office.

"I want the best and most experienced pilots that we have," the commanding general of the air force told his Hercules squadron leader.

Benny Peled was familiar with most of the names on the list.

"We'll call Michael Golan, Arnon Shechori, Ariel Luz, and Avraham Levitan," said the squadron leader. (Names have been changed for security reasons.) "Get going."

CHAPTER TWENTY-FOUR

Mercedes 220D

Midday. In another few minutes, the ministerial team would convene in the prime minister's office. The chief of staff summoned the head of Field Security Department in Intelligence Branch, Colonel "Yitzhak Aligo."

"Yitzhak. We're staging an operation at Entebbe, and its success depends on secrecy. . . ."

Aligo, a veteran intelligence officer, nodded. He needed no further explanation.

"We have already been working two days, and nothing is out," General Gur added. "There's no reason why we can't keep it that way for another day or two."

The colonel wondered how many men were party to the secret, and exactly who they were. One thing didn't worry him, however—Jonathan Netaniahu's boys knew how to keep their mouths shut. Yitzhak Aligo was far more concerned about ministers and their assistants, though he could do little to prevent leaks from the civilian-political echelon. But everyone in Israel was concerned about leaks. The espionage services of both the United States and the Soviet Union had augmented their intelligence efforts in the Middle East, including Israel. A Soviet spy ship had been an almost permanent fixture off the coast of Israel, obviously to intercept as much radiotelephone and radio traffic as possible. The ship departed in April 1976, but that did not .mean that the Russians had abandoned their efforts. Probably they were using more sophisticated electronic means.

"All right, let's hear the plan," the prime minister said.

Justice Minister Zadok entered and sat down as General Gur moved over to an enlarged map of Entebbe Airport. "Gentlemen, the plan I will now present is viable, though it isn't final because of some important data that we still lack."

The four ministers turned to study the map, which showed Old Terminal, the runways beside it, and various other buildings.

"Mota, what is the very latest that a decision can be made if we want to operate on Saturday night?"

"In my opinion, not later than three o'clock Saturday afternoon."

Gur completed his presentation, leaving the prime minister as convinced as he himself was that the plan was feasible, yet there was still no need to decide immediately. Rabin now suggested that final approval should wait till the next day, Saturday, after evaluation of the night rehearsal and examination of any new data that would be supplied in the meantime by the intelligence community.

Shimon Peres was anxious about the delay and pressed for a decision, but he could not change the general consensus. The dangers were still great and most of the men were conservative about the mission.

"Would it be possible to take Idi Amin as a hostage?" a minister ventured.

The other men in the room smiled, not quite sure whether their colleague was joking. "I know a few Ugandans who would be glad to be rid of him," someone commented.

"Where will the planes refuel?" another minister wanted to know.

"Either Entebbe or somewhere else," Gur replied.

The chief of staff's answer was totally unexpected. The very thought of refueling Hercules aircraft at Entebbe seemed incredible at that moment. However, General Gur did not want to expand on the theme: "The idea isn't complete and we're still working on it."

The discussion continued without any excitement or tension, though some of the men present were finding it difficult to digest what they had just heard. Until this session, the military solution had been only wishful thinking, yet that had changed literally overnight.

"What happens if our men run into Ugandans?"

"We have the defense minister's permission to shoot at them, but we will do our utmost to prevent it happening."

"Perhaps we should offer the terrorists half the prisoners they want in return for the women and children. . . ."

"Certainly not! They wouldn't agree!"

Rabin brought the discussion back on course: "At this stage, I must stress that there is still no certainty about the chances of the operation. Our intelligence data are still limited, and we must therefore continue to function on two planes: negotiation with the terrorists as if we have no military option, and preparation of the military option as if there is no negotiation.

"I want to make it clear to anyone who doesn't yet know that we stopped Asher Ben-Natan in Paris and instructed him not to talk to Poniatowski about the plan. Meanwhile, Gandhi went to Paris this morning and should be about to meet the French team at this hour. Preparations must of course continue here while Gandhi acts in Paris."

Peres seemed impatient: "I suggest that we arrange ourselves in such a way that a decision can be made not later than two o'clock tomorrow afternoon. Everything must be done to prevent leaks. Secrecy is an essential precondition. I'm sure the whole world is listening."

Zadok suggested: "It would be worthwhile to convene the government today, to empower us or the Ministerial Defense Committee to make the decision."

Allon spoke up at last: "For a decision, we still need data on refueling. But my opinion is that in general principle, rescue of the hostages with the danger of a number of losses is preferable to the release of forty terrorists. We must decide now to empower the security forces to prepare everything as though we are going for the military option."

Rabin said finally: "I want to state in closing this discussion that, at this hour, there is no certainty about the possibility of staging the operation. The information at our disposal is extremely limited; the risks are great. We don't even have the deployment of the Ugandans on the spot. I propose that we treat the operation as a possibility, together with the negotiation which will continue."

The prime minister and his colleagues left the Cabinet Room silently, betraying nothing by their expressions. The only record was handwritten, without copies.

Two of the participants were in no hurry to leave. Chief of Staff Gur and Foreign Ministry Director General Avineri stayed to talk.

"Mota, how do you feel about it?" Professor Avineri asked.

"If I solve the problem of the flight back, it will be easier to take Entebbe than it would be to capture Lod Airport in Israel, because the surprise will be total."

"And if it doesn't work?"

"If it doesn't work, we won't have much to worry about in the future. This will be the last stand."

A little after midday, two men in civilian clothes appeared in a Tel Aviv used-car lot and pointed: "That old Mercedes over there. . . ."

"The idea of the Mercedes is really very simple," Yossi Yaar explained to Yoni Netaniahu. "Every officer in the

Ugandan army, from company commander on up, has a black or dark green Mercedes. Every Ugandan soldier who sees such a car approaching automatically jumps to attention."

Yoni smiled. He had never been a great advocate of Israel's military assistance to Africa, but this Friday afternoon he was finally prepared to admit that the great efforts were paying a dividend.

"To surprise the Ugandans on duty on our way to Old Terminal even more than they will be already, we use a Mercedes. We might just gain a few more seconds that way."

As Yossi finished explaining to his commanding officer, a Mercedes drove through the gate into the camp.

"Good God," exclaimed Yossi, "they've brought a white one. . . ."

Air force General Benny Peled relaxed. Through the past week, he had prodded his colleagues—General Staff officers and the chief of staff himself—to mount an operation at Entebbe. Now, the complete plan was laid out before him and he was satisfied. Nevertheless, he asked the aides sitting across the table from him to prepare alternatives, no matter how absurd, to cover every eventuality as the planes came in to land at Entebbe.

—What happens if the landing lights are extinguished suddenly?

—How do we land in the dark?

—What do we do if the planes are fired on while on the ground?

—How do we take off if we don't gain control of Entebbe tower?

Benny had answers for almost all the problems, and the ones still unsolved were given to two squadron leaders—one a pilot and the other an intelligence man. Instructions were flowing out of air force headquarters to the leader of a Hercules squadron on a base somewhere in Israel.

Lockheed Aircraft Corporation had begun to develop a new generation of transport plane in 1951. The result was the Hercules, or C-130, which was put at the top of the Israeli air force transport-aircraft roster shortly before the 1973 Yom Kippur War. One enthusiastic journalist wrote: "The Hercules can even reach Siberia."

The C-130A model in service in the IAF was used for transport and paratroopers. Its operational range is 2,400 miles, fully loaded. Its maximum airspeed is 365 miles per hour, and its maximum altitude, 23,000 feet. The Hercules can cope with 700 yards of runway, or with bumpy terrain if necessary. It can carry ninety-two soldiers or seventy-four stretchers.

The air force also had Boeing 707s, which were mostly used to carry soldiers to and from Sinai for home leaves. At noon on Friday, the American CIA—so the authors were told—discovered that two IAF Boeings were parked at Lod Airport, swarming with fitters and painters. Different insignia were being painted on the planes. The authors later learned that a coded cable was at that time on its way from Tel Aviv to the CIA in Washington: THERE ARE INDICATIONS OF OPERATIONAL ACTIVITY IN ISRAEL, THOUGH IT IS DIFFICULT TO ASSUME THAT ISRAEL WILL OPERATE IN UGANDA. . . .

General Zeevi had been sitting at this table in the Quai d'Orsay for three hours.

"We are not responsible for people imprisoned outside of Israel whose release is demanded by the terrorists," Gandhi clarified. "We are also not going to agree to release more than forty, and we will decide the composition of the group. I suggest that arrangements be made here so we can work around the clock," said the Israeli general.

The French team listened to the Israeli statement of position without reacting. Ambassador Gazit and General Zeevi understood that the French were not empowered to decide anything. That prerogative was reserved to the

foreign minister and president of France. Having discussed as much as could be done in the first session, Gazit
and Zeevi returned to the embassy. Meanwhile, Gad
Yaakobi had granted an interview to the French Europe 1
radio station. He was confronted with one question: "How
does the government of Israel justify its submission to
terrorists, after all its declarations of recent years that
there can be no surrender to extortion?"

Yaakobi explained that, given the fact that there were
more than one hundred innocent Israelis in the hands of
terrorists who enjoyed the full cooperation of Idi Amin,
there was no alternative but to negotiate. Then, choosing
his words carefully, the transport minister added: "However, the decision of the government of Israel should under
no condition be viewed as a change of policy. The government continues to uphold the principle of no surrender
to terrorists."

Once the interview was over, and the microphone
turned off, Yaakobi told the reporter: "It's clear that,
neither in an interview nor even to you off the record, am
I at liberty to say at this stage everything that is being
done. Remember what I'm saying, and don't come to me
with complaints afterwards. . . ."

At 5:15 P.M., the senior officers retraced their steps to
Shimon Peres' office. Mota Gur was not present. Yekutiel
Adam, head of Staff Branch, was now the senior man. He
reviewed the situation as of that hour, including the fact
that most of Israel was dismayed at the government's
capitulation and that the state of preparations in the force
assigned to the mission was excellent: everything was pro-
ceeding quickly and to his complete satisfaction. Teams
from the air force, paratroop command, Intelligence
Branch, medical corps, and others had been hard at work
for twenty-four hours, supervising every little detail.

"*Nu*," Peres turned in traditional Jewish fashion to one
of the generals, "what do you think about it?"

"It's a gamble. If it succeeds it's exceptional. But, God forbid, if something happens, if a missile hits one of the planes, it will be a terrible tragedy."

"You understand that if we give in today, they'll ask us to evacuate Kadoum [on the West Bank] tomorrow in exchange for hostages, and the next day they'll want the Golan Heights. . . . Kuti, what do you think? Are you satisfied with the operation?"

"Yes. We've learned a lot in the past few days:

—There are three doors to Old Terminal.

—The terrorists are standing guard in twos or threes, mostly by the doorways.

—The other terrorists are in a side room, which used to be the VIP Room.

—Ugandan soldiers are on the second floor of Old Terminal.

—The control tower is roughly the height of a four-story building, and it commands a view of the whole area.

"Success depends on us knowing exactly where the terrorists and the hostages are. Everything depends on intelligence."

Shimon Peres was smiling as he welcomed the former ambassador of the United States to the United Nations, Professor Daniel Patrick Moynihan. Peres made no attempt to hide his anxiety over the outcome of the negotiations: "Who are we negotiating with? Idi Amin?"

Moynihan, known to be friendly to Israel and a sworn enemy of Arab and international terrorism, listened attentively. "Idi Amin personally greeted the hijackers at Entebbe Airport when the French plane landed. He ordered his soldiers to help them and to guard the plane, to give them whatever they needed, including explosives."

In a ninety-minute conversation, the two exchanged views on the nature of international terrorism, on the cooperation between Palestinians and Baader-Meinhof, on South Americans, and the Japanese Red Army. Moynihan agreed with the defense minister that negotiation under these conditions was fraught with peril. He also doubted Amin's credibility. In fact, in late 1974, Moynihan publicly called the Ugandan a "murderer." Now he laid out for Peres his theory of the terror internationale, fed from various sources.

"Have you no effective way to rescue the hostages?" Moynihan asked. Peres felt distinctly uncomfortable. He did not want to deceive his visitor, yet could not tell him anything.

"Look, Mr. Moynihan, I am minister of defense. There are colonels to deal with current military matters."

Moynihan got the impression that this was a subject better not discussed. As they parted at the door of his office, Peres volunteered: "One thing I can tell you. On Sunday, it will all be over. . . ."

"It will all be over very quickly, if we operate precisely as we should," Yoni Netaniahu said. He was giving a late afternoon briefing to the commanders of secondary units and their men. Apart from short sorties to the General Staff to get the most up-to-date intelligence data and planning details, Yoni had spent the day with his soldiers. Now they were on a deserted landing strip somewhere in Israel. Nearby stood an air force Hercules. Some distance back from the runway, men were filling sandbags to build a high wall. An officer was measuring it and checking the width of openings.

"Exactly as it is there," he said.

The sandbag rampart precisely matched the dimensions of the outer wall of Old Terminal, given the known data. There were three openings in the wall, exactly as in Entebbe. There was a side room, set back somewhat from the main wall. The Hercules was parked 1,500 yards from the sandbag model. Its distance had been determined to keep it out of range of small-arms fire and well away from Uganda army or terrorist bazookas. Barrels marked the shortest route from the Hercules to Old Terminal. Various types of vehicles were repeatedly rehearsing the descent from the plane's ramp and the fast drive to the sandbag wall.

Soldiers stood in the gaps in the wall armed with carbines and dummy grenades held ready in their hands— these were the "terrorists." Paratroops leaped from vehicles to "eliminate" them.

Yoni Netaniahu and Yossi Yaar watched intently, analyzing every move.

"Where would it be reasonable to expect the first encounter?"

"What if they open fire?"

Yoni studied the running soldiers, as they bent double and raced between the "terrorists" and the "hostages"— for whom no substitutes had been supplied.

"That high control tower bothers me," Yoni told Yossi. "It commands the whole area. That's dangerous! We'll assign two jeeps to hit it."

"The most important thing is speed," Yoni called time after time to his running men. "There isn't a second to waste! A hand grenade takes only four seconds to explode. Run all the way till it's over! Kill the terrorists!"

The Mediterranean twilight was already on them as the white Mercedes made its first appearance beside the parked Hercules. Soldiers backed it into the plane so that its nose faced the rear, then they rehearsed the drive down the ramp and over to Old Terminal.

Tzur Ben-Ami won the job of driver of the old Mercedes taxicab. Yoni had a soft spot for the boy. As Tzur took his place at the wheel, Yoni remarked to Yossi: "Look what a nice kid, and what we're sending him to do. . . ."

At that moment, as the sun sank below the horizon marking the beginning of the Jewish Sabbath, the talks between the Israeli and French teams at the Quai d'Orsay;

between the French ambassador in Kampala and the government to which he was accredited; between the Somalian ambassador, Dr. Wadia Hadad, and the terrorists in Entebbe—all were progressing swiftly. General Zeevi was placing a proposal on the oval table in Paris for the exchange of the hostages and prisoners from Israel. His draft was written in Hebrew, but Ambassador Gazit promptly translated into French:

—The transfer will be at a military or civil airfield in France or Djibouti. Under no circumstances will it be in Uganda.

—The hostages will leave Entebbe in an Air France plane. The terrorists will leave Israel in an El Al plane.

—The two groups, terrorists and hostages, will not meet on the ground at the airfield where the exchange is carried out. (To avoid any morale problems or emotional outbursts.)

—At both airports of departure, Entebbe and Lod, a check will be made by Frenchmen, against lists.

—Because of time differences, the takeoff of both planes from the two airports will be upon receipt of a go-ahead from Paris.

—No terrorist will disembark before a count and confirmation by the receiving party.

—A check will be made at the airfield of the exchange of the inside of the aircraft, by French representatives and the receiving party.

—Identification of the hostages will be by authentic documents.

—If anybody is missing, the process of exchange will be halted.

At 9 P.M., Jean Sauvignard called Yigal Allon and told him that France considered herself responsible for the whole affair. Perhaps, if the plan was a good one, it would be possible to gain a few days' extension. Anything. . . .

The phone rang in Michael Golan's home. He had only

returned from the marina half an hour ago, after spending hours out on a boat sailing under the fierce sun.

"Come to squadron immediately," the clerk said in a nervous voice.

It was as if an electric shock brought Michael back to full alertness, the fatigue of the day forgotten.

"Honey! Get me pajamas, cigars, and a book!"

Michael Golan was remembering the first day of the Yom Kippur War, when he had rushed to his squadron in answer to an urgent call. Now, he raced his car out to an air base somewhere in Israel, consumed by burning curiosity: what could require his presence on a Friday night, on the Sabbath?

"It must be horsemeat," Dr. Hirsch joked, raising a smile from the other hostages who were struggling to chew their midday meal, which was suddenly cut short. Dora Bloch was turning red in the face and choking. A lump of meat had lodged in her throat. Her immediate neighbors gathered around to help, and Ilan thumped her on the back in the hope of dislodging the morsel. Dr. Hirsch tried to fish it out. Hadassa David, a nurse by profession, took her by the arm and led her to the toilet area, where she stuck her finger into Dora's mouth, hoping to induce vomiting. Nothing helped. Dora was doubled over by a fit of uncontrollable coughing.

Dr. Hirsch called the Ugandan doctor, who promptly ordered her transfer to the hospital. An ambulance appeared and Dora was lifted inside. Ilan started to climb aboard, intending to stay with his mother, but the German girl noticed and waved him out of the car: "Your mother is strong enough without you. You stay here!" Ilan kissed his mother and the ambulance drove away.

Mulago is one of two hospitals in the Ugandan capital of Kampala. It contains an emergency receiving ward, clinics, and a pharmacy; the wards and operating theaters are in separate buildings. In the past, Mulago was staffed by a majority of European doctors and nurses, backed up by a quiet and efficient army of black nursing assistants. In recent years, the Europeans departed one by one, giving up their places to Ugandan doctors.

The ambulance drove over the bumps, installed to slow down traffic at the entrance to the hospital, and delivered Dora Bloch to the emergency ward.

By nine o'clock that evening the terrorists were distinctly nervous. One of them grabbed Yosef Hadad. "If you don't give us the letter you're supposed to write, we'll kill a few of you."

Again Michel Bacos stepped into the breach, calmly suggesting that nothing was to be gained by delaying any longer.

Jeanette Almog wrote out the text and Ilan Hartuv delivered the declaration requested by Idi Amin to Michel Bacos. "I have the letter they wanted, Captain. I would like you to come with me to deliver it."

Antonio Degas Bouviet had the guard duty outside Old Terminal. Ilan called out to him: "We have a letter for Idi Amin, but if you like, we'll give it to you."

The Peruvian studied Ilan's face, then, after a long pause, said: "Idi Amin did say that it would be a good thing to do. I will give it to the deputy president of Uganda, who will get it read over the radio."

Meanwhile Wilfried Böse came out of the VIP Room and walked over to join Bouviet, Hartuv, and Bacos. Ilan read the text out to the two terrorists, but Böse didn't like it: "They'll say we got it from you at gunpoint."

The Peruvian laughed and ordered Ilan to seal the letter. Taking the envelope from the Israeli, he called over a Ugandan officer, apparently the commander of Entebbe Airport. The Ugandan accepted the letter: "Don't worry. Idi Amin isn't here, but we'll look after you. . . . Your lives are in danger unless Israel returns the prisoners."

His gratuitous afterthought sent a shiver down Ilan Hartuv's spine.

The ambassador of Israel in Washington intended to spend the upcoming Sabbath with his family. Late Friday afternoon, Washington time, he received an unexpected message from Tel Aviv: DO NOT LEAVE THE EMBASSY OVER SHABBAT. That was all. Ambassador Dinitz muttered to himself. "What can they be cooking up in Tel Aviv?"

"You realize that failure of an IDF operation will mean the end of this government?" The questioner was Amos Aran, director general of the Prime Minister's Office and a close personal friend of Rabin's, who had come over to his home for a short chat.

Rabin listened, but did not reply immediately. Finally, he said: "I know! I know! But the question right now isn't the government. It's human lives, a lot of them!"

When Aran left, Rabin picked up a transcript of a conversation between Burka Bar Lev and Idi Amin. Only one sentence interested him at that moment: "I want to tell you in the name of the Palestinians that, if there is any aircraft noise over the airfield other than at the times set by us, they'll blow up the terminal!"

Anyone glancing at the prime minister's face would have seen his anxiety.

Michael Golan was late. He burst into the briefing room of his transport squadron, and looked through the heavy haze of cigarette smoke at the men seated there. In a distinct break with regular practice, there was a liberal sprinkling of khaki and olive green among the uniforms of the men seated on long benches. Michael wondered what soldiers were doing here in an air base. His eyes moved to the green duty board hanging on the back wall of the room. Apart from his own name, he could see those of other veteran pilots, navigators, and flight engineers chalked up in neat columns.

The commanding general of the air force gave the briefing in person.

"Gentlemen, we are operating tomorrow at Entebbe."

Benny Peled didn't raise his voice, and he spoke as if talking about the details of an afternoon hike. Having thrown his first bombshell, he looked around the room to measure reaction. There was little surprise. Most of the men present had already guessed why they were here.

"Gentlemen, I want you to know that all the communications equipment of Russia, the United States, Egypt, and Syria is listening—they are impatient to know what will happen. If we cannot keep this mission a tight secret, it will fail!"

The general went on to detail the operation, the crews, takeoff, flight paths to Entebbe, refueling, and the return journey. It was an exhausting briefing.

When it was over, the briefing room emptied in a flash. Pilots, navigators, and flight crew clustered on the plaza outside to talk among themselves about what they had heard. Some minutes had passed when Yossi, the squadron leader, called a few of them back: "The ground-force boys are demanding a rehearsal." His pilots were astounded. A number of Hercules aircraft flying around on a Friday night would arouse the suspicions of half of Israel. Finally they reached a compromise. One pilot would take up a single Hercules, to demonstrate takeoff and landing for the chief of staff.

At a party in the home of Tel Aviv Mayor Shlomo Lahat, the subject of Entebbe, of course, overshadowed everything else.

"What do you think," Mayor Lahat whispered to one of the journalists there, "won't we send the army to save them?"

"You really think it's possible?"

"Logistically," said the mayor, who was himself a retired IDF general, "I don't see any problem. We could
even get farther than that."

His companion was stubborn: "Do you know something,
or are you just making small talk?"

"Me? I don't know a thing," said Lahat sorrowfully,
"and I'm afraid that there isn't anything to know, more's
the pity."

The newsman tried the deputy defense minister of
Israel: "Talik, what do you say? Are we going to give in,
or do we rescue them by force?"

Yisrael Tal did know the secret. Though taken by surprise by the blunt question, he did not give anything
away: "You're asking me? You journalists know everything. I don't know anything. Go ahead, you tell me. . . ."

Conversation turned to a critical article in today's
Maariv, written by Ephraim Kishon, in a frontal attack
on the helplessness displayed by the government of Israel
over the Entebbe hijacking. Almost everybody congratu-
lated Kishon. Then, as it was long after midnight, the last
of Shlomo Lahat's guests bid him goodnight and started
for their automobiles.

Yoni Netaniahu sat in the front seat of the Mercedes,
to the right of the driver. Yossi Yaar occupied the rear
left-hand seat. Two of his advance team stood aside and
watched the rehearsal, as their nine comrades sat, uncomfortably jammed in the Mercedes.

Time and again, the car raced from the belly of a parked
Hercules and hurtled towards the sandbag model of Old
Terminal. Everything was to scale, and each man knew
which door was his target.

"The Ugandan soldiers might just try to stop the car,"
Yoni told his eight companions. "We stop for nothing!
The boys who follow will take care of the Ugandans!"

Time after time the soldiers repeated their race from

the car into Old Terminal. They rehearsed the braking of
the car, the leap out, the shots at the terrorists until it
seemed as if they had been doing only this for a week.
They ran between marked barrels, dummy targets, and
their comrades who had been placed to represent the
hijackers and Ugandan troops.

Yoni's small force would take most responsibility for
the charge. Altogether, fewer than fifty men took part in
the rehearsal. Then, after they had the attack down pat,
a new detail was added: collection of the hostages from
Old Terminal and transportation of the wounded—just
in case!

"The hostages are quite likely to be in shock and running all over the place." Yoni tried to paint the scene at
Entebbe Airport. "We have to be ready for a situation
where they'll run out of our hands and vanish. As soon
as we are in control, we form two lines—a sort of corridor
from the building to the plane, which will approach the
area. If they run, it will have to be within our cordon
into the aircraft."

In an aside to Yossi, Yoni added: "I want you to think
of all the possibilities. We daren't miss one. A mistake
could end in tragedy."

At 11:15 on Friday night, the chief of staff arrived.
He was just back from a two-hour flight in a Hercules,
during which he cross-examined the pilot on every conceivable aspect: takeoff and landing on lit and darkened
runways. Now Mota Gur watched soldiers erupting from
the Hercules, racing to the model of Old Terminal. Gur
kept his eyes on his watch: fifty-five minutes from simulated landing of the Hercules to takeoff, ostensibly with
hostages and wounded on board. The Hercules of course
still stood on the runway, but was now packed with
soldiers substituting for its planned passengers.

Yoni turned to Mota Gur: "How does it look to you?
What chances do you give us?"

The ground-force commander was convinced that the

rehearsal had been perfect, but he had no intention of appearing arrogant to his supreme superior: "I'm confident that there are no problems—but we must go on rehearsing and drilling it."

Gur asked him, "Don't you think you've got too many men on the jeeps?" even though it was evident that the chief of staff was pleased.

General Gur phoned Shimon Peres, at home in north Tel Aviv, as soon as he left the base.

"Shimon," he said, "we've just done a rehearsal. It's okay. There's no point in me coming over now—it's late. Now it's a job that can be done!"

CHAPTER TWENTY-FIVE

"The Eyes
of All the World"

The exercises on a deserted runway somewhere in Israel ended long after midnight, and Yoni ordered the men who would take part in the real event to prepare their equipment and personal weapons. His soldiers retired to their huts, cleaned carbines and submachine guns, prepared shrapnel and smoke grenades, torches, ropes, and personal medical kits.

Seated in his office with Yossi, Yoni spent the rest of the night going over every possible eventuality that could interfere on the ground in Entebbe.

"How will the hostages themselves know that we're not attacking them?" Yossi suddenly asked.

"No problem," said Yoni after a moment of thought. "Each squad will have a bullhorn. The man carrying it will keep on announcing 'This is *Zahal* [the IDF], lie down!' until the shooting stops."

"When do we take the hostages out of the building?"

"Not before we've eliminated the last of the terrorists. First we must kill those bastards."

Both the lieutenant colonel and the major were convinced that casualties would be heavy, both among their own men and among the hostages. Yoni understood that the General Staff had taken this into account, and were preparing to deal with it. All he had to worry about was the ground operation itself, its speed and efficiency.

In the lean-to camp garage, a team of mechanics were working over the Mercedes. The car was not in good mechanical shape, but by cannibalizing their other vehicles, they succeeded in replacing worn parts and improving the car's performance. When the mechanics were finished, two soldiers started painting. In less than an hour, the Mercedes was as black as the cars that serve Ugandan officers from the rank of major on up.

In the hour before dawn, while darkness still covered Israel, a convoy of vehicles issued out the gate of Yoni Netaniahu's home base toward an air base somewhere in central Israel. There were a number of Land Rovers, an armored personnel carrier, a gray Peugeot pickup truck, and a few Israeli-made "Rabbi" field cars. At dawn, they parked in an out-of-the-way corner of the military base. On the runway alongside them stood four Hercules transport planes. Air force ground crew were going in and out of the planes, stripping equipment not needed for this flight, and loading other equipment. Within the hour the column of vehicles vanished into the four planes. Each vehicle faced the rear, pointing down the still-open ramp. Air-force dispatchers supervised the lashing of each one with easily detachable cables.

The stench from the washrooms of Old Terminal was becoming unbearable. No water flowed from the faucets, and the lavatory basins were clogged. Ugandan soldiers brought water to fill roof tanks, but the pipes were blocked.

Many of the hostages were already up at 5:30, but many others were lying around feeling as though they were about to die. With the last of their strength, they dragged themselves to the washroom, vomiting on the floor as they went. All the passengers, except for the five religious families that hadn't touched their portions, had become ill from the meat served on Thursday. Without water in the faucets, the situation seemed desperate indeed.

Two harried doctors worked hard to ease their patients, yet it seemed hopeless. Some were moved to a nearby clinic. The others lay, between sleep and wakefulness, hoping for salvation. Breakfast went back to the Ugandan kitchen almost untouched. There was little conversation in Old Terminal that morning.

"My impression is that nothing has leaked so far," the chief of staff said at the nine o'clock meeting in the defense minister's office. Both Peres and Rabin looked very relaxed—Gur's late report had been very encouraging.

None of the men in the room harbored any more doubts about mounting an Entebbe rescue mission. All that remained to be done was the updating of operational detail.

"What do we do about the French aircrew?"

"We offer to bring them with us."

"I suggest that we hold a press conference, this afternoon, with Capucci and Okamoto, to talk about the negotiations. That should catch the attention of the world, and serve as a nice diversion."

"Let's not exaggerate. Too much deception can be counter-productive!"

The defense minister still wanted to check whether the operation could be brought forward by one hour, to give the force one more hour of darkness in case anything went wrong. But nothing could be done about it now, since the ground mission had been set for 11 P.M. with a precise timetable that coordinated other activities.

The eighteen Cabinet ministers were carefully instructed not to say a word over the phone, nor even to discuss anything with their families.

Prime Minister Rabin arrived at his Tel Aviv office close to ten o'clock. Few soldiers were to be seen in the

General Staff compound, though the underground "pit" was buzzing with activity. Since everyone in the command bunker, officers and men alike, was party to the big secret, their chances of getting home for a few hours this Sabbath day were nil. Apart from them, and the units comprising the mission force, the officer corps of the IDF—like many other citizens of Israel—was convinced that the government would decide, within the coming day, to release convicted terrorists in return for the Entebbe hostages.

Froike Poran, Rabin's military secretary, placed a last report on the prime minister's desk. The report from Israeli intelligence agents was most impressive. Here were the answers to a number of the questions that had troubled Yitzhak Rabin yesterday, and without which he might have withheld final approval for the mission. At 11:15, he opened the last team discussion. The atmosphere in the room seemed more optimistic. General Gur spread out maps, drawings, a detailed operational plan, and a precise timetable. For thirty minutes, he described every stage of Operation Thunderball, using a map on which the flight paths of the Boeings and Hercules were already plotted in red. When he finished, Peres, Allon, and Gur were in agreement: the operation had to be approved.

But Gur suddenly said: "It would be good to know what the prime minister thinks of it."

Yitzhak Rabin almost trumped his companions' cards during the discussion of the Cabinet meeting which convened shortly after. From one of his comments, it could be deduced that he was indirectly supporting continued negotiation. He repeated that the operation was dangerous, that it could involve a great many losses, and that its failure would be a terrible blow to the armed forces.

Shimon Peres exploited the slight air of bewilderment in the room to say a few words of his own. His eyes passing from face to face around the table, he spoke with considerable pathos, though quietly: "If we capitulate, we will become a doormat. Our image will be harmed as it never has been before. So far we have never hesitated to risk human lives when there was a chance of saving others. We preached to the whole world not to give in to extortion. If we succeed, and I think we have more than a fair chance of succeeding, this nation will straighten its back, and other nations will be encouraged to follow the same path. Between the almost certain rescue of one hundred or more Israelis by military action, and the danger to innocent people in humiliating and doubtful negotiations—there is no other way but to accept the first alternative. That's the way we have behaved over all the years. The eyes of Israel and of all the world are on us."

Rabin sighed, rubbed his hands, then asked: "When do the planes have to go?"

Peres didn't doubt that the question was also an answer. The others were also sure at that moment that the prime minister was leaning in favor of Operation Thunderball.

"They have to take off from central Israel for an airport in the south at 1:50 P.M.," the chief of staff replied. The foreign press was later to claim that the "airport in the south" was Ophir at Sharm el-Sheikh, the southern tip of Sinai.

Dr. Yosef Michaeli again checked the medical equipment laid out along the runway. He had been alerted yesterday at noontime, and warned to stand by. Now he stood with the twenty doctors and medical corpsmen watching small detachments of soldiers collecting in various places around the airfield. They sat on the ground and alongside runways, listening to final briefings. One of the units was only hearing now, for the first time, where they were due to go in the very near future. The actual revelation of their destination confirmed their guesses and in fact relieved their nervous tension. For some of them it was their first combat mission, and they were happy to have been chosen. They made a final check on weapons and personal equipment before filing into the waiting aircraft. Paratroops and Golani infantrymen waited for the last preparations to be completed. Within the planes, air force ground crews lashed the last equipment into place, paying particular attention to the vehicles.

Close to 2 P.M. the great doors of the four Hercules aircraft swung shut. The roar of engines filled the still air. In another four minutes, they would be airborne.

Four minutes before the appointed time for the session of the Ministerial Defense Committee, its members were already in their places in the Cabinet Room, where some of them had in fact been for several hours this Saturday morning. The others who were not members of the team had no idea why this meeting had been called, although they assumed that the exchange of terrorists for hostages was to take place shortly. The maps and sketches strewn across the table soon dispelled that idea. Ministers Peres, Allon, Yaakobi, Hillel, Zadok, Rabinowitz, Bar-Lev, Galili, Burg, Shem-Tov, and Hausner sat through Mota Gur's third briefing—some in growing astonishment.

"It is a very bold operation," the prime minister added at the end of Gur's presentation.

"We cannot delay decision," said Shimon Peres, "because hundreds are already party to the secret."

Rabin said: "It's not a decision to take lightheartedly. This is the army's first mission outside the Middle East."

"How many losses are we likely to sustain?" Galili asked. Mota Gur did not hesitate: "There could be scores. . . ."

Rabin shrugged his shoulders. "It has become clear that negotiation under the prevailing conditions entails no less danger, and perhaps more than the proposed mission."

Peres agreed: "The terrorists turned down any suggestion of an exchange in a place other than Entebbe. According to a still unconfirmed source, they have also demanded from France, apart from the release of prisoners, five million dollars. . . . It's impossible to negotiate that way. They also intimated that their list of prisoners demanded from Israel is not final. . . . We alerted Shlomo Avineri to tell the German ambassador he should wait until we know what the terrorists say about the place for exchange. That is also the French opinion."

Rabin plucked a square of paper from the holder in front of him, and wrote: "I think the planes can start out."

The time was 2:35 P.M. as he passed the note to Shimon Peres. The defense minister glanced at it, and nodded to the prime minister in a gesture that clearly confirmed: they are on their way!

Both men smiled. The clock would not be turned back now.

"Gentlemen, it seems we are going on a mission to Entebbe. . . ."

The Cabinet Room was stuffy and hot as Gur presented facts, surveyed intelligence, noted the order of battle and mode of operation.

"I'm relaxed enough about the landing," the prime minister summed up. "On the basis of up-to-date intelligence, I'm also not worried about takeoff and refueling. In any event, the main question is going to be how long it takes for the boys of the first plane to gain control over the terrorists. That's what will decide it!"

Rabin scanned the faces in the room. Many of the ministerial assistants were busily scribbling on papers—keeping their records for history.

"Gentlemen," the prime minister said, "I recommend the operation. The forces are on their way, and are about to take off. If the government decides against within the next minute or so, they can be brought back and it won't be a tragedy."

Rabin was now completely calm, relaxed, and even smiling. He no longer doubted that, in a minute or two, all hands would be raised in favor of the military option at Entebbe.

"Gentlemen, who is in favor of the decision which I

shall now read? 'The government resolves to approve implementation of a rescue operation of the hostages held in Entebbe, by the IDF, according to the operative plan submitted to the government by the defense minister and the chief of staff.' Gentlemen, who is in favor?"

Eighteen hands rose and stayed up for a moment as if the ministers wanted to relish this ceremonial and historic occasion.

Interior Minister Burg pulled out a copy of the Bible, and opened it to the portion of the week: Numbers 21:1-4. In an emotional voice, while his colleagues were already on their feet, ready to disperse, he began to read: "And when King Arad the Canaanite, which dwelt in the south, heard tell that Israel came by the way of the spies; then he fought against Israel and took some of them prisoners. And Israel vowed a vow unto the Lord, and said, If thou wilt indeed deliver this people into my hand, then I will utterly destroy their cities. And the Lord hearkened to the voice of Israel, and delivered up the Canaanites; and they utterly destroyed them and their cities: and he called the name of the place Hormah."

The minister of the interior looked up: "That is how they will be destroyed tonight in Entebbe. . . ."

CHAPTER TWENTY-SIX

"Mercedes on Way to Bilbi"

Shimon Peres came out of his office and turned homeward. Yitzhak Rabin was also planning to go home for a few hours' rest. The decision was made. The planes were airborne. Now, there was nothing to do but wait—and it was going to be a long night for both men.

"Well, if there's going to be a tragedy, God forbid," Rabin observed to his aides as he got up to leave, "I know that I will be the target for criticism. Me, and nobody else!"

He was already at the door when Eli Mizrahi called him back. Gandhi was on the line from Paris. The prime minister didn't want to talk to him, realizing that open telephone lines could spell catastrophe. "What am I going to tell him?" Rabin pleaded with his assistants, who thought he should answer the call. "I can't tell him the truth. . . ."

At the Paris end, General Zeevi was angry and excited. He told Rabin that he did not understand. "What's going on? After all, tomorrow is Sunday. The ultimatum expires at midday and, so far, I don't know what is being done about it."

The prime minister pretended not to understand what Zeevi was talking about at first. "Gandhi," he enunciated clearly, "you ask me what to do? Right now you are the man who has to give us answers. Go back to the French one more time, and ask them what's happening in Uganda. Ask them whether they have any answers to our proposals in principle. I don't have enough to convene the ministerial team, or anything to discuss."

Yitzhak Rabin repeated his previous instructions, that there would be no exchange in Entebbe under the patronage of Idi Amin—a man who could not be trusted. He went on to tell Zeevi that he personally would agree to Paris, or even Cairo. "I want you to understand that it isn't the number of terrorists to be released that counts, but rather the list of names. Capucci isn't the main thing for me. I'm far more concerned about releasing someone who has committed murder. . . ."

Finally, Rabin took pity on Gandhi, and tried to hint that this would not be the final word: "You know what? I'll contact you again later. Perhaps I'll have something to tell you."

Replacing the receiver, the prime minister of Israel muttered: "Gandhi will kill me. . . ."

The foreign minister had a problem of his own to solve. Yigal Allon knew that West Germany wouldn't forgive Israel if she gave up her anarchist prisoners before finding out about the military expedition to Entebbe. He also knew about Ambassador Fischer's frantic phone calls. What he didn't yet know was how to solve the problem without telling the Germans what was happening.

When the formula finally materialized, he sat with Avineri and they drafted a cable to Ambassador Meroz in Germany:

"Get in touch with Foreign Minister Genscher immediately, to deliver the following:

"A. Updating of negotiation through agency of the French, and detailing of Israeli position regarding preference to be given the technique of exchange.

"B. Delivery of information regarding French position in accepting Israeli view, and which clearly understands that Israel is negotiating with the terrorists on foundation of willingness to release terrorists from prisons in Israel, but not prisoners held in other countries. In other words: Israel negotiates only in her own name.

"C. France promised to take care of extension of ultimatum as much as possible.

"Genscher must understand from our explanation that the government of Israel is not putting pressure on the government of Germany, and that in our opinion the Germans have no reason to rush in accepting decisions."

"That piece of diplomatic double-talk should hold them a few hours more, without spilling the beans," Allon said.

Through the Mercedes' windows Yoni Netaniahu scanned the faces of his men. Most of them, despite the thunder of the engines, were asleep, sprawled on the canvas benches that passed for seats in a military transport. A few had removed their shirts to get some relief from the heat. Yoni opened the door, only to find that some of the boys were lying under the car wheels. "All I need is for the Mercedes to start traveling inside the plane," he said.

From the cockpit of the second Hercules in formation, Michael Golan looked down at the sea, and was astonished to see a long convoy of ships, most of them heading for the Suez Canal. The pilot of the lead plane was making an effort to steer well clear of the ships below. No point in being spotted now! Golan held course behind the leader.

He was not particularly worried. The only danger at this stage was from the shores of Egypt and Saudi Arabia, but before long the four Hercules transports would have passed well on their way south. The planes, observing radio silence, slowly gained height as the terrain below became mountainous.

Michael Golan wasn't pleased. In his cockpit, he could hear the broadcasts of aircraft crossing African airspace. He said nothing, yet from what he heard they would run into heavy clouds, rain, and hail as they neared the equator. Bad weather could affect the timetable. He had to be over Entebbe Airport and coming in to land on the dot of 11:03 P.M. Who the hell needed clouds, rain, and hail now?

Looking back from the cockpit, Michael could see the vehicles lashed into place and the sleeping soldiers sprawled under now-dimmed lamps along the benches.

"The guys are recharging their batteries," he remarked to his second pilot.

In the lead Hercules, the Mercedes rocked Yossi and Yoni from side to side as the plane bucked through turbulence, but the two men were already sleeping. Fatigue had finally overcome.

Stomach poisoning got the better of the four pills a day that Hana Cohen swallowed on doctor's orders. There was no improvement in her condition. Amin had visited earlier and had informed the hostages that he expected the answer of the government of Israel by midnight. No one, at this point, had much hope that the hijackers' demands would be met.

"Perhaps prayer will help us," Hana whispered to her husband.

The five families of observant Jews congregated in a corner to recite Sabbath afternoon and evening prayers. Though they prayed in lowered voices, the ancient words were clearly heard across the silent room.

"Out of the depths have I cried unto thee, O Lord. Lord, hear my voice."

Sara Davidson and Wilfried Böse were once again deep in conversation.

"Do you really think that your friends, the Arabs, could have hijacked the plane without someone like you?"

"True, it's a question of talents."

"And if Israel releases the terrorists you want, who is there to guarantee that you will free us?"

"We will play fair."

"Is hijacking of planes fair play?"

"Of course! You must differentiate between the hijacking and the negotiation to settle the affair."

Thick clouds swirled around the planes and heavy rain beat down on the cockpit windshields. From long experience, Michael Golan knew that their situation, although unpleasant, was not particularly dangerous. Clouds, rain, and hail hampered accurate navigation, yet he was still able to see the other aircraft flying nearby through the darkness. From his radar scope he could place them precisely, though he could not communicate with them.

In the lead plane, a man whom we shall call "Natan Aloni" pored over a large-scale drawing of Entebbe International Airport. Colonel Aloni commanded a standing-army unit of paratroops. Having awakened from a short nap, he was again puzzling over the difficulties that might crop up on the ground, where there would be little time to find solutions.

Operation Thunderball was not a stroke of genius, nor the invention of one man, but rather the work of many men in a number of teams in the short space of forty-eight hours. Under the pressure of time, each officer and man in the force had become thoroughly aware of his own role, yet he knew next to nothing about the other components of the mission. There had simply been no time for full-scale briefings of the entire force.

Natan Aloni now turned to a typewritten sheet summarizing all stages of Operation Thunderball.

"OPERATION THUNDERBALL"

Information:

1. *Ground:* Entebbe International Airport, located on the banks of Lake Victoria, has two runways, a long one and a short one. There are two terminals: New and Old. Old Terminal contains two hallways, in one of which, the western, the hostages are located. It has three entrances, identifiable by covered walkways that lead to them. In a side room, on the east side, is a rest area for the terrorists. On the second floor are Ugandan troops. The airport has two control towers, one of which is close to Old Terminal. Airport control and flight supervision are in New Terminal.

2. *Enemy:* The hostages are permanently guarded by two terrorists in the passenger hall and apparently two more outside. Other terrorists are in the rest room or not present on the spot. The terrorists are dressed European-style, carrying weapons such as Kalashnikov carbines, Scorpion submachine guns, and hand grenades.

   There are eighty or a hundred Ugandan troops in the area of the terminal, some on the second floor. Ugandans may also be in the old control tower and in other areas of the airport.

   It is possible that the Ugandans are equipped with recoilless rifles and bazookas, apart from their personal arms, which include FN rifles, Kalashnikovs, and Uzzi submachine guns.

Objective:

3. An IDF force will raid Entebbe International Airport, Uganda, and will liberate the 105 passengers of an Air France plane.

Method:

4. *General:* An IDF force will reach Entebbe by air, and will raid Old Terminal on foot and with the help

of vehicles, and will gain control over the airport in order to permit landing and takeoff of the planes without hindrance.

5. *Stages:* A. Flight from Israel to Uganda.
   B. Landing at Entebbe International Airport.
   C. Raid Old Terminal, where terrorists are located.
   D. Kill terrorists.
   E. Transfer hostages to aircraft.
   F. Refuel and take off.

6. *Forces and Assignments:*

Force A will land in the first plane and will move at speed to Old Terminal where the hostages are being held. Force A will strike the terrorists and Ugandan soldiers (if necessary) and will afterward secure the area of the terminal against attack.

Force B will move quickly to the second floor of Old Terminal, to prevent Ugandan soldiers and/or terrorists from opening fire on IDF soldiers and the hostages.

Force C will secure freedom of movement between Old Terminal and a Hercules, which will then approach the terminal to collect the hostages.

Force D will move quickly to New Terminal and will gain control over the control room, to permit the landing of additional aircraft, if necessary, and the takeoff of planes that participated in the mission.

Force E will secure the runway for the Hercules aircraft and will prevent attack on the parked planes.

Force F will secure the parking area of Ugandan air force MIGs, and will prevent their takeoff or any counter-offensive use of them.

Force G will erect blocks and ambushes, according to detailed plan, to prevent the sending of reinforcements of army or terrorists, from the airport area or any other place.

The document went on to detail aspects of maintenance, control and communications, medicine, and administration, but—with the planes now nearing Ugandan airspace— Natan Aloni was solely interested in the operational detail. His nerves were tightening with the well-known pre-combat feeling.

Yitzhak Rabin's tension could no longer be concealed. He was at home in north Tel Aviv. In the street below, his two cars and bodyguards were waiting impatiently to return to his office. At the door, Rabin turned back and called his wife.

"Leah, I'm going to the office, but before I go I would like you to know that we're operating tonight to free the hostages. Don't say a word to anybody, or even hint that you know anything. I'll phone when it's over."

He arrived at the Defense Ministry in record time, making a vain effort to wipe the signs of nervousness from his face. He sat in Shimon Peres' office with the other ministers, waiting for the first report from a landfall 2,187 miles away from Tel Aviv.

To the left of the minister's desk, above the battery of telephones, stood a small intercom. It was now linked into the command net of Operation Thunderball. Amid the growing tension, Defense Ministry spokesman Naftali Lavi had news for Shimon Peres.

"Burka Bar Lev has arrived in the ministry. He was called in case we need to phone Idi Amin tonight."

"Don't bring him here," Peres ordered. "He knows nothing about the operation, and he mustn't know at this stage. Let him wait in a room somewhere nearby."

Cigar smoke swirled around the oval table where the Israeli and French teams had just ended yet another session. In the Quai d'Orsay, the clocks recorded 8 P.M. Rehavam Zeevi again praised the relations between the two teams, then pressed the French again to get another deferment of the ultimatum, which was now due to expire at 1 P.M. Israel time the next day. Behind the facade of self-control, Zeevi was still wondering why no further instructions had arrived from Tel Aviv, but he was certain that something would turn up during the night—and at the right moment to prevent any killing tomorrow.

Squadron leader Yoel Asif, at the controls of the lead Hercules, decided that they would have to fly through the storm. Their mission was planned to split-second precision, and there could be no delays. He kept a close eye on the flashes of lightning over Lake Victoria on the approaches to Uganda.

Yoni Netaniahu had been up for an hour and alerted his men to buckle on their battle gear. When a bell rang in the depths of the Hercules to signal imminent landing, Yoni was walking down the line of his troops. The aircraft hurtled in towards Entebbe Airport at 350 miles an hour.

Yoni shook hands with each man and wished him good luck.

The soldiers climbed onto two jeeps stowed in the rear of the cabin. Yoni opened the front door of the Mercedes, and climbed in next to the driver's seat. Yossi took the left-hand spot on the second bank, and Tzur Ben-Ami was in position at the wheel. Six more soldiers piled into the car. Receiving the signal, Tzur and the other two drivers started their engines.

An unidentified aircraft circled Entebbe at thirty thousand feet. That, as the foreign press would later report, was an Israel air force Boeing, carrying Generals Peled and Adam, among a passenger list of senior officers, each of whom had specific duties to perform. For at least part of the way, Peled had flown the plane himself, but now he was leaning over maps and listening to radios, earphones clipped tightly to his head. This aerial command post, so far from home, was the connecting link between Entebbe and Tel Aviv.

Entebbe International control tower received a routine request for permission to land.

In the cockpit of the second Hercules, Michael Golan was straining to see out through the Plexiglas windshield. They were through the storm, clear of the thunder and lightning, and approaching Entebbe. He noted with satisfaction that, so far, the four aircraft had kept within the strict instructions given them before departure from Israel.

"The planes are over 'Jordan,' " was reported to the chief of staff a few minutes before 11 P.M. He studied a sketch spread out on his deck. "Jordan" was the code name for Lake Victoria.

Shortly before, General Gur had convened all those generals who were still unaware of the preparations for Operation Thunderball. Despite the jittery atmosphere as the clock hands crept towards 11 P.M., Mota Gur was smiling like a magician who has just pulled something out of his hat. His audience had expected details of an exchange of terrorists for hostages. They listened openmouthed as the chief of staff told them that the planes were already well on their way to Entebbe.

Now, back in his own office, Mota Gur waited for the first report from "Bilbi," the code name of Old Terminal. Once the planes crossed "Jordan," the ground forces would go into action at "Bilbi."

Entebbe Airport was visible in hazy moonlight. Michael Golan could see, in the distance, the lights of the airport runway. They were on in expectation of a passenger plane due to land.

Raindrops pattered on the windshields of the Hercules transports.

Yoni Netaniahu closed the Mercedes door and poked his weapon through the open window. Yossi was doing the same thing behind and to the left of him.

At 11:03 P.M., only thirty seconds behind plan, the wheels of the first Hercules touched down on the long asphalt runway of Entebbe International. After seven hours of silence, Yoel Asif turned on his radio to say four words: "I am on 'Yuval.' "

His craft rolled down the runway code-named "Yuval" in the direction of Old Terminal. Fifteen hundred yards from the building, the Hercules braked to a stop. The cars had descended the heavy ramp while the plane taxied to the destination. When Yoel turned to look in the cabin behind him, it was already empty. Peering through the cockpit windows, he saw a black limousine followed by two Land Rovers racing across the tarmac.

The battle for "Bilbi" would begin within seconds.

CHAPTER TWENTY-SEVEN

"I Repeat,
Transgressors Eliminated..."

At 11 P.M., Captain Michel Bacos stood beside the mattresses of Hana and Pasco Cohen. Yaakov and Zippy Cohen sprawled, fast asleep, on a bench at their sides. The Frenchman held a glass of water in his hand, and bent over to wake Hana.

At that moment Claude Silvers called out to Wilfried Böse, asking him to douse the lights in Old Terminal to allow the ailing hostages a good night's sleep. Böse refused, shrugging his shoulders as if to indicate the impossibility of granting such a request, and turned back to his station by the right-hand door.

Uzzi Davidson reached page 136 of his book.

Lisette Hadad tossed and turned on her hard mattress, trying to fall asleep.

The lead Hercules was still taxiing slowly along the runway as a dozen soldiers leaped out and dispersed, several yards apart, on either side. Each of them turned to a

nearby runway beacon and placed mobile flashlights alongside them—a precaution in case the control tower shut off
the power before the other three planes landed. More
soldiers charged out of the belly of the plane as it stopped
moving, taking positions around it to combat any possible
Ugandan reaction.

Colonel Natan Aloni was standing by the ramp of the
first Hercules as it dropped open to allow in a flow of cool
night air. At a distance, he could see the control tower—
code-named "Aviva." With the stream of air came an
army of tiny tropical flies and mosquitoes which beat
against the faces of waiting infantrymen. The temperature
was 60°.

Aloni, a veteran soldier, had correctly estimated that
the hard work would be over as soon as the plane had
landed safely. They had already come several hundred
yards down the runway, and no one had opened fire. From
here on, he was confident that Operation Thunderball
could proceed exactly as planned. Shouting "Forward," he
ran in the direction of "July"—New Terminal. The force
under his command had to seize the control tower to
ensure a clear takeoff at the end of the raid.

The mobile beacons placed by paratroops from the first
plane were already illuminating the area next to runway
"Yuval."

It was cramped and uncomfortable inside the Mercedes.
As the pilot swung the nose of the plane around, Tzur
Ben-Ami pressed down on his accelerator and the car
leaped forward. Old Terminal was over to the right bathed
in a pool of light. The nine men in the Mercedes knew its
location, approximately 1,500 yards away, from rehearsals
the day before.

Yoni shouted to the other drivers to keep in line, then
ordered Tzur to drive slow enough not to arouse suspicion.
Ten or fifteen seconds had already elapsed since they had

left the plane, and the Mercedes was approaching the old control tower when Yoni and Tzur spotted two figures a couple of hundred yards from them.

"Pay attention now," Yoni ordered as his men gripped their weapons. The Mercedes moved straight ahead, the two Land Rovers close behind. Rain was spattering the windshield.

The two Ugandan guards were now only fifteen yards from them. During rehearsals, Yossi had insisted that Ugandan troops would not stop a Mercedes, and would certainly never fire on it; after all, these were the cars their officers used. Now, therefore, he was no less surprised than his comrades when one of the Ugandans signaled the car to halt. They were only four yards away.

The Mercedes crawled one yard nearer. This soldier could endanger the entire mission, but there was no mistaking his uplifted right arm.

A pistol poked out the right-hand window. The Ugandan fell, but wasn't dead. Nobody had heard the shot that hit him.

"Right, step on it," ordered Yoni.

Tzur Ben-Ami responded immediately.

Michael Golan steered straight into the pool of light that was Entebbe. He glided in to land and taxied straight to his preset offloading point, behind a twenty- or thirty-foot-high hillock next to one of the runways. Flicking on his microphone, Michael confirmed: "I am at 'Katie.' "

Four flight controllers were on duty in the tower. Five minutes earlier, a passenger plane had asked permission to land. Now, something strange was happening to the radar screens—so foreign journalists were told later. The dancing white spots known as "snow" obscured their entire radius of sweep. Having little choice, the controllers sat back to wait patiently till the electronic disturbance abated.

"There's another light plane in the air," one of the controllers remarked, his voice clearly heard over the radios in the Hercules' cockpits. The men were instantly panicked.

Brigadier Dan Shomron had another worry. When the first Hercules braked at its assigned spot, Shomron jumped off the ramp to choose a location for his command team. The sudden silence of the Ugandan airport hit him hard. For one terrible moment, he was sure that the hostages must have been moved from Old Terminal—a fear reinforced by the memory of a crack United States army detachment that reached an American prisoner of war camp in Vietnam only to find it empty. The silence persisted as the second Hercules trundled along the runway to its parking spot.

In the defense minister's office far off in Tel Aviv, the silence seemed almost painful. The ministers sat along the walls and around the desk, some smoking, others leaning toward the intercom as if their attentiveness might coerce it into speech. But the intercom wouldn't cooperate.

Asher Ben-Natan's bottle of Napoleon brandy still stood on the desk. No one touched it. Military secretaries Braun and Poran sat with poised pens, ready to record any word coming from the intercom.

Somebody coughed, and Yitzhak Rabin turned toward him, instantly indignant, in tacit reproach for disturbing the moment.

Shimon Peres closed his eyes and his companions got the impression that he was offering up a silent prayer. He knew that the next ten or twenty seconds were the most critical of all—for the hostages, for the soldiers on the ground in Entebbe, for the army, and for the government of Israel.

Not far from Peres, Mota Gur was listening over his intercom to the command net on the ground in Entebbe. He could hear the first reports coming in to Dan Shomron, but was waiting for a clear picture from his head of Staff

Branch, Yekutiel Adam. In the past there had been occasions when Mota had been grateful for his deputy's characteristic lack of loquaciousness, but right now he was dying to know what was happening in Entebbe.

The Israeli air force Boeing had just landed at Nairobi. The plane appeared to be an El Al jet on a scheduled flight from Johannesburg to Tel Aviv, via Nairobi. Inside the craft, doctors were installing the last items of equipment, ready for what was to come.

Kenyan security men moved in to surround the plane.

The third Hercules was a few feet above the runway when the lights went out. Pilot Ariel Luz was shocked, but only for a fraction of a second. He made a hard landing and let his plane roll forward, hoping to spot the beacons placed by the paratroops from the first plane. Then he applied his brakes, but the heavy craft only rolled to a stop on the grass beside the asphalt runway.

Michael Golan was puzzled. Only a moment ago, the runway lights had been on; now it was pitch dark. He was worried that Ugandan soldiers could creep out from the terminal buildings to attack the three planes already on the ground.

Kuti Adam, circling above in another plane, was desperate for news. He could hear Dan Shomron, could listen to reports from the teams spreading out over the airport, could grasp that the aircraft were landing without difficulties so far—but he knew nothing about the most critical stage of all. Operation Thunderball would stand or fail by what happened to the Mercedes and its companion Land Rovers. If the terrorists or Ugandans realized there were Israelis in the cars, Old Terminal could become a charnel house. Yoni Netaniahu and his men had seconds in which to reach all three entrances to the building—and Kuti Adam still had no word of them.

The fourth Hercules came in to land between the paratroop torches. In the third plane, the pilot was in a cold sweat. Beyond his windows, he saw that his front wheels had stopped three feet from a six-foot-deep trench. Three feet more and Operation Thunderball would have been over for him, his crew, and his passengers.

The Mercedes and its two Land Rover escorts were now speeding into the area between the old control tower and the terminal, close enough to see the covered walkways at the entrances, exactly as described in their preliminary briefing.

Three or four seconds ago, the second Ugandan—the one who hadn't been shot—had vanished from sight. Now he surfaced again, close to the control tower. He hadn't panicked, and he opened fire immediately. A paratroop sergeant in one of the Land Rovers loosed a burst from a Kalashnikov and the Ugandan fell.

"Faster," Yoni shouted.

Tzur Ben-Ami pressed the pedal down as far as it would go. Then the Mercedes jerked to a stop, its four doors already swinging back hard on their hinges, as the occupants shot out from the car. The spot could not have been better chosen—near enough to Old Terminal for a fast entry, but just far enough not to alert the terrorists unnecessarily.

Yoni, Yossi, and their team raced like men possessed toward the three entrances to Old Terminal.

"Those soldiers must be organizing a revolution against Amin," Jaaber commented on hearing two or three shots in the distance outside the building. This was the burst that had cut down the second Ugandan sentry.

Michel Bacos was washing his hands.

Yitzhak David straightened up on his mattress.

Lisette Hadad pulled her blanket over her head and

rolled off the mattress onto the floor. Yosef Hadad grabbed a nearby chair and lifted it over his head.

Jean Jacques Maimoni, who was sitting at the far end, lifted his mattress over his body.

Yossi was the first to reach the doorway. The distance from the Mercedes took him at most three seconds. Yoni ran alongside, with the others close on his heels. Behind the rail that ran the length of Old Terminal, Yossi spotted a terrorist who had come out of the building. He fired. The terrorist bent over and ran back in the direction of the doorway.

Wilfried Böse heard the shot and came out to see what was happening. Yossi shot again, but missed. Böse leaped backward and pointed his carbine in the direction of the hostages.

"Retreat!" shouted Böse, turning his head. Yossi shot him.

"Get in," yelled Yoni. "Through the doors!"

Jaaber stood at the far end, gesturing at the terrorist girl in an unmistakable question: "What's going on?"

The girl threw her hand grenade on Jean Jacques' mattress.

Sara Davidson threw herself flat on the floor, then crawled with Uzzi and her two sons toward the corridor to the washrooms. It wasn't far, and it offered the protective sanctuary of a wall. The washrooms were already crowded with terrified hostages who had pressed themselves flat to the floor.

Hana Cohen had lost sight of her son Yaakov. In the chaos, she didn't notice that he wasn't running with her husband and daughter into the corridor. The three of them sprawled on the floor, Pasco Cohen covering his two women with his own body.

Yaakov Cohen tipped over the bench on which he had been sleeping, and covered himself with a mattress.

Ilan Hartuv ran for the corridor.

Yossi raced under the awning and up to the first door. To his horror, he found it was locked. In a fraction of a second, he spun around and hurtled toward the second entrance. He could still hear Yoni egging the others on: "Forward! Forward!" A terrorist suddenly appeared in Yossi's way. He pressed hard on the trigger of his gun— but nothing happened. Empty magazine! Three soldiers hurtled past and into the second doorway. Yossi switched magazines in record time and jumped in after his men. Coming through the doorway, he noticed the terrorist girl standing inside the hall to the left of the door. Another instant and Yossi would have shot her, but the man behind him beat him to it. Hit by a burst, she spun onto the floor near a window. Beyond the group of hostages, who were hugging the floor, a terrorist aimed his Kalashnikov down at the spread-eagled bodies. One of the French crewman screamed: "Don't shoot!"

The terrorist hesitated a second, and it was his last. From ten yards away, Yossi fired a burst that killed him outright.

Across to the right another terrorist managed to fire. He loosed three or four shots that echoed around the hall, then dropped. Amnon Ben-David hit him. He tried to rise and Amnon shot him again.

The paratroopers who had burst through the two open doorways could now take in a sight of utter confusion. A mad mixture of people, beds, mattresses, blankets, overnight bags. The hostages were terrified. After all, it had happened in fifteen seconds—far too quickly for anyone to grasp!

Ron Vardi and his comrades clung to the sides of a command car as it careened across the empty space to the new control tower. Off to one side was a fire station. As Ron watched, it was suddenly pitch black. Somebody had killed the airport lights. At the foot of the tower, the combat team could hear the crackle of shots from elsewhere on the field, but their target was deserted. The four flight controllers were no longer at their stations. An officer scanned the panels, searching for a switch that would restore light to the runways.

Lieutenant Shlomo Lavi raced at the head of his force, riding in two Rabbi field cars, into the Ugandan air force parking area. According to plan, his men were to prevent any attempt by the MIG pilots to get their craft airborne and attack the departing Hercules. Shlomo's mission proceeded smoothly. In minimum time the area was secure, without opposition.

Around the field, men of the Golani and the paratroop detachments were already deployed across main access routes and roads to block any reinforcements from a nearby army camp almost within earshot of Entebbe International.

At the center of the airport, Dan Shomron was losing patience. Still not a word from Yoni Netaniahu, though he could hear the crackle of light-arms fire—rarely a good sign.

Yoni's Land Rover team headed straight for the second floor. Their mission was to secure the building against any attempt to interfere with the transfer of hostages to the aircraft. The first soldier racing up met two Ugandan soldiers on the stairs. They froze. Above them, on the second floor, were more of their comrades. There was some resistance, but it was over in less than a minute and the Israelis were free to mount guard on the roof, where they could survey the entire surrounding area.

The force now inside Old Terminal had a rough idea of the number of terrorists, all of whom had to be taken care of if the evacuation was to proceed safely. While Yossi and his squad went in to the passenger hall, another team ran along the front of the building to the old VIP

Room at the far end. As they arrived, the terrorists off
duty came tumbling into the corridor.

Two white Europeans came out of a nearby room. For
a split second Ilan Gonen held his fire, thinking that these
must be passengers off the Aerobus.

"Who are you?" Ilan shouted in English.

No answer. The two men continued their slow walk.

In the defense minister's office, shots could be heard
over the intercom. Were it not for the tension and anxiety,
Rabin, Peres, and the others might have found time to
marvel at the wonders of modern technology that could
let them listen to a battle two thousand miles away. Yet,
apart from a few crisp orders issued by Dan Shomron, and
terse conversations between the plane and the ground below, there was no way of knowing how things were going
or whether the hostages were safe. Amos Aron was sending a message to President Ford over the phone to Ambassador Dinitz in Washington: AT THE TIME OF DELIVERY
OF THIS MESSAGE, OUR FORCES. . . . Dinitz listened in
astonishment.

It was only at 11:07 P.M. that Kuti Adam's voice finally
came through in the chief of staff's private bureau and the
defense minister's room elsewhere in the building.

"Everything's okay. You'll have a precise report immediately."

Everything's okay?

What had happened at Entebbe?

Were the hostages safe?

Were the terrorists dead?

What about casualties?

The prime minister and his defense minister leaned forward, almost unable to bear the tension, praying to hear
Dan Shomron's voice.

Mota Gur no longer hesitated. He called Dan directly.

"What's happening there?"

"Everything's all right. I'll report later. I'm busy now."
Again, everything's all right. . . . What's all right?

Yosef Hadad held the chair over his head as protection
against terrorist bullets. A bullet hit his chair, and he
thought his end had come. Out of the corner of his eye,
he could see Böse lying in a pool of blood.

Pasco Cohen lay on top of his wife and daughter, with
more hostages on top of him. He lifted himself for a moment to make sure that Zippy wasn't suffocating. A bullet
penetrated his thigh, then tore an artery near his bladder.

"I'm wounded," he told Hana quietly, "look after the
children."

As Pasco collapsed on the floor of the corridor, Jean
Jacques Maimoni panicked at the sight of the hand grenade that had landed on his mattress. The boy jumped to
his feet and ran, bent over, toward the washroom corridor.
Two bullets hit his back and sent him sprawling on the
floor, dead. Yitzhak David, who lifted his body in an attempt to pull Jean Jacques down, took a bullet in his
shoulder.

"Who are you?" Ilan Gonen yelled again. But the two
Europeans went on walking, as though all the hubbub and
chaos had nothing to do with them. The soldier pointed
his gun barrel at them. Spotting the flash of a grenade fuse,
he let loose a burst, then dropped flat on the floor. The
grenade exploded in the corridor, tearing the bodies of the
two Europeans but not harming the paratroopers.

Sara Davidson thought she could hear voices speaking
Hebrew. They were coming nearer! A loudspeaker boomed
through the enclosed space: "This is *Zahal*—the IDF!
We've come to take you home! Lie on the floor and wait
for instructions! This is *Zahal*!"

Yosef Hadad shouted in a voice clearly heard throughout Old Terminal: "They're ours! They're ours!"

Somebody else lifted a head to call: "Israeli soldiers? Israeli soldiers!"

Baruch Gross peeked into the hall from the washroom corridor and almost stopped breathing. Before him stood an Israeli soldier. There could be no mistake! But the man's gun was pointing at him. Baruch didn't lose his head: "*Yisrael!*" he shouted the Hebrew word, "*Yisrael!*" The gun barrel turned, and it seemed to Baruch that his life was also turning.

"Lie on the floor," boomed the bullhorn, "we have come to get you and it will be all right!"

Thirteen-year-old Benny Davidson couldn't believe it. Only at noon he had jokingly told his parents and brother that "the army will come to free us tonight at midnight." So he had said it—so what? He didn't mean it, and certainly didn't believe it. And now, one hour before midnight, Israeli soldiers had appeared in Old Terminal. Sara Davidson dropped on top of Ron, while Benny mumbled a prayer.

Hana Cohen didn't lose her head. She was too good a nurse for that. Tearing Pasco's shirt, she bandaged the wound, but the makeshift dressing turned red. The wound was deep. Pasco was losing too much blood.

Yossi ran through Old Terminal checking to see that all the terrorists were dead. Then he called a sixteen-year-old hostage named Michael, and asked him to identify them. Once that was done, Yossi reported to Brigadier Dan Shomron, somewhere on Entebbe's field. Shomron passed the news on to Yekutiel Adam in the Boeing. Adam relayed the message to General Gur. "The transgressors are eliminated," he said quietly. "I repeat, transgressors eliminated."

Four words were all it took to relieve the tension in Shimon Peres' study. A smile flittered across Yitzhak Rabin's face, and Shimon Peres' eyes sparkled. But they still didn't know very much.

The men in the room could now allow themselves a few words of quiet conversation, but their voices were muted. Suddenly the phone rang; General Zeevi from Paris. He was still waiting for new instructions. Who the hell could negotiate this way? Could he please speak to the prime minister?

This time Rabin told Gandhi that there was no more need for French mediation, and he hoped that the general would forgive him for not saying anything sooner. As a military man of many years' standing, Gandhi could understand Rabin's earlier predicament. And he would be delighted to accept the honor of personally informing President Giscard d'Estaing.

On the second floor of Old Terminal, paratroops checked room by room, looking for terrorists or Ugandan troops. Their instructions were to allow the Ugandans to escape, provided of course they didn't offer resistance. Scores of black troops made use of the opportunity to get away, and quickly.

Almost all the Israeli vehicles were now headed toward the old control tower. First place was given to the half-track armored personnel carrier, from which a torrent of lead from bazooka rockets and machine-gun bullets poured onto the tower. Its occupants had been firing on the Israelis for the past few minutes, and the paratroopers could not but admire the courage of the unknown defenders. Finally it seemed that stage two could begin: the hostages could be moved out to the plane that would take them home.

Only now did Yossi realize that he hadn't heard Yoni's voice for at least sixty seconds. He scanned the interior of Old Terminal, but there was no sign of his commanding officer. Running from the building, he found Yoni almost immediately. He lay unconscious on the ground by the building, a doctor and a corpsman in attendance, trying to save his life. He had been shot in the very first minutes after leaving the Mercedes—a bullet in the back, fired from

the old control tower, the place that had worried him during yesterday's rehearsal. Yoni had dropped to the ground,
mortally wounded, a moment after guiding his men to
target.

Yossi, startled to realize that he was now in command
of the main force in Operation Thunderball, begged the
doctor: "Do everything you can!"

Inside the lead Hercules, Dr. Yosef was getting anxious.
He knew that the aircraft now made a huge static target
as it sat being filled with fuel. It was vulnerable even without the flashes of firing that the doctor could see through
the small portholes. With him were nine more doctors and
orderlies, waiting up front for the hostages, praying they
weren't wounded—but ready to do their jobs if they had to.

Yitzhak David rubbed his shoulder. Blood was pouring
from it. Ilan Hartuv suddenly noticed the sticky red
stream, and raised his voice over the din: "Our leader is
hurt. Someone come and bandage him." Michael helped
Ilan bind the wound and brought him over to the mattress
where, until yesterday, his mother had slept. It was empty,
but next to it lay Ida Borowitz, her son Boris stooping
over her.

Ida's body was covered with blood. Nobody had noticed
her die, but the body of a terrorist lay beside her. Had he
shot her? Had he decided to die with one of the hostages?
Boris hugged the dead body of his mother and wailed:
"*Imaleh, Imaleh*—Mother, Mother!" There were tears in
the eyes of the people around him, yet the time had not
yet come to mourn the dead.

Sergeant Hershko Surin was due to begin demobilization
leave the next day, Sunday. His three years of conscript
service were almost over. Twelve hours before ending his
military career, Hershko dashed into Entebbe Old Terminal. Climbing the stairs to the second floor, he met two
Ugandans. One of them was faster than Hershko. Sergeant
Surin dropped to the ground, wavering between life and
death, his body paralyzed.

By the outer wall of Old Terminal, a doctor labored to save Yoni Netaniahu. It was useless. The brilliant young lieutenant colonel who had come home to serve his people was dying. Yossi Yaar and the others lifted him gently onto a stretcher. For a moment it seemed that Yoni's will to live might overcome. He raised his head as though wanting to say something—then dropped back on the stretcher.

CHAPTER TWENTY-EIGHT

"Mount Carmel,
Mount Carmel"

Yossi ordered his men to collect the casualties strewn across the floor. The bodies of Ida Borowitz and Jean Jacques Maimoni were laid on stretchers, as were the ten people injured in the course of the lightning-fast raid. Bullhorns summoned all the hostages back from corridors and side rooms into the main hall. The stunned men, women, and children shuffled in. The paratroopers had to slap a few to bring them out of shock.

The pilot of the first Hercules started his engines and began to move his craft slowly and cautiously toward Old Terminal, stopping 500 yards away. Yossi ordered his men to prepare the evacuation of the wounded and the hostages, although shots were still being exchanged between Israeli soldiers and Ugandans. When it seemed that the gunfire had finally stopped, Yossi picked up a bullhorn and instructed the hostages to check and see that all members of their families were accounted for.

Uzzi Davidson collected together Sara, Benny, and Ron. Yitzhak David, lying on a stretcher, grasped his wife's hand.

Ilan Hartuv was very worried. His mother was still in Mulago Hospital, but what could be done about that?

Outside the terminal, soldiers took position in two lines, forming a funnel straight to the gaping hatch of the Hercules. Yoni's solution for shock and panic would still be used, even if he wasn't there to supervise it. Yet there was another reason: no one wanted a hostage to run into an engine.

Command cars, jeeps, Rabbi field cars, and a Peugeot pickup truck pulled into the area in front of the building as the 104 hostages were started moving toward the waiting plane. There was some panic. Families clung together and rushed for the vehicles. One young girl came out dressed only in bra and panties, as there had been no time to dress. A soldier threw her a blanket, and she wrapped it around herself as she scrambled onto a command car. Shots were still being fired.

Eighteen minutes had passed since the Mercedes began its journey across Entebbe Airport. Now Yekutiel Adam's voice boomed out from a radio in the General Staff "pit," and from the intercoms in Gur's and Peres' rooms: "Mount Carmel. I repeat, Mount Carmel!"

The prime minister and defense minister knew now that the tough part of the mission was almost over. "Mount Carmel" was the code word denoting the start of evacuation from Old Terminal.

Defense Ministry spokesman Naftali Lavi dialed the home of a military correspondent of one of the daily papers. "It's worthwhile to stay awake tonight," he said—but refused to elaborate.

"What's happening?"

Naftali could not explain, so he merely said, "They'll trade terrorists for hostages tonight."

The journalist couldn't swear to it, but there seemed to be a note of mockery in the spokesman's last remark.

*   *   *

The 500 yards now appeared secure, so Yossi gave the signal for the vehicles to move. Across the way, the engines of the Hercules were holding to a steady, muffled roar. Hostages who hadn't found places on the vehicles began to walk toward the plane.

Hana Cohen swept Zippy up in her arms and began to run. Yaakov caught up with her and ran alongside. Pasco, lying on a stretcher, waved weakly to his son as he was lifted inside the Hercules. A team of doctors and orderlies set to work at once to save his life, pushing Hana, who wanted to help, gently aside. Before she even found a seat, she could see a blood-transfusion bag in place as the precious fluid dripped into Pasco's body. The wound was evidently more serious than she had realized.

Dr. Yosef leaned over the stretcher that bore the unconscious body of Lieutenant Colonel Jonathan Netaniahu. There was nothing more that could be done. Yoni was dying, and the doctors were powerless to prevent it happening.

Soldiers helped hostages off the vehicles by the ramp of the Hercules, guiding them across the 500-yard walk. Their stunned charges were encouraged to move at a brisk pace, yet there was no need for panic.

Inside the cockpit, the pilot and his crew were already making their pretakeoff instrument check. Behind them, at the bottom of the ramp, officers and men of the Thunderball force quietly asked each hostage to check that all his family were accounted for. When Captain Bacos approached the ramp, an officer politely asked him to check his family—the crew of Air Force 139. No one was missing. Only Ilan Hartuv remained silent. He was leaving his mother behind in a Ugandan hospital, with no way to save her—but what else could he do? It would be futile to remain in Entebbe. Now, in the doorway of the Hercules, he could only hope that the president of Uganda would extend his protection to Dora Bloch. Still stunned by the events of the last half hour, Ilan pressed forward into the belly of the plane. Like the others, he was still finding it difficult to believe that the week of captivity was nearly over.

Far away across the airport, Lieutenant Shlomo Lavi and his men detailed to guard the Ugandan MIGs were firing at Ugandan soldiers coming from the direction of the terminal. The opposition was heavy enough to force Lavi's team into equally heavy return fire.

Michael Golan, in the cockpit of the second Hercules, was still behind the hillock next to a runway. The MIGs were parked in a lower area of the airport and he couldn't see them, although he did notice flames and a column of smoke ascending into the night sky. It was Shlomo Lavi's men blowing up eleven MIGs—seven 21s and four 17s. Perhaps half the order of battle of the Ugandan air force was now smoke and ashes.

A spirited radio conversation began between Michael and the other three pilots. Minutes ago an attempt had started to refuel the Israeli planes from Entebbe Airport storage tanks. They had brought three pumps and a group of men who had served in Uganda and knew exactly where the airport fuel stocks were kept. One of the planes was already linked up, but the pump was supplying fuel at low pressure. It seemed as if the process was going to take 45 minutes, and the pilots were growing nervous. Finally, the Golani detachment commander radioed a suggestion to Dan Shomron to stop the refueling: "We have succeeded. Why should we take more risks here?"

Kuti and Benny heard the conversation and agreed, ordering immediate takeoff. Never mind reloading the pumps! All of them together are only worth ten thousand dollars! Let Amin have them. Get those planes airborne!

The lead Hercules, with its load of dazed hostages, lumbered onto the long runway, gathered speed, and climbed heavily into the night. In the cockpit, the hands

of the clock indicated 11:43; precisely forty minutes after
the first plane landed at Entebbe.

" 'Hear, O Israel . . .' " One of the passengers recited the
ancient prayer, and Baruch Gross picked up the refrain.

The men in Tel Aviv sighed with relief. Prime Minister
Rabin was beaming from ear to ear. Peres led the group
across the building to the chief of staff's suite. General
Gur, tired but happy, was sitting at his desk, surrounded
by senior officers and staff generals. On the table were a
number of bottles of *kiddush* ceremonial wine—the contribution of the army chief rabbinate. Peres shook Mota's
hand warmly.

Yitzhak Rabin went back to his own building, where
Cabinet ministers, opposition leaders, and the Foreign Affairs Committee chairman were waiting. Handshakes all
around. Smiles and beaming faces.

Mota Gur asked the operator to get his home. Rita Gur
and the children were asleep when the phone rang. Rita's
husband, who had "lied like never before in my life" over
the last three days, now told his wife about the operation
in Entebbe for the first time. She didn't seem surprised.
Putting down the receiver, Mota couldn't understand her
unemotional response.

Two or three minutes later, Mota's daughter phoned
him. "Daddy," she said in growing excitement, "We didn't
understand what you said. . . ." Mota patiently explained
a second time. When the call was over, Rita Gur and her
daughter took an atlas off the bookshelf.

"Where's Entebbe?" young Miss Gur asked.

In the embassy of Israel in Paris, two more senior staff
members were brought into the secret, so they could type
the now-translated messages to the president and foreign
minister of France. Zeevi was under orders from Yitzhak
Rabin to come home immediately after delivering the news.

He ran to his hotel to collect his suitcase, then returned to the embassy to instruct Ambassador Gazit: "Please inform our French colleagues that the negotiation was sincere, and we didn't try to deceive them even for a minute."

Gandhi sat back in the ambassador's car as it raced out of Paris, bound for Geneva. Two drivers alternated at the wheel, in order to get the general to an El Al plane due to take off for Israel in the early hours of the morning.

"If we tried to sum up now," Gur said at 1 A.M. on Sunday, "I would say the operation proceeded exactly as planned. I hope that the casualty list will also show that it was an achievement. Yoni has been injured, and perhaps another from the force. Among the hostages, there are also few casualties. It was an impressive achievement, but it wouldn't have been possible without the performance of one man. I don't know whether, on occasions like these, you can apportion the percentages of success to every one who had a part in it, but if so, then I'm sure that we would have to credit most of the percentages to the minister of defense. He pushed in favor of the operation in spite of great opposition."

Again the wine glasses were raised.

Now Yitzhak Rabin was ready to phone Golda Meir. She was spending the night with her daughter at kibbutz Revivim in southern Israel.

"Golda, I know it's late, but I think it's worth waking you. . . ."

Rabin described the night's events to the former prime minister, who was overjoyed. Then he phoned the president of Israel, the speaker of the Knesset, and the two chief rabbis.

In a very happy mood, Defense Minister Peres summoned Burka Bar Lev and ordered him to phone Idi Amin. Since he knew that the call would be heard by a great many people, Peres decided to wring a little retribution from the Ugandan, and perhaps sour his love affair with the terror organizations. " 'Thank you for your cooperation,' tell him that," he said to Burka. "I think it worthwhile to make some people believe that Amin helped rescue the hostages."

It seemed that Idi Amin had been shaken awake. Even now, long after the landing at Entebbe, he knew absolutely nothing about the raid.

"Who's there?" the president asked.

"Burka Bar Lev. B as in Bomba. A as in Airplane. . . ."
Finally Amin understood.

Bar Lev: "Sir, I want to thank you for your cooperation, and I'm very grateful."

Amin: "Have I done anything?"

Bar Lev: "I only want to thank you, sir, for your cooperation."

Amin: "What have I done?"

Bar Lev: "Exactly what you wanted to do!"

Amin: "Uh, uh, what's happened?"

Bar Lev: "What's happened? I don't know."

Amin: "Can you tell me?"

Bar Lev: "No. I don't know. I was asked to thank you for your cooperation."

Amin: "Can you tell me about the proposal you wanted to make to me?"

Bar Lev: "I have been asked by my friend, with high connections in the government, to say 'thank you very much for your cooperation.' I don't know what it means, but I think that you do."

Amin: "I don't know because I'm only just back this minute from the conference in Mauritius to solve this problem before the ultimatum expires tomorrow morning."

Ber Lev: "I understand. Okay, sir. . . . Thank you for your cooperation, and perhaps I'll call you again tomorrow morning. Do you want me to call you tomorrow morning?"

Amin: "Yes."

Bar Lev: "All right. Thank you, sir. Shalom."

Amin: "Okay. . . ."

Bar Lev immediately shared the conversation with Peres, who phoned Rabin. The prime minister roared with laughter.

At Nairobi Airport, Hana Cohen noticed that her husband's condition was not improving, although he was being given a lot of blood. One of the doctors told her that Pasco would be taken off the plane to get treatment in Nairobi, and would then be flown to Tel Aviv in a Boeing. When Hana protested that she wanted to be with him, the doctor said: "Impossible. Your husband will be home before you." Hana believed him and stayed in the Hercules, which shortly took off for Israel.

Uzzi Davidson stood all the way from Nairobi to Israel in the cockpit. He gave up his seat in order to be the first to see the shores of Israel. His legs were aching.

Some of the aircrew got busy making bikini pants from first aid dressings for the young girl who came aboard in bra and panties. She was shivering, as were many of the others.

They needed many more blankets, since the high altitude made for lower temperatures. The pilots opened sheets of aluminum foil to cover their passengers, who were still exhausted and in shock. Lemonade and candy were handed out, and some of the tired soldiers tried to start a group sing, but the hostages couldn't cooperate. They still had to absorb what had happened—and they knew that their rescue had cost lives. Deep inside the plane lay the stretchers of Ida Borowitz and Jean Jacques Maimoni. Ida's son Boris was grief-stricken, and Sara Davidson had understood that the soldiers had suffered casualties as well. When she asked one of them whether they had sustained any losses, he didn't answer. . . . He didn't need to. Sara could see the sorrow on his face.

In Washington, the celebrations on the eve of the Bicentennial of American independence were in full swing when

Ambassador Dinitz delivered his message to President Ford:

> Mr. President. We have a common interest in the war on terror. After Israel arrived at the recognition that she was unable to rescue the passengers on the plane at Entebbe peacefully from the hands of the hijackers, the government of Israel resolved on a military operation. Instructions were issued to avoid losses of life as far as possible. I hope, Mr. President, for understanding of the motives for the action.

Having delivered the formal message, Dinitz was now in a position to tell the President of the United States that the operation was a complete success.

Early evening in America was late night in West Germany. When Foreign Minister Dietrich Genscher received the telephoned message from Ambassador Yohanan Meroz, he crowed with joy, then boomed: "If Yigal Allon was here beside me now, I would kiss him."

A French wire services teleprinter in Kampala was chattering away: THREE UNIDENTIFIED PLANES LANDED AT ENTEBBE . . . THERE WERE SHOTS. . . . In newspaper, radio, and television offices in Tel Aviv, Washington, Buenos Aires, Tokyo, Sydney, and Bonn, duty editors gazed in amazement at the message from the heart of East Africa.

Shimon Peres and Mota Gur bent over a sheet of paper, preparing an official communiqué to be released by the military spokesman. Menachem Begin scanned their draft, and asked them to replace "liberate" by "rescue."

At 3 A.M., *Galei Zahal*, the broadcasting station of the Israeli Defense Forces, announced: "IDF forces tonight rescued. . . ."

The insistent ringing of a telephone woke Professor
Yosef Gross, chairman of the committee of relatives of
the Entebbe hostages. Defense Ministry spokesman Lavi
was on the line. It took several minutes before Professor
Gross was able to grasp what it was all about, then, he
cried.

At 4:20 A.M. the chief of staff knocked on the defense
minister's door. "Shimon, I have bad news. Yoni Netaniahu
is dead, after receiving a bullet in the back. It came from
the control tower."

Next day, the defense minister recorded in his diary:
"I couldn't hold it back. That broke me. I cried. . . ."
The next day the Knesset chose to change the name of the
rescue mission to Operation Jonathan.

High over Africa, Michael Golan was fuming—even
though the mission was a success. He had heard Israeli
radio broadcasts over his earphones, and the planes were
still withing range of anyone who wanted to hit them. Why
the hell couldn't Tel Aviv wait a few hours? He didn't
know that the French wire service in Kampala had already
informed the whole world.

Up ahead in the lead Hercules, Uzzi Davidson was
still standing in the cockpit, waiting to see Israel. His eyes
were damp as he spotted Sharm el-Sheikh on the horizon,
and his heart was full of pride in his country as the four
Hercules aircraft swept low over Eilat in the victory
gesture usually reserved to fighter pilots. Down below he
could see people standing in the streets, clapping.

Early in the morning, at an airbase somewhere in central
Israel, the Hercules landed. The hostages were led into a
security briefing by Intelligence Branch head Shlomo Gazit.
The bodies of the dead were removed and the wounded
were rushed to the hospital. The hostages were still dazed,
and Prime Minister Rabin and Defense Minister Peres

could get little from them in answer to their questions.

Almost three hours after their "unofficial arrival" in Israel, the passengers back from the death trap in Entebbe got ready for their emotional reunion with their families and friends. They had told what they could of their traumatic week, and in return had been warned what not to say about the events of the past night. They had shaken off some of their shock, though it was now replaced by growing emotion as they finally realized that they were home—safe—thanks to a miracle. They were ready to face Israel and the world.

It was mid-morning when an Israeli air force Hercules rolled to a stop on the apron at Ben-Gurion Airport, and the ramp slowly dropped onto the tarmac. Led by Captain Michel Bacos, beaming from ear to ear, the Entebbe hostages filed out into the arms of their relatives, and onto the television screens of a world breathless with excitement at the renewed knowledge that the age of the impossible was not over—that men with resolve in their hearts were still prepared to take risks for the sake of freedom and human dignity. Indeed, in America, it seemed as if the Entebbe rescue was a gift offered to prove on Independence Day what the founding fathers of the United States really meant 200 years ago when Thomas Jefferson wrote: "certain inalienable rights . . . life, liberty, and the pursuit of happiness. . . ."

Ben-Gurion Airport was packed with a happy throng of thousands, come to welcome the hostages back from hell. All Israel was jubilant. No longer was this the anxious country of yesterday, still remembering the trauma of Yom Kippur, 1973, and wondering about its ability to defend its own interests. People were laughing and greeting strangers as if they were beloved relatives. Fifty-three minutes in Entebbe—and three million Israelis were rejoicing.

A woman reporter knocked on a door in Natanya early

in the morning, to tell the Maimoni family about the Entebbe rescue. "I'm not happy yet," said the mother, tears rolling down her cheeks. "I have a premonition of evil, and I won't believe he is safely out of Uganda until I actually see my Jean Jacques with my own eyes."

Amid the laughter and babel of voices at Ben-Gurion Airport, the desperate cries over a loudspeaker went almost unheard: "Rabbi Tzemel to the Officers' Club please!" "Would the Borowitz and Maimoni families please come to the Officers' Club."

Outside the excitement reached a peak. Men rode on their friends' shoulders, and an aged Yemenite blew the *shofar*—the ceremonial ram's horn trumpet associated with festivals. Flags were hoisted and circles formed to dance wild horas on the tarmac of the airport apron.

Inside the Officers' Club the air force chaplain, Rabbi Tzemel, was telling the bitter news to the relatives of Jean Jacques Maimoni and Ida Borowitz. Mr. Maimoni wept bitterly, but through the din beyond the walls no one heard him.

Hana Cohen, on arrival in Israel, rushed to the hospital to look for her husband. They told her he hadn't arrived yet. She waited for hours until someone informed her that he was hospitalized in Nairobi. "He'll be home in a few days," they told her. Relatives took Hana, Yaakov, and Zippy Cohen home to Hadera. At four in the afternoon, soldiers knocked on her door. As gently as possible, they broke the news that Pasco Cohen had passed away in Nairobi.

The next morning, Entebbe Old Terminal was deserted. Only a disarray of mattresses, blankets, scraps of food, and remnants of clothing remained as evidence that this miserable place had served as housing for over a hundred people over the last week.

Idi Amin counted the bodies of his soldiers, and told hypocritical lies over the international telephone lines to

Israel and the world, in a vain effort to shake off any suspicion of partnership with the terrorists.

In Old Terminal, strewn among the upset furniture and bedding, were the bodies of six terrorists—including the girl known as Halima. They would probably be buried in Kampala, the city that had served as a dumb witness to the drama and tragedy of the hijacking. Four or five of the terrorist team were still alive, simply because they hadn't been in Old Terminal on the night of retribution. Perhaps some of them chose to desert, or maybe they were already seeking other targets for revenge.

Idi Amin's greatest revenge was exacted from seventy-five-year-old Dora Bloch. While he told newspapermen, through clearly heard tears, in telephone conversations, that he hadn't cooperated with the terrorists, he ordered his secret police to execute Dora Bloch. It was the third day of her hospitalization in Mulago Hospital. She did not know, on that morning of July 4, 1976, that her son Ilan Hartuv and her fellow passengers on Air France 139 were already on Israeli soil. She was the only Israeli left in Uganda, and it was to her that Idi Amin turned. At 9:30 A.M., four stockily built men burst into her ward, trapped the confused old woman, and dragged her, screaming, out of the building. Dora Bloch was not silent. She called for help and fought for her life, but she had no chance. The four secret policemen gagged her with a rag and dragged her to a waiting car. Later investigation by the British embassy revealed that from the hospital they drove to a sugar plantation near Kampala, where she was executed by pistol shot. Afterward, the murderers tried to burn her body, but the flames did not completely consume her—and the remains were buried on the spot.

While Idi Amin threatened neighboring Kenya with military retaliation for allowing refueling of the Israeli aircraft at Nairobi, Jerusalem approached Washington to obtain aid for the Kenyans. The Israeli representative who asked the Kenyan authorities how much Israel owed for aircraft fuel and medical services was in for a pleasant surprise: the answer—no charge! That was Kenya's contribution to the rescue of the hostages, the Kenyans told the Israeli.

Amin knew he had become a laughingstock. Now he was scared that the Israelis wouldn't be satisfied with their raid on Entebbe, but would also want revenge for the slaying of Dora Bloch. His primitive reaction was expected —an attempt to make his peace with Israel. He phoned Israel, and even told the press, that he wanted to make an arms deal because he was short of spare parts for all kinds of weapons earlier bought in Israel. Then he called to say that he wanted to return the Westwind executive jet which he had received years before from Israel Aircraft Industries, but never bothered to pay for. He was afraid that Israel knew the plane had been put at the service of Wadia Hadad, to fly the terrorist boss from Mogadishu to Kampala and back during the prolonged Entebbe negotiations.

He gave a flat refusal to the PLO representatives in Kampala who wanted to stage a large, demonstrative funeral for their comrades, the hijackers of Air France 139. Amin ordered their burial without any unnecessary ceremony.

Twenty Ugandan soldiers paid with their lives for their president's cooperation with the hijackers. But that wasn't enough for Idi Amin. He ordered the execution of the four flight controllers of Entebbe International. He accused them of cooperating with the Israeli assault force simply because they didn't detect the approaching planes and didn't warn the army or contact his office. The execution was carried out on the spot, at the airport, the four unfortunate men tied to trees. Nobody listened to their protestations that they hadn't seen the approach of the Hercules because their radar was covered with electronic "snow." Their execution in fact prevented any Ugandan attempt to investigate how the planes landed. A committee of investigation, appointed by Idi Amin and including the Libyan ambassador, reached a deadlock on the first day and ceased its deliberations.

Israel celebrated the victory over international terrorism and the rescue of the hostages. It was rejoicing mingled with grief, as are most of Israel's victories and successes. The country had to escort three of the hostages, Sergeant Hershko Surin, and Lieutenant Colonel Jonathan Netaniahu to their last resting places. Yoni's past commander spoke at the graveside, and his words sounded like a last will and testament. The young officer, almost the same age as Yoni, and with no less combat experience, said:

"A nation fights over the trenches of its life, and loses not only the best fighters and officers of today, not only the leaders of future legions. We lose along the roads of battle the elite, those with the potential for our spiritual creativity, the poets and the writers, the thinkers and scientists, the pillars of future impetus in all areas of life and society.

"Our Yoni—we saw him torn between the lust for knowledge and the sense of mission, the satisfaction of military deeds; Yoni of the history and philosophy books— Plato, Marx, and Klausner; Yoni who looked at the history of Israel not as a collection of facts, but as a source of personal commandments to action; we saw him in battle, in the crucible of fire, in courage and wisdom. But we must remember that beyond it all is the unquenchable Israeli spirit which was put to the test at Entebbe. The spirit stood the test, but at a heavy price, yet with straight back. All these things, we can, if we want it, adopt to ourselves and bequeath to those who follow us.

"Through all the Yonatans, from the Maccabees to our own Yoni, the rebirth and sovereignty of Israel were and are dependent on a few sons, and their willingness to grasp the sword. The death of the sons, painful as it may be, is a part of our lives and of our ability to stand fast."

The next day, Jean Jacques Maimoni and Ida Borowitz were laid to rest in cemeteries near their homes. Over the grave of Ida Borowitz, Transport Minister Gad Yaakobi said: "There is no rejoicing for the people of Israel but that it is mingled with sorrow."

Epilogue: One Family

Evening on Tel Aviv seafront, September 9, 1976.

Darkness has already fallen, but the waves are still visible from windows above the shore. At this early hour of night, there is little to differentiate between the foam of the Mediterranean as it pounds on the beach below the banqueting hall of a Tel Aviv hotel, and the waves of Lake Victoria, two thousand miles away on another continent.

The hall is already full. People have come from all over, and no one is absent; in the first seconds it is difficult to recognize them. They are dressed in their best, barbered or coiffeured, relaxed, happy, yet sad.

Sad because not all of their number made it. There are people in mourning: Hana, widow of Pasco Cohen; the parents of Jean Jacques Maimoni; the sons of Dora Bloch; the relatives of Ida Borowitz—and the comrades of Sergeant Hershko Surin and Lieutenant Colonel Jonathan Netaniahu.

Happy because the army of Israel brought them back from captivity in an operation that thrilled the entire world. Happy because the threat of death no longer hovers over them.

Handshakes, kisses, hugs, and tears. "We're like one big family," says Sara Davidson. "In Entebbe we were reborn."

"There was a miracle in Entebbe," Chief Rabbi of Israel Shlomo Goren says in his blessing to the hostages restored to life. "It was a miracle from the Lord Almighty, Blessed be His name."

Deep in the crowd, Uzzi Davidson comments: "But this time the Lord Almighty needed a little help from the IDF."

Postscript

Wadia Hadad continues to build his infrastructure of terror, financed by millions of dollars, and backed by countries such as Libya and Iraq. Israel has been fighting the war of terrorism since 1948, but Hadad has made the struggle much more difficult. Hadad constantly seeks new recruits as well, mostly in Germany and Scandinavia, and his minions resort to crime to reinforce his immense treasury. So great is the wealth at his disposal that he has invested it in Europe, and he finances his operations in great part from interest and dividend income. Experts estimate that the group now controls something over one hundred million dollars. The astounding thing was that the group had its beginnings in a coup that brought $5 million in ransom money from Lufthansa, in return for release of a 747 hijacked to Aden in February 1972. At that time, Hadad was operations officer of the Popular Front for the Liberation of Palestine, led by George Habash.

The vast sum of money was dazzling. He decided not to transfer it to the PFLP, but to keep it—so he said—in the operations division. This act resulted in a violent argument, which in turn led to a rift. The rift was not ideological, as has usually been the case when terror groups split up, but financial. Two of the participants in the Aden hijacking, the same men who achieved publicity some years later for their part in organizing the Air France hijacking to Uganda, joined their commander. They paid with their lives when the IDF released the hostages. One of them was an Iraqi—Abd-el Abd Razak el-Abed. When the group began operations, he was sent to Europe, and operated mostly in the north and west of the continent. He was also called Abu Danada. It is now known that he played a key role in the sending of the three Japanese killers—from the "Red Army"—to Lod Airport, where they killed 26 people, including 16 pilgrims from Puerto Rico. The second was Faiz Jaaber from Hebron, who also held a senior position under Hadad—until he met his death at Entebbe.

Part of the Lufthansa money was used to pay the Red Army, as a means of convincing them to send their men to Lod. Wadia Hadad realized that large sums of money were an essential precondition for contacts with other terror groups and experts. Without it, he could not establish the infrastructure that also was essential. The money that it took to establish him as a focal point for other groups came from a number of sources (aside from the Lufthansa ransom). At first there were large-scale robberies, including banks, in Lebanon. There also were contributions from Iraq and Libya, and smaller sums from the South Yemen Republic (Aden).

Another important source of funds was Europe—and the means lay in two kinds of smuggling. To Europe: narcotics. From Europe to the Middle East: expensive stolen cars. The man in charge of the car-stealing net was Faiz Jaaber, who was operating out of West Germany. With the help of local criminals and Arab youngsters, he stole cars and smuggled them out from one of the ports.

The income was colossal, though it didn't begin to compare with Iraqi and Libyan contributions.

It is known that Hadad's men invested their funds in a number of economic endeavors, including Arab financial houses that promised a regular return. Inside Europe they prepared cover addresses and hiding places, including hotels, restaurants, and cafés. These served his operatives who went to Europe, and men of other terror organizations who were receiving cooperation and aid from Wadia Hadad.

They also acquired sophisticated equipment for forging documents in Germany, which was transferred to one of their centers in Iraq. With its help, the organization could produce documentation for anyone in need, including those Europeans tempted into accepting invitations to the group's camps in the Arab states. Camps such as these exist in Iraq, Libya, and South Yemen. The existence of a camp near Aden recently came to public attention when Israel arrested a young Dutch girl, Ludwina Jansen, who had been trained there and sent to Israel on a reconnaissance mission prior to an operation at Lod Airport. The girl, arrested by the *Shin Bet* while her Air France plane was making a transit stop at Lod, said that she arrived at the camp together with another young Dutchman, Marius Niverberg. Both were members of a Dutch group that numbered thirteen trainees.

The recruitment of Europeans into Wadia Hadad's organization was done in the most innocent fashion—unlike the link with Baader-Meinhof before the Air France hijacking, when the German group was promised that success would result in release of their members from German prisons, and in large cash rewards. In that case, Hadad's men in advance identified Wilfried Böse as suitable to lead the hijack team. At that time Böse was in Baghdad, living at Hadad's expense. The other recruitments were made ostensibly in the name of "international revolution." Professional recruiting agents operate in students' clubs and universities throughout Europe. They look for leftist youths of extremist convictions, and when they find sufficiently zealous candidates, they begin by offering a special Middle East seminar. For the most part they do not mention weapons or sabotage training, nor do they suggest the possibility of terror action in Israel or against Israeli targets. The trip to the Middle East is of course paid by the organization.

Those who accept the invitation soon find that the seminar is not so abstract, and that it does include weapons training. There is talk of the left and of revolution, but this is mostly "revolution" in Israel. Films are shown of the refugee camps, and the participants are told that until Israel is put in her place there can be no world revolution. The first stage of revolution must be war on Israel.

The senior recruiting officer in Hadad's group is thirty-six-year-old Tiasir Koba'a, born in Qalqiliya, which is now in Israeli hands. In the 1960s he was chairman of the Palestinian Students' Association. After finishing his studies in a Nablus high school, he went to Cairo University, where he became active in an extremist group—*Kaumion el-Arab*—and was chosen as secretary of the students' association. He took part in anti-Israel conferences, and contended that his hatred stemmed from the fact that his family was killed when the IDF took Qalqiliya in the War of Independence. Qalqiliya, of course, wasn't taken in 1948, and was in Jordanian hands until 1967, when it escaped the war unscathed—but this was irrelevant.

In December 1967, he was sent to the West Bank in order to provoke strikes among the local population. Arrested by the authorities, he was sentenced to three years in prison in Israel. Three French attorneys, who refused to say who sent them or paid for their tickets, wanted to defend him at his trial. When he was released in January 1971, he was deported to Jordan. But his name came up before that, during the first plane hijacking by terrorists (the El Al plane from Rome that was landed in Algeria). He was on the list of terrorists whose release was demanded as ransom for the plane, passengers, and crew. Israel agreed to a deal, but Koba'a was not included in it. Upon arrival in Jordan, he was sent directly to Lebanon, where he joined Habash's group, then found his was to Hadad's faction. His student experience stands him in good stead. It is known that he instructed his recruiting agents to look for candidates from those countries that have good relations with Israel, and where the population tends to sympathize with her: Holland, Denmark, and the other Scandinavian countries, for example, are areas of high priority. This is on the assumption that youngsters from those countries will arouse less suspicion when they are sent on missions in Israel, or against Israeli targets outside the Middle East.

Worldwide echoes and reactions to the Entebbe raid showed that public opinion in the West and in parts of the Third World were in favor of waging a war on terrorism. Governments were another matter. They, like most international bodies and agencies, were too apathetic and hesitant to take the necessary steps. Terrorism, after all, is not the sole preserve of Palestinians in particular or Arabs in general. Most countries of the world have experienced it in one form or another. Some constantly suffer from their own domestic variety: suffice it to mention the Red Army in Japan, Baader-Meinhof in Germany, the IRA in Ireland and England, the seemingly crazed fringe groups in the United States, Turkey or various South American countries. Yet, for all their supposed local causes, the subversive groups now bear the stamp of an international consortium, in which one helps the other in an effort that threatens to strike at the very heart of a free society. They share finances, manpower, and weapons. They enjoy direct or indirect involvement of other countries—such as Uganda and Libya.

Almost constant capitulation to terrorist extortion of funds and the release of convicted murderers and saboteurs from prison will not reduce acts of terrorism. The attitude of "give them what they want this time, then they'll go away and leave us alone" has only served to encourage acts of depravity. The terrorist knows that, as long as he is not hit by a bullet, the worst he can expect is a few weeks or months of imprisonment before he is released as the payoff for yet another kidnapping or hijacking.

A successful fight against terrorism calls for a series of actions that cannot bear fruit immediately. Since Entebbe, Israel does not make do with her own preparations, but tries to persuade other governments and countries of the need for such an organization. She seeks decisions in international bodies to provide for trial and extradition of hijackers. She seeks sanctions and boycotts against countries that aid and abet terrorists. Transport Minister Gad Yaakobi told an aviation conference in Washington that, since 1968, all the terrorists who struck at civil aviation have been freed, except for those imprisoned in Israel. Eighty-five terrorists and murderers, responsible for twenty-nine hijackings and attacks on four airports, have been released without completing their sentences, mostly without even being brought to trial. This despite the fact that they caused the deaths of more than two hundred civilians.

Wadia Hadad's organization, and the others, do not see Entebbe as the end of their war. Two events were soon to serve as proof of that. On August 11, 1976, two terrorists attacked a group of El Al passengers at Istanbul Airport. They threw hand grenades and fired their machine guns indiscriminately. Four passengers died and twenty-eight were wounded. The two assailants turned themselves over to the authorities, safe in the conviction that it was only a matter of time till they would be released. Three weeks later, on September 4, other terrorists hijacked a KLM plane on a flight from Nice, France, to Israel, after refueling in Tunisia. Again, as on previous occasions, they were demanding the release of terrorists from Israeli prisons in return for the lives of the hostages, not one of whom was an Israeli. This time they decided to negotiate while the plane was still in the air. But Israel decided not to respond to calls from the plane. With no other choice, they landed on Cyprus and, a few hours later—hours in which they could not establish contact with their head-quarters because of electronic interference—decided to surrender. Like their predecessors in the trade of hijack-ing, they were sure that no harm would come to them. And so it was. Libyan representatives took them under their wing and they disappeared.

From the beginning it was clear that the main aspect of the war against terror at this stage would be strikes against Wadia Hadad's group, which had succeeded in spreading an efficient net over the countries of Europe. Various intelligence services now agreed to cooperate, even without the knowledge of their governments, against this terror group. While governments were still guided by politi-cal interests, these intelligence services, or men in them, had an interest in smashing the international terror that threatened to destroy civil aviation and the innocent people who used its services. It was a good omen, indicating that beneath the surface there was a willingness to cooperate—even if it was primarily intelligence-oriented.

The terror organizations, their leaders, suppliers, and supporters—both active and passive—must be under con-stant surveillance. Resolute action depends on excellent intelligence. Countries must be willing to trade critical information in the fastest way possible. Experience has shown that Interpol, the international organization of police forces, is not the tool for the job. Quite apart from its commitment to noninvolvement in politics, information transmitted through Interpol in the past has leaked to Arab countries, who have gladly handed it on to the terror groups.

In a conversation with the authors of this book, Lieutenant General Mordechai Gur said that the Israeli Defense Forces devote a negligible percentage of their effort to the ongoing campaign against terror, and that—in his opinion—there is no point to mounting a massive offensive on this front. Arab terror will continue to be a cancer as long as the political problem that it purports to represent is not solved, but it can certainly be kept "on a back burner."

The IDF is convinced that terrorism is not a cause of major difficulties, and in no way compares with the scale and scope of battle between armies. Terror, in its present guise, evidences a fierce desire on the part of its practitioners to avoid clashes and evade contact, so it cannot rightly be considered guerilla warfare.

Mota Gur supports a counter-terror policy that can be summed up in a phrase borrowed from the rifle range: "Fire when ready!" In other words, take action when it suits you, where it suits you, and against whomever necessary. The Entebbe rescue itself is proof that the army of Israel has the power, the boldness, and the imagination.

Israel is aware that the general staffs of the Jordanian and Egyptian armies discussed the operational lessons to be learned from the IDF raid at Entebbe. They may have drawn the right conclusions, and then again they may have been wrong. Whichever way, Israel does not doubt that the Ugandan expedition—however successful it was—is no more than one battle in an ongoing war.

ABOUT THE AUTHORS

Yeshayahu Ben-Porat, 45, was born in Vienna. He is a graduate of the Sorbonne and the Hebrew University, and is currently senior political correspondent of *Yediot Aharonot*. The books he has co-authored include *Embargo, The Secret War, The Spy Who Came from Israel*, and *Kippur*. He is also a popular television personality in Israel.

Eitan Haber, 36, was born in Israel, and has covered all the major events of the 1960s and '70s for *Yediot* and for the IDF's *Bamachane* magazine. His work has taken him to the United States, Scandinavia, and Cyprus. Haber is co-author of *From Our Military Correspondents, Thus We Won, The Paratroops, Diary of the First Combat Squadron, Kippur*, and *A Dictionary of Israeli Security*.

Zeev Schiff, 43, was born in France, and is a member of the editorial board of *Haaretz*. He is widely regarded abroad as Israel's foremost military commentator, and is frequently quoted in the British and American press. He covered the Vietnam War for *Haaretz* and has written about European installations of NATO and the men who run the Pentagon. Schiff is co-author of *Fedayeen* and *A Dictionary of Israeli Security*, and is author of *La Guerre Israelo-Arabe, Wings Over Suez*, and a history of the Israeli army. His book *October Earthquake* won him the Sokolov Prize, Israel's most coveted award for journalism.

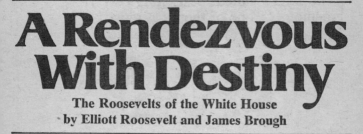

MORE SAVAGE — MORE SHOCKING than Helter Skelter!

THE GANG

by Herbert Kastle
author of Cross-Country and Ellie

THEY WERE HER MEN:
- Bert, a writer who was determined to turn his fictional fantasies into hard action for the first time in his life.
- Manny, a big, handsome stud going downhill, desperate to prove his manhood again.
- Mark, Manny's teen-age son, who crossed over the generation gap to join his elders in a world of x-rated kicks and kills.

SHE WAS THEIR WOMAN:
- Celia, six feet of breath-taking female, dedicated to satisfying every passion of these three men, so long as she could hold them together.

THEY WERE THE GANG
Bound together by violent lust and hate, no law of God or man could stop them!

A DELL BOOK $1.95 (2786-06)

BESTSELLERS
FROM DELL

fiction